OXFORD IB DIPLOMA PROGRAMME

RIGHTS AND PROTEST

COURSE COMPANION

Mark Rogers
Peter Clinton

OXFORD
UNIVERSITY PRESS

OXFORD
UNIVERSITY PRESS

Great Clarendon Street, Oxford, OX2 6DP, United Kingdom

Oxford University Press is a department of the University of Oxford. It furthers the University's objective of excellence in research, scholarship, and education by publishing worldwide. Oxford is a registered trade mark of Oxford University Press in the UK and in certain other countries

British Library Cataloguing in Publication Data

Data available

978-0-19-831019-8

10 9 8 7 6 5 4

Paper used in the production of this book is a natural, recyclable product made from wood grown in sustainable forests. The manufacturing process conforms to the environmental regulations of the country of origin.

Printed in India by Manipal Technologies Ltd

Acknowledgements

The publishers would like to thank the following for permissions to use their photographs:

p20: Peter Magubane ; p21(B): Drum Social Histories/Baileys African History Archive/Africa Media Online; p21(C): Drum Social Histories/Baileys African History Archive/Africa Media Online; p21(T): Martin Gibbs/Africa Media Online; p23: Jock Leyden/Natal Daily News ; p27: Hulton-Deutsch Collection/Corbis; p29: The Star © 1999 - 2015 Independent Online; p32: Drum Social Histories/Baileys African History Archive/Africa Media Online; p33: Jurgen Schadeberg/Getty Images; p34: DeAgostini/Getty Images; p37: Alain Nogues/Sygma/Corbis; p38: Drum Social Histories/Baileys African History Archive/Africa Media Online; p40: Federation of Free States of Africa; p42: Mike Abrahams/Alamy; p43: JH Jackson/Cape Argus; p45: Hulton-Deutsch Collection/Corbis; p46: The Star © 1999 - 2015 Independent Online; p49: JH Jackson/Cape Argus; p50: Drum Social Histories/Africa Media Online; p52: Jurgen Schadeberg/Getty Images; p53: Jurgen Schadeberg/Hulton Archive/Getty Images; p57: Drum Social Histories/Baileys African History Archive/Africa Media Online; p60: Graeme Williams/South Photos/Africa Media Online; p63: Drum Social Histories/Baileys African History Archive/Africa Media Online; p66: Drum Social Histories/Baileys African History Archive/Africa Media Online; p72: Roshan Dadoo; p76: Drum Social Histories/Baileys African History Archive/Africa Media Online; p78: Roshan Dadoo; p81: Peter Magubane; p83: Drum Social Histories/Baileys African History Archive/Africa Media Online; p86(BL): David Turnley/Corbis; p86(BR): Drum Social Histories/Baileys African History Archive/Africa Media Online; p86(CL): Drum Social Histories/Baileys African History Archive/Africa Media Online; p86(CR): Gille de Vlieg/South Photos/Africa Media Online; p86(T): UWC-Robben/Island Museum Mayibuye Archives; p87: Sipa Press/Rex Features; p91: Keystone-France/Gamma-Keystone/Getty Images; p92(BL): Drum Social Histories/Baileys African History Archive/Africa Media Online; p92(BR): Drum Social Histories/Baileys African History Archive/Africa Media Online; p92(TL): Drum Social Histories/Baileys African History Archive/Africa Media Online; p92(TR): Drum Social Histories/Baileys African History Archive/Africa Media Online; p93: Eli Weinburg, UWC-Robben/Island Museum Mayibuye Archives; p97: Juda Ngwenya/Reuters; p98: Drum Social Histories/Baileys African History Archive/Africa Media Online; p100: Punch Limited; p102: Keystone/Hulton Archive/Getty Images; p104: Keystone Pictures USA/Alamy; p106: IDAF/Rex Features; p108: Punch Limited; p109: Rob Crandall/Alamy; p113(B): Keystone Pictures USA/Alamy; p113(T): Punch Limited; p115: Rob Crandall/Alamy; p119: Dea Picture Library/Getty Images; p120: Adrienne de Jongh; p121: The Art Archive/Alamy; p129: Everett Collection Historical/Alamy; p134: Mary Evans; p137: Ella Mahler Collection/Oklahoma Historical Society; p141: Bob Adelman/Corbis; p144: John Frost Newspapers/Alamy; p149: Bettmann/Corbis; p150: Bettmann/Corbis; p152: Pictorial Press Ltd/Alamy; p153: Everett Collection Inc/Alamy; p154: Flip Schulke/Corbis; p155: Reprinted by arrangement with The Heirs to the Estate of Martin Luther King Jr c/o Writers House as agent for the proprietor New York, NY ©1953 Dr Martin Luther King Jr ©renewed 1983 Coretta Scott King; p157: Bettmann/Corbis; p158: Everett Collection Inc/Alamy; p164: Bettmann/Corbis; p166: Corbis; p178: The Protected Art Archive/Alamy; p179: Bettmann/Corbis; p181: Everett Collection Historical/Alamy; p184: White House Photo/Alamy; p185: Bettmann/Corbis; p187: David J. Frent/David J. & Janice L. Frent Collection/Corbis; p189: Marion S Trikosko/Stock Montage/Getty Images; p194: Corbis.

Cover illustration by Karolis Strautniekas, Folio Illustration Agency.

Artwork by QBS Learning and OUP.

The authors and publisher are grateful for permission to reprint the following copyright material:

We are grateful to the authors and publishers for use of extracts from their titles and in particular for the following:

Ralph D. Abernathy: Brief excerpt from pp. 179-81 from AND THE WALLS CAME TUMBLING DOWN. Copyright (c) 1989 by Ralph David Abernathy. Reprinted by permission of HarperCollins Publishers.

I Callinicos: *Oliver Tambo: Beyond the Engeli Mountains* (2004) pp 220–21. David Philip Publishers, Cape Town, South Africa. Reproduced by permission of New Africa Books.

***The Rise and Fall of Jim Crow: Jim Crow Stories: The Ku Klux Klan* (1866)** http://www.pbs.org/wnet/jimcrow/stories_events_kkk.html. Reproduced by permission of WNET.org.

Interview with Dave Dennis, conducted by Blackside, Inc. on November 10, 1985, for *Eyes on the Prize: America's Civil Rights Years (1954-1965)*. Washington University Libraries, Film and Media Archive, Henry Hampton Collection.

'Fifty-six Africans killed', from The Guardian, 22 March 1960 http://www.theguardian.com/century/1960-1969/Story/. Copyright Guardian News & Media Ltd 2015.

Scott Ellsworth: extracts from *The Encyclopedia of Oklahoma History and Culture*. Reproduced by permission of Scott Ellsworth.

Martin Luther King, Jr.: speech made on 5 December 1955 at the Holt Street Baptist Church. Reprinted by arrangement with The Heirs to the Estate of Martin Luther King Jr., c/o Writers House as agent for the proprietor New York, NY. Copyright © 1955 Dr. Martin Luther King Jr. © renewal 1983 Coretta Scott King.

Cynthia Lee: 'A single act of kindness becomes part of civil rights lore' from a UCLA publication, 10 May, 2011. UCLA Newsroom newsroom.ucla.edu/stories/civil-rightsactivists-still-remember-203453. Reproduced by permission of UCLA.

T Lodge: *Mandela, A Critical Life* (2006), p.57. Oxford University Press. By permission of Oxford University Press.

T Lodge: *Black Politics in South Africa since 1945*, (1983). Longman. London. Reproduced by permission of Professor Tom Lodge.

Rian Malin: A letter to the editors of the *New York Review of Books*, 21 March 2013. Reprinted by permission of Rian Malin.

Nelson Mandela: The Authorized Portrait © copyright Nelson R. Mandela, 2006 edited by M Maharaj and A Kathrada. Reprinted by permission of PQ Blackwell Ltd.

B Martin: *Justice Ignited: The dynamics of backfire* (2006) Rowman & Littlefield. Reproduced by permission of Rowman & Littlefield.

Excerpts from Montgomery City Code (1952), Chapter 6, Sections 10 and 11 IIT Chicago-Kent Library Blog, blogs.kentlaw.iit.edu/library/exhibits/montgomery-1955/images-documents/montgomery-city-code/. Alabama Department of Archives and History, Montgomery, Alabama. Reproduced by permission.

K Shillington: *Encyclopedia of African History*. Vol. 1–3 (2005) p1444. Taylor and Francis, New York. Reproduced by permission of Taylor and Francis Group LLC Books.

E Sisulu: *Walter and Albertina Sisulu: In our lifetime* (2002) David Philip Publishers. Cape Town, South Africa. Reproduced by permission.

Robert Weisbrot: Freedom Bound: A History of America's Civil Rights Movement. Copyright © 1990 by Robert Weisbrot. Used by permission of W.W. Norton & Company Inc.

We have made every effort to trace and contact all copyright holders before publication, but if notified of any errors or omissions, the publisher will be happy to rectify these at the earliest opportunity.

Links to third party websites are provided by Oxford in good faith and for information only. Oxford disclaims any responsibility for the materials contained in any third party website referenced in this work.

Course Companion definition

The IB Diploma Programme Course Companions are resource materials designed to support students throughout their two-year Diploma Programme course of study in a particular subject. They will help students gain an understanding of what is expected from the study of an IB Diploma Programme subject while presenting content in a way that illustrates the purpose and aims of the IB. They reflect the philosophy and approach of the IB and encourage a deep understanding of each subject by making connections to wider issues and providing opportunities for critical thinking.

The books mirror the IB philosophy of viewing the curriculum in terms of a whole-course approach; the use of a wide range of resources, international mindedness, the IB learner profile and the IB Diploma Programme core requirements, theory of knowledge, the extended essay, and creativity, activity, service (CAS).

Each book can be used in conjunction with other materials and indeed, students of the IB are required and encouraged to draw conclusions from a variety of resources. Suggestions for additional and further reading are given in each book and suggestions for how to extend research are provided.

In addition, the Course Companions provide advice and guidance on the specific course assessment requirements and on academic honesty protocol. They are distinctive and authoritative without being prescriptive.

IB mission statement

The International Baccalaureate aims to develop inquiring, knowledgable and caring young people who help to create a better and more peaceful world through intercultural understanding and respect.

To this end the IB works with schools, governments and international organizations to develop challenging programmes of international education and rigorous assessment.

These programmes encourage students across the world to become active, compassionate, and lifelong learners who understand that other people, with their differences, can also be right.

The IB learner Profile

The aim of all IB programmes is to develop internationally minded people who, recognizing their common humanity and shared guardianship of the planet, help to create a better and more peaceful world. IB learners strive to be:

Inquirers They develop their natural curiosity. They acquire the skills necessary to conduct inquiry and research and show independence in learning. They actively enjoy learning and this love of learning will be sustained throughout their lives.

Knowledgable They explore concepts, ideas, and issues that have local and global significance. In so doing, they acquire in-depth knowledge and develop understanding across a broad and balanced range of disciplines.

Thinkers They exercise initiative in applying thinking skills critically and creatively to recognize and approach complex problems, and make reasoned, ethical decisions.

Communicators They understand and express ideas and information confidently and creatively in more than one language and in a variety of modes of communication. They work effectively and willingly in collaboration with others.

Principled They act with integrity and honesty, with a strong sense of fairness, justice, and respect for the dignity of the individual, groups, and communities. They take responsibility for their own actions and the consequences that accompany them.

Open-minded They understand and appreciate their own cultures and personal histories, and are open to the perspectives, values, and traditions of other individuals and communities. They are accustomed to seeking and evaluating a range of points of view, and are willing to grow from the experience.

Caring They show empathy, compassion, and respect towards the needs and feelings of others. They have a personal commitment to service, and act to make a positive difference to the lives of others and to the environment.

Risk-takers They approach unfamiliar situations and uncertainty with courage and forethought, and have the independence of spirit to explore new roles, ideas, and strategies. They are brave and articulate in defending their beliefs.

Balanced They understand the importance of intellectual, physical, and emotional balance to achieve personal well-being for themselves and others.

Reflective They give thoughtful consideration to their own learning and experience. They are able to assess and understand their strengths and limitations in order to support their learning and personal development.

A note on academic honesty

It is of vital importance to acknowledge and appropriately credit the owners of information when that information is used in your work. After all, owners of ideas (intellectual property) have property rights. To have an authentic piece of work, it must be based on your individual and original ideas with the work of others fully acknowledged. Therefore, all assignments, written or oral, completed for assessment must use your own language and expression. Where sources are used or referred to, whether in the form of direct quotation or paraphrase, such sources must be appropriately acknowledged.

How do I acknowledge the work of others?

The way that you acknowledge that you have used the ideas of other people is through the use of footnotes and bibliographies.

Footnotes (placed at the bottom of a page) or endnotes (placed at the end of a document) are to be provided when you quote or paraphrase from another document, or closely summarize the information provided in another document. You do not need to provide a footnote for information that is part of a 'body of knowledge'. That is, definitions do not need to be footnoted as they are part of the assumed knowledge.

Bibliographies should include a formal list of the resources that you used in your work. The listing should include all resources, including books, magazines, newspaper articles, Internet-based resources, CDs and works of art. 'Formal' means that you should use one of the several accepted forms of presentation. You must provide full information as to how a reader or viewer of your work can find the same information. A bibliography is compulsory in the extended essay.

What constitutes misconduct?

Misconduct is behaviour that results in, or may result in, you or any student gaining an unfair advantage in one or more assessment component. Misconduct includes plagiarism and collusion.

Plagiarism is defined as the representation of the ideas or work of another person as your own. The following are some of the ways to avoid plagiarism:

- Words and ideas of another person used to support one's arguments must be acknowledged.

- Passages that are quoted verbatim must be enclosed within quotation marks and acknowledged.

- CD-ROMs, email messages, web sites on the Internet, and any other electronic media must be treated in the same way as books and journals.

- The sources of all photographs, maps, illustrations, computer programs, data, graphs, audio-visual, and similar material must be acknowledged if they are not your own work.

- Works of art, whether music, film, dance, theatre arts, or visual arts, and where the creative use of a part of a work takes place, must be acknowledged.

Collusion is defined as supporting misconduct by another student. This includes:

- allowing your work to be copied or submitted for assessment by another student

- duplicating work for different assessment components and/or diploma requirements.

Other forms of misconduct include any action that gives you an unfair advantage or affects the results of another student. Examples include, taking unauthorized material into an examination room, misconduct during an examination, and falsifying a CAS record.

Contents

YOUR GUIDE FOR PAPER 1

The middle years of the twentieth century saw an explosion of protest by non-White people of the United States and South Africa against the racist policies of segregation and discrimination followed by their governments. This struggle for rights, freedom and justice is a defining part of the modern history of the two countries.

The first of two case studies in this book focuses on the civil rights movement in the US. Coverage begins in 1954 with the Brown versus Board of Education decision. The book proceeds to examine some of the landmark moments in the struggle for rights, such as the Montgomery bus boycott and the Freedom Summer. The climax of

the study is the passage of the Civil Rights Act in 1964 and Voting Rights Act in 1965.

In South Africa, the focus of the second case study, the election of a National Part government in 1948 was followed by a tightening of existing legislation and the imposition of an even harsher racial system known as apartheid. The Black majority responded with a series of non-violent, mass-based protests against the authorities. The peaceful protest of the 1950s was then transformed into armed struggle in the aftermath of the Sharpeville massacre of 1960. The culmination of the study is the Rivonia Trial, in which life imprisonment terms were handed down to Nelson Mandela and his codefendants in 1964.

Historical concepts

The content in this unit is linked to the six key IB concepts.

- The move from petty apartheid to grand apartheid
- The move from peaceful protest to armed struggle

- Sporadic change from segregated schools throughout the southern United States in 1954 to many, but not a majority of schools desegregated by 1965.
- Segregated public facilities legal through out the southern states; the Civil Rights Act of 1964 makes such segregation illegal
- Presidential support for civil rights and civil rights legislation rises

- Was there any real difference between petty apartheid and grand apartheid?
- To what extent were the various protests and campaigns against apartheid successful?
- Was the ANC taken over by the South African Communist Party?
- Did Chief Luthuli authorize the use of armed struggle?
- To what extent did the goals of Malcolm X and Martin Luther King, Jr. differ?
- In what ways were the views and methods of the NAACP, SCLC, SNCC, and the NOI different?

- Nature and characteristics of the apartheid system
- Limitations to the success of anti-apartheid opposition
- Dr Martin Luther King, Jr. remains key civil rights leader throughout the period
- Segregationist opposition to civil rights employs economic, political, and violent means throughout the 1950s and 1960s

Key concepts

Change · Perspectives · Continuity · Significance · Causation · Consequence

- Why did the National Party government implement apartheid laws?
- What factors determined the various strategies employed by the anti-apartheid movement?
- Why did states such as Virginia practice Massive Resistance after Brown v. Board of Education?
- What were the reasons why SNCC, the SCLC and CORE used the tactic of nonviolent protest?
- Why did segregationist fight hard to maintain Jim Crow laws and practices?

- What events/actions/individuals/organizations were most significant in shaping the apartheid system and the response of the Black majority to this system?
- What were the impact of non-violent resistance by civil rights protestors?
- What were the significant contributions the United States Supreme Court and the Presidency to the rights of African Americas?
- What was the importance of the Civil Rights Act of 1964 and the Voting Rights Act of 1965 to civil rights?

- What was the impact of the apartheid system on the lives of South Africans?
- What were the results of the Sharpeville massacre?
- What were the results of the Rivonia Trial and the jailing of the leaders of Umkhonto we Sizwe?
- What response from the United States government did Freedom Riders hope to catalyze?
- How did overt and visual opposition to civil rights actions effect the views of the American public?
- What were the immediate and lasting effects of the violence by law officers during the Selma to Montgomery March in 1965?

History is an exploratory subject that fosters a sense of inquiry. It is also an interpretive discipline, allowing opportunity for engagement with multiple perspectives and a plurality of opinions. Studying history develops an understanding of the past, which leads to a deeper understanding of the nature of humans and of the world today.

"Rights and protest" is a prescribed subject for Paper 1 of your IB History examination. This book focuses not only on helping you to cover and understand the content relating to this topic, but will also help you to develop the skills necessary to answer the source questions.

The content of this prescribed subject may also be relevant to the topics that you are studying for Paper 3.

This book includes:

- analysis of the key events in each case study

- activities to develop your understanding of the content and key issues

- links between the content and historical concepts (see previous page)

- timelines to help develop a chronological understanding of key events

- a range of sources for each topic

- practice source questions along with examiner's hints

- links to theory of knowledge (TOK).

How to use this book

This first chapter will explain how to approach each question on the IB Paper 1; there will then be source exercises to try throughout the book which will give you the opportunity to practise your Paper 1 skills.

Where you see this icon, you will find extra help answering the question, either at the end of the chapter or next to the question itself.

Preparing for Paper 1: Working with sources

As historians, our training and discipline is based on documentary evidence.

— David Dixon

When you work with sources you are practising a key component of historians' methodology. Paper 1 skills are the skills that historians apply when they research a question and attempt to draw conclusions.

In Paper 1 you will:

- **demonstrate** understanding of historical sources

- **interpret and analyse** information from a variety of sources

- **compare and contrast** information between sources

- **evaluate** sources for their value and limitations

- **synthesize** evidence from the sources with your own detailed knowledge of the topic.

ATL Thinking skills

Read the following comment on sources and then answer the questions that follow.

> The practice of history begins with evidence and with sources. The availability of sources is often the key determinant of what becomes most popular, because some areas, for example nineteenth-century France, benefit from a greater volume of documents than others, such as ancient Germany. Whereas historians of early modern and medieval popular culture face a constant battle to find material ... those concerned with modern political history face a veritable forest of official documents – more than any one person could marshal in a lifetime. It is vital, therefore, that students of history become aware of the scope of historical sources, and the methods which historians use to order them.

> Black J and Macraild, D M. 2007. *Palgrave Study Skills – Studying History*. 3rd edn, page 89. Macmillan. Basingstoke, UK

1 According to Black and Macraild, what makes certain historical subjects more popular than others?

2 What problems do contemporary historians face?

Following the catastrophe of the First World War the new Bolshevik government in Russia published all the Tsarist documents relating to the outbreak of the war. This led to other European governments publishing volumes and volumes of documents – in what became known as the "colour books" – but in most cases attempting to demonstrate how their country had **not** been responsible for causing the war. Historians have subsequently had vast quantities of documents to use as more government and military sources were declassified and released. However, as recent historiography has revealed, there is still no consensus among historians as to the key causes of the First World War.

3 In pairs discuss whether each generation of historian can move closer to "historical truth" and can be more objective because they are further away in time from an event and have more sources to work from.

4 Listen to this discussion on the historiography of the causes of the First World War: http://www.bbc.co.uk/programmes/b03srqz9?p_f_added=urn%3Abbc%3Aradio%3Aprogramme%3Ab03srqz9

What different interpretations do historians have on the causes of the First World War? What factors have affected their interpretations?

Following on from your discussions for question 3 and 4, get into small groups and consider *what is the role of the historian?* To what extent do you agree that the key role of historians is to bring us closer to historical truth? Or do historians, selection of evidence and use of language tell us more about their own eras and societies than those of the past?

What can you expect on Paper 1?

Paper 1 has a key advantage for students as the question format is given in advance; you can predict the nature and style of the four questions on this paper. This means that you can also learn and practise the correct approach for each of these questions and maximize the marks you attain technically. The majority of marks on this paper are awarded for skills.

This book deals with the prescribed topic of global war. As this is an IB prescribed topic you will need to ensure you have learned all of the content in this book which is linked to each sub-topic from the bullet point list set down in the syllabus:

Case studies	Material for detailed study
Case study 1: Apartheid South Africa (1948–1964)	**Nature and characteristics of discrimination** ● "Petty Apartheid" and "Grand Apartheid" legislation ● Division and "classification"; segregation of populations and amenities; creation of townships/forced removals; segregation of education; Bantustan system; impact on individuals **Protests and action** ● Non-violent protests: bus boycotts; defiance campaign, Freedom Charter ● Increasing violence: the Sharpeville massacre (1960) and the decision to adopt the armed struggle ● Official response: the Rivonia trial (1963–1964) and the imprisonment of the ANC leadership **The role and significance of key actors/groups** ● Key individuals: Nelson Mandela; Albert Luthuli ● Key groups: the African National Congress (ANC); the South African Communist Party (SACP) and the MK (Umkhonto we Sizwe—"Spear of the Nation")

Case study 2:	Nature and characteristics of discrimination
Civil rights movement in the United States (1954–1965)	• Racism and violence against African Americans; the Ku Klux Klan; disenfranchisement
	• Segregation and education; Brown versus Board of Education decision (1954); Little Rock (1957)
	• Economic and social discrimination; legacy of the Jim Crow laws; impact on individuals
	Protests and action
	• Non-violent protests; Montgomery bus boycott (1955–1956); Freedom Rides (1961); Freedom Summer (1964
	• Legislative changes: Civil Rights Act (1964); Voting Rights Act (1965)
	The role and significance of key actors/groups
	• Key actors: Martin Luther King Jr; Malcolm X; Lyndon B Johnson
	• Key groups: National Association for the Advancement of Colored People (NAACP); Southern Christian Leadership Conference (SCLC) and Student Non-violent Coordinating Committee (SNCC); the Nation of Islam (Black Muslims)

The four sources on the examination paper will be a selection of both primary and secondary sources. The length of each source may vary – but the total length of the paper should not exceed 750 words in total. One of the four sources will be a "visual" rather than text-based source, for example a photograph, cartoon, table of statistics, graph or map.

This book will thus give you plenty of practice with a wide range of different sources on the topic of rights and protest.

How to approach the source questions on Paper 1

Refer to the guidelines below when attempting the source-based questions in each chapter of the book.

First question

This is in two parts. It is made up of a 3-mark and a 2-mark component – giving you a possible total of 5 marks. It is assessing your *historical comprehension* of the sources. You do not need to give your own detailed knowledge in your response.

This is the only question that asks you to **explain** the content and meaning of the documents

Part a

The 3-mark question asks you to comprehend, extract and possibly infer information. Here are some suggestions for answering this question:

• Write: firstly …, secondly …, thirdly … to ensure that you make at least three separate points.

• Do not repeat the same point you have already made.

• Do not overly rely on quotes – make your point and then briefly quote two or three words of the source in support.

Part b

• You should try to make two clear points for this question.

• For each point, refer specifically to the content of the source to provide evidence for your answer.

For parts a and b you should not need to bring in your own knowledge; however your contextual understanding of the topic and sources should enable you to understand more clearly the content and message of each source.

Second question

As you know, historians need to use and evaluate sources as they research a historical era or event.

For the second question, you need to evaluate one source in terms of its "value" and "limitations" by examining its origin, purpose and content. This question is worth 4 marks.

To find the origin and purpose look carefully at the provenance of the source:

For origin	**Who** wrote it/said it/drew it?
	When did the person write it/say it/draw it?
	Where did the person write it/say it/draw it?
	What is the source – a speech/cartoon/ textbook, etc.?
For purpose	**Why** did the person write it/say it/draw it?
	Who did the person write it/say it/draw it **for**?
For content	Is the language objective or does it sound exaggerated or one-sided?
	What is the tone of the source?
	What information and examples do they select or focus on to support their point?

From the information you have on the origins of the source, and what you can infer about the document's *purpose*, you must then explain the value and limitations the source has for historians researching a particular event or period in history.

The grid on pages 7 and 8 gives you an idea of the kinds of values and limitations connected with different primary sources.

> **Examiner's hint:** *Note that value and limitations given in the grid are general or generic points that could be applied to these sources. However, your contextual knowledge and the specific provenance of any source that you get in the examination will allow you to make much more precise comments on the value and limitations of the source that you evaluate in a document question. Notice also that the value of the source will always depend on what you are using it for.*

What are the values and limitations associated with secondary sources?

The most common secondary source that you will have to deal with is one from a text book or historian. Again the key questions of "What is the origin of the source?" and "What is the source's purpose?" need to be addressed in order to work out the value and limitation of the source in question.

Here are some points you could consider regarding the value and limitations of works by historians and biographers:

Source	Values	Limitations
Historians	• are usually professionals or experts in field • have the benefit of hindsight which is not present in contemporary sources • may offer sources based on a range of documents; the more recent the publication, the more sources will be available	• might have a broad focus to their work or might have a very specific and narrow focus • might be an expert in a different region or era from the one they are writing about • may be influenced by their nationality, racial background, experience, politics or context
Biographers	• will have studied the individual in question in much detail • may provide sources that have value due to tone, use of language and expression • sometimes have the benefit of hindsight	• might have become too involved with their subject and have lost objectivity • may focus on the role of the subject of their biography at the expense of other individuals or factors • might not have direct access to the subject and/ or other relevant sources (the place and date will be key here) • may have limitations due to tone, use of language and expression

ATL Thinking skills

Consider the following provenance:

Tom Lodge, a South African historian who is professor of peace and conflict studies at the University of Limerick in Ireland. *Mandela: A Critical Life* **(2006).**

1 Using the points on the previous page, consider the value and limitations of this source for a student analysing Japanese history in this period. [Remember to research Lodge's credentials as a historian of South Africa.]

2 How would a school history textbook differ in value and limitations compared to the work of a historian?

ATL Communication and thinking skills

Task 1

Find a biography of one key figure from the period of history that you are studying. With reference to the questions above, analyse the value and limitations of the source in providing extra insight into the role and impact of this individual.

Task 2

What questions would you ask about an **autobiography** to assess its values and limitations to your research?

ATL Thinking skills

Read the following extract:

Part of the problem for historians is defining what a source is. Although primary sources are usually closest, or indeed contemporary, to the period under observation, and secondary sources those works written subsequently, the distinction is actually quite blurred. Once we move away from simple cases [such as politicians' diaries, or cabinet minutes] which are clearly primary, difficulties do arise. Take Benjamin Disraeli's novel of 1845, *Sybil; or the Two Nations*. This is first and foremost a piece of fiction … For historians … however, Sybil is something of a primary source: it typifies the milieu [social setting] of the young Tory Radicals of the day [of whom Disraeli was one] …

Black J and Macraild, D M. 2007. *Palgrave Study Skills – Studying History*. 3rd edition, page 91. Macmillan. Basingstoke, UK.

Note: Disraeli was a 19th-century British Conservative Party leader, and British Prime Minister from 1874–80.

Question

What is the problem with trying to define sources as "primary" or "secondary"?

Examiner's hint: *Note that for the purposes of evaluation, a source has no more or less intrinsic value to historians just because it is primary or secondary.*

Always focus on the specific origins and purpose of a source – not whether it is primary or secondary. You do not need to give this distinction in your answer.

ATL Communication and thinking skills

Read the following statements. Why would these statements be considered invalid by examiners?

- A limitation of this source is that the translation could be inaccurate.

- This source is limited because it doesn't tell us what happened before or after.

- This source is limited because it is biased.

- This textbook was written over 70 years after the event took place so it is unlikely that the author had first-hand experience. This is a limitation.

- A value of this source is that it is an eyewitness account.

- This source is only an extract and we don't know what he said next.

- This is a primary source and this is a value.

- As it is a photograph, it gives a true representation of what actually happened.

Refer back to the examiner's hint on page 5 regarding this table.

Source	Values These sources:	Limitations These sources:
Private letters (audience – the recipient) Diaries (audience – personal not public at the time of writing)	• can offer insight in to *personal* views or opinions • can indicate the affects of an event or era on an individual • can suggest motives for public actions or opinions • can, through tone, use of language and expression give insight into perspective, opinion or emotions	• only give individual opinion, not a general view or government perspective • may give an opinion that changes due to later events or may give a view not held in public • might have the motive of persuading the audience (in the case of private letters) to act in certain way • may have limitations because of tone, use of language and expression
Memoirs to be published (audience – public)	• can offer insight into *personal* views, suggest motives for public actions and might benefit from hindsight – an evaluation of events after the period • might show how the individual *wants* his or her motive or actions to be viewed by the public	• may revise opinions with the benefit of hindsight, i.e. now the consequences of actions are known • might be written because the author wants to highlight the strengths of his or her actions – to improve the author's public image or legacy • may have limitations because of tone, use of language and expression
Newspapers, television or radio reports Eyewitness accounts	• could reflect publicly held views or popular opinion • might offer an expert view • can give insight into contemporary opinion	• could be politically influenced or censored by specific governments or regimes • may only give "overview" of a situation • might only give a one-sided narrow perspective • could emphasize only a minor part of an issue • may have limitations because of tone, use of language and expression (Note that eyewitnesses are not useful just because they are at an event; each eyewitness will notice different aspects and may miss key points altogether, which could be a limitation)
Novels or poems	• could inform contemporary opinion • might offer insight into emotional responses and motives	• could provide a "dissenting" voice, i.e. not popular opinion • could exaggerate the importance of an event or individual • could have political agenda • may have limitations because of tone, use of language and expression

Statistics	• can offer insight into growth and decline • might suggest correlations between indicators, e.g. unemployment and voting patterns • might suggest the impact of an event or its results over time • make comparisons easier	• are gathered for different purposes (e.g. political, economic) and could be deliberately distorted • might relate only to one location or time period • might suggest incorrect correlations; there could be another causal factor not included in some sets of statistics
Photographs	• can give a sense of a specific scene or event • can offer insight into the immediate impact of an event on a particular place, or people's immediate response • might offer information on the environment	• are limited as we cannot see beyond the "lens" • might distort the "bigger" picture because of their limited view • might be staged • might reflect the purpose of the photographer; what did he or she want to show?
Cartoons or paintings	• can inform public opinion as cartoonists often respond to popularly held views • can portray the government's line when there is censorship	• could be censored and not reflect public opinion • often play on stereotypes (particularly cartoons) and exaggeration • could be limited to the viewpoint and experience of the cartoonist or artist (or the publication the cartoon or painting appears in) • may have limitations because of tone, use of language and expression
Government records and documents Speeches Memoranda	• might show the government's position on an issue • can offer insight into the reasons for decisions made • might reveal the motives for government policies • can show what the public has been told about an event or issue by the government • might be a well-informed analysis	• often do not offer insight into the results of policies and decisions • might not reveal dissent or divergent opinion • might not show public opinion • can be used to keep sensitive information classified for many years • may not explain the motives for a decision or political purpose • may have limitations because of tone, use of language and expression

ATL Research skills

Find primary sources of the types listed in the grid above for the topic that you are currently studying. Using the notes in the grid above, analyse the values and limitations of each of these sources.

For the sources that you have assessed, also look at the content and the language being used. How does the tone, style or content help you to assess the value and limitations of the sources?

Third question

This will ask you to **compare** and **contrast** two sources. Your aim is to identify similar themes and ideas in two sources, and to also identify differences between them. It is marked out of a total of 6 marks.

The key to this question is *linkage*, i.e. you are expected to discuss the sources together throughout your response. The examiner is looking for a *running commentary*. At no time should you talk about one source without relating it to the other. "End-on accounts" – where you write about the content of one source followed by the content of the second source – do not score well.

How do you approach this question?

You must find **both** similarities and differences. This is best presented as two separate paragraphs – one for comparisons and one for contrasts. Here are some tips:

- You could practice using highlighter pens – highlight the similarities in each source in one colour and the differences in another colour.

- You must make sure that you mention **both** sources in every sentence you write. The skill you are demonstrating is linkage.

- Always be clear about which source you are discussing.

- Find both the more "obvious" similarities and differences, and then go on to identify the more specific comparisons and contrasts.

- Deal with similarities in your first paragraph and differences in your second.

- Ensure that each point you make is clearly stated. If you quote from the sources, make this brief – quote only two or three words to support your point.

- Do not introduce your answer or attempt to reach a conclusion. This is not necessary and wastes time.

- Do not waste time explaining what each source says.

- Do not discuss **why** the sources are similar or different.

Examiner's hint: *Note that you must make more than* **one** *comparison and more than* **one** *contrast. You should attempt to identify* **six** *points of linkage as this is a 6-mark question. This might mean there are three points of comparison and three points of difference. However, there might not be balance – there could be two points of comparison and four points of contrast, or four points of comparison and two points of contrast.*

How to draw comparisons/show similarities

Both Source A and Source B …

Source A suggests … ; similarly, Source B suggests …

Source A supports Source B …

Like Source B, Source A says …

In the same way that Source B argues … , Source A points out that …

How to draw contrasts / show differences

Source A suggests … ; however, Source B says …

Source B disagrees with Source A regarding …

Source A claims … as opposed to Source B which asserts …

Source B goes further than Source A in arguing … while A focuses on…

Examiner's hint – what *not* to do: *The focus of this question is* **how** *the sources are similar or different – it is asking you to look at the content of the source. This question is* **not** *asking you* **why** *the sources might be similar or different.*

Do not use grids, charts or bullet points – always write in full paragraphs.

It is **not** *a full valid contrast to identify what is simply mentioned in one source but not the other (i.e. "Source A mentions that … played a role, whereas Source B does not mention this" is not developed linkage).*

Question Three will be assessed using generic markbands, as well as exam specific indicative content. The markbands are:

Marks	Level descriptor
5–6	• There is discussion of both sources. Explicit links are made between the two sources. • The response includes clear and valid points of comparison **and** of contrast.
3–4	• There is some discussion of both sources, although the two sources may be discussed separately. • The response includes some valid points of comparison **and/or** of contrast, although these points may lack clarity.
1–2	• There is superficial discussion of one or both sources. • The response consists of description of the content of the source(s), and/or general comments about the source(s), rather than valid points of comparison or of contrast.
0	• The response does not reach a standard described by the descriptors above.

Examiners will apply the "best fit" to responses and attempt to award credit wherever possible.

Fourth question

This is worth the most marks, 9 of the total of 25. It requires you to write a mini-essay. The key to this question is that an *essay* is required – not a list of material from each source. However, you are required to *synthesize* material from the sources with your own knowledge in your essay.

How do you approach this question?

It is recommended that you plan your answer as you would any essay question. The difference here is that you will use evidence from the sources as well as from your own detailed knowledge to support your arguments.

- First make a brief plan based on the sources and group them into either those which support the point in the essay title and those which suggest an alternative argument, or group them under themes if the question is open, e.g. "Examine the reasons for the

changing alliances...". Add the sources to the grid as shown below.

- Then add your own knowledge to the grid. This should be detailed knowledge such as dates, events, statistics and the views of historians.

- When you start writing, you will need to write only a brief sentence of introduction.

- When using the sources, refer to the them directly as Source A, Source E and so on.

- You can quote briefly from the sources throughout the essay but quoting two or three words is sufficient.

- Use *all* the sources.

- Include own detailed knowledge

- Write a brief conclusion which should answer the question and be in line with the evidence you have given.

Sources that suggest X	Sources that suggest other factors
Source A	Source B
Own knowledge: events, dates, details	Own knowledge: events, dates, details
Source D	Source C
Own knowledge: historian	Own knowledge: events, dates, details
Source E	Source A makes more than one point, can be used to support more than one argument or theme
Own knowledge: events, dates, details	

▲ Planning grid for the fourth question – mini-essay

The Fourth question will be assessed using generic markbands, as well as exam specific indicative content. The markbands are:

Marks	Level descriptor
0	• The response does not reach a standard described by the descriptors below.
1–3	• The response lacks focus on the question. • References to the sources are made, but at this level these references are likely to consist of descriptions of the content of the sources rather than the sources being used as evidence to support the analysis. • No own knowledge is demonstrated or, where it is demonstrated, it is inaccurate or irrelevant.
4–6	• The response is generally focused on the question. • References are made to the sources, and these references are used as evidence to support the analysis. • Where own knowledge is demonstrated, this lacks relevance or accuracy. There is little or no attempt to synthesize own knowledge and source material.
7–9	• The response is focused on the question. • Clear references are made to the sources, and these references are used effectively as evidence to support the analysis. • Accurate and relevant own knowledge is demonstrated. There is effective synthesis of own knowledge and source material.

Examiners will apply the "best fit" to responses and attempt to award credit wherever possible.

Here is a summary of the key points for each question with the kind of language that is useful when answering each question.

First question, part a

Remember you have to show your understanding of the source and come up with three points. Here are some useful sentence starters:

> This source says that …
>
> Secondly …
>
> It also suggests that …

First question, part b

Always start with your key point.

> One message of this source is …
>
> This is supported by … *here refer to specific details in the source.*
>
> Another message of the source is …
>
> *You need to make a separate point, not an elaboration of the first point: you need two clear points about the message of the sources.*

Second question

This question is assessing your ability to analyse a source for its value and limitations by looking at its origin and purpose and content.

> Make sure that you use the words "origin", "purpose" or "content" in each of your sentences to ensure that you are focused on what the question needs, e.g.
>
> A value of the source is that its author …
>
> A value of the purpose is that it …
>
> The language of the content of this source indicates that …
>
> The content also seems to focus on, or use, examples which are …
>
> On the other hand, there are also limitations to using this source for finding out about … This is because (*explain here how origin and purpose can cause problems for the historian*) **or**
>
> A limitation of the origin is …
>
> A limitation of the purpose is …
>
> The content of this source makes it less valuable because …

Third question

This is designed to assess your cross-referencing skills.

When comparing two sources you could use the following structures:

> Sources A and B agree that …

> Moreover, the two sources are also similar in that … This is supported by … in Source A and … in Source B …

For a contrasting paragraph:

> Source A differs from Source B in that Source A says … while Source B argues that …

> Another difference between the two documents is that …

> Moreover, Source B goes further than Source A when it suggests/says that …

Fourth question

This is a mini-essay and is assessing your ability to synthesize sources with your own knowledge as well as your ability to give supported arguments or points that address the specific essay question.

Use your essay writing skills and vocabulary for this question.

In addition, as you are using sources as well as your own knowledge, you could use the following to help tie in the sources to your own knowledge:

> As it says in Source C …

> This is supported by the information given in Source …

> Source A suggests that … and this is supported by the fact that in the Soviet Union at this time …

> Historians have argued that … This viewpoint is supported by the information in Source E concerning …

How should I distribute my time in the Paper 1 examination?

A key issue for this paper is managing your time effectively in the examination. If you do not work through the questions efficiently you could run out of time. You must allow enough time to answer the fourth question; after all this is worth the most marks on the paper.

You will have one hour to complete the paper. At the beginning of the examination you have five minutes reading time when you are not allowed to write anything.

We recommend that you use your five minutes reading time to read through the questions first. This will give you an initial understanding of what you are looking for when you read the sources. Read through the questions and then begin to read through the sources.

How much time should I spend on each question?

Some examiners have suggested that the time you spend on each question could be based on the maximum number of marks that the answer could receive. The following is a rough guide:

First question, parts a and b	10 minutes	5 marks
Second question	10 minutes	4 marks
Third question	15 minutes	6 marks
Fourth question	25 minutes	9 marks

1 APARTHEID SOUTH AFRICA (1948–1964)

In May 1948, the Whites-only electorate of the Union of South Africa voted the Herenigde Nasionale Party (more usually known as the National Party or the NP), led by Dr DF Malan, into power. The margin of the NP victory was exceptionally narrow. In fact, the ruling United Party (UP) of sitting Prime Minister Jan Smuts won the majority of the popular vote, but the electoral system was weighted in favour of larger, rural constituencies where the NP managed to out-perform its rivals. This meant that Malan was able to form a coalition government with the smaller Afrikaner Party (AP) of Nicolaas Havenga.

Despite the narrowness of the NP mandate, the decision of the White voters of South Africa was momentous. The NP would remain in power for more than four decades. During this period, it would implement an extreme version of racial segregation known as *apartheid*, a word which means "apartness" in Afrikaans. Malan and his successors enacted a series of legislative measures designed to reinforce the dominance of the minority White population over the other peoples of South Africa. They also sought to engineer the complete separation of the different racial groups in the country. Their actions resulted in an explosion of opposition to the apartheid system among the non-White peoples of South Africa, and growing disgust and opposition to the country from the international community, leading to diplomatic pressure and trade sanctions. In the 1980s, with South Africa in a state of deepening political and economic crisis, a section of the NP leadership made the decision to begin dismantling the apartheid system. The country completed its transition from apartheid to non-racialism with its first fully democratic elections in 1994. These were won handsomely by the African National Congress (ANC), the party which had been at the forefront of Black opposition to the apartheid system since the NP first won power in 1948.

Nelson Mandela, the ANC leader who had spent 27 years in apartheid prisons, became South Africa's first ever Black president.

The focus of the case study in this chapter is on the crucial early years in the history of apartheid South Africa. It begins with the NP triumph in 1948 and ends in 1964, when the state completed its crackdown on opposition and dissent by handing down terms of life imprisonment to Nelson Mandela and other leaders of the ANC. The apartheid system erected during these years amounted to an emphatic denial of the political and economic rights of the majority of the population by a small White minority. The story of this period is of the protest against this discrimination, first by peaceful means and later through armed struggle.

1.1 The origins of apartheid

The origins of apartheid

Note: The origins of apartheid is not included as a bullet point in the *IB History: Rights and Protest* syllabus, and it will therefore not be examined. However, it is indispensable to an understanding of the apartheid system and it is strongly recommended that it is studied by students. A country profile of South Africa and a discussion of its history prior to 1948 can be found on pages 118–128. Before proceeding with the rest of this case study, you may find it useful to gain some basic knowledge of South Africa and its pre-1948 history.

The idea of apartheid is based on one basic assumption about the nature of humankind. This is that the various ethnic groups, or races, that constitute humanity are essentially different from one another. Each ethnicity has a set of common physical characteristics that distinguishes it from other racial groups. The argument continues that there must be a natural hierarchy of the races, because some groups will possess certain biological traits which make them inherently superior to others. The apartheid theorists took it for granted that the evident cultural achievements of the White race were proof enough of its superiority, and that it therefore enjoyed a position right at the apex of the pyramid of the races in South Africa. They similarly believed that Black people had achieved nothing of any note and that they were therefore at the bottom of the racial pile. Other groups, including Coloureds and Indians, occupied the intermediate spaces in the hierarchy. According to the apartheid vision, government should acknowledge the reality of these fundamental racial differences. Fundamental racial inequalities should be reflected in its policies, which should be designed to promote the interests of the superior White race while keeping all of the races separate.

Expressed in this way, the idea of apartheid was in many respects similar to the various **social Darwinist** philosophies (such as Nazism) that were popular in Europe in the first part of the 20th century. What made it different is the way in which it sought justification in **Calvinist** scripture and reasoning as well as through science. According to the Calvinist logic, God created the different races and it was therefore his wish that they should remain separate. It was the destiny of his chosen people, the Afrikaners, to rule in South Africa and ensure that this divine will was enforced.

The manner in which this sense of Afrikaner exceptionalism developed is an issue that has long interested historians. The traditional account identifies its roots in early Afrikaner history, specifically in the experiences of the *trekboers* who lived on the colonial frontier. These pious Dutch colonists, cut off from Europe and therefore isolated from its modern intellectual currents, cultivated an Old Testament world view which led them to draw analogies between their experiences and those of the biblical Israelites. Slavery was a part of their everyday life and so racial inequality was taken for granted. They encountered powerful Xhosa kingdoms, and the ensuing clashes contributed to a growing feeling of animosity

Social Darwinism

A philosophy popular in the late nineteenth and early twentieth centuries, which applied Darwin's theories of natural selection to human society. Social Darwinists argued that "survival of the fittest" is a basic law of human nature and that "superior" races should aim to dominate "inferior" ones.

Calvinism

The austere theology of the sixteenth century religious reformer John Calvin, who argued that humankind is divided between the elect, or those who have been chosen (or pre-destined) by God for salvation, and those who have been condemned to eternal damnation. Calvin advocated a stern and moralizing approach to society and government.

between the Boers and the Black people of the region. Afrikaners grew to equate Africans with the biblical "sons of Ham", condemned by God to be "hewers of wood and drawers of water" (Joshua 9:21). The British decision to abolish slavery in 1833 led some Boers to undertake the famous Great Trek to their "promised land", where they would be free of the interference of the foreign, ungodly British. The fortunate coincidence that many of the lands where they settled had been extensively depopulated as a result of the Mfecane earlier in the century reinforced this sense of divine deliverance. The famous victory of the Boers against the Zulu at the Battle of Blood River in 1838 affirmed that the Boers were indeed "God's chosen people". Following this battle, they made a solemn covenant with God which, if honoured, would allow them to triumph over their enemies. The Blood River victors vowed to bring civilization to Africa in return for God's favour and protection. Their subsequent history – the establishment of the two Boer Republics; the struggle with the British culminating in the South African War; the establishment of the Union of South Africa and the introduction of a segregationist system by Smuts and Hertzog; and finally the NP victory of 1948 – may be interpreted in this way as the slow unfurling of Afrikaner destiny. Apartheid would be the final triumph, the fulfilment of the Blood River pact between God and his chosen people.

TOK connections

Constructing historical myths and reading history backwards

Some historians, most notably André du Toit, have challenged the so-called Calvinist myth about the origins of apartheid. Du Toit argues that the assumption that the 19th-century Boers had a sense of their own special destiny is a fiction generated by Afrikaner nationalists in the 1930s. They did this in order to rally Afrikaners around the cause of nationalism and help the NP gain power. Du Toit points to the activities of the Afrikaner Broederbond (a semi-secret organization with close links to the NP) in organizing the centenary celebrations which commemorated the Great Trek and the Battle of Blood River. Popular re-enactments of these events were used to project the attitudes and values of modern Afrikaner nationalists onto the historical *Voortrekkers*. Du Toit argues that those who took part in the Great Trek were in fact poorly educated frontier farmers with little interest in theology. They were simply escaping the unwelcome interference of a foreign power and had little sense the journey that they were undertaking held any religious significance.

The supposition that Afrikaners had regarded themselves as "God's chosen people" from a very early point in their history, and that the apartheid system was a natural outgrowth of this collective self-image, is a good example of how easy it can be to fall into the trap of "reading history backwards". Considering that du Toit argues that this so-called Calvinist myth is a 1930s Afrikaner construction, it seems quite odd that many pro-British historians of the liberal school (such as CW de Kiewiet) were just as keen as Afrikaner nationalists to lend their authority to this train of thought. The explanation is quite simple, however. The "Calvinist myth" suggests that racial discrimination in South Africa, and ultimately the apartheid system itself, had uniquely Afrikaner roots. However, recent research indicates that the firm foundations for a system of segregation had already been put in place in South Africa by the late 19th century, if not earlier. Moreover, it was not the Afrikaners who were responsible for this, but the British.

Segregation in early practice

There is an alternative view of the origins of racism and segregation in South Africa. This argues that it can be found not in the Calvinist mentality of the Afrikaners but in the character of early British rule in the Cape. The position runs contrary to the frequently held assumption that British administration in South Africa was paternalistic and liberal, the paramount concern being to protect the interests of Africans. The history of the Cape Colony tells a rather different story. Following the establishment of British rule, new urban settlements were built on the far eastern frontier. The largest of these towns were East London and Grahamstown. Contact with the Xhosa was fairly frequent, as Africans travelled to farms and cities in search of work. As time passed, the attitudes of the newly settled British became increasingly racist. Their mindset was reflected in the 1853 constitution of the Cape Colony, which distinguished between two types of people, "civilized" and "uncivilized", without referring specifically to their racial identities. However, the latter category obviously referred to the Xhosa population, who would henceforth be subjected to certain punitive laws. These included the requirement that they should carry passes. These were documents they would be obliged to produce when travelling outside the immediate vicinity of their residence or employment. Passes would be used to regulate the movement of Black people, but could also prevent them from leaving their jobs and seeking work elsewhere. From an early point in time, then, the connection between segregationist laws and economic forces was obvious.

Residential segregation, which was supported by the imposition of curfews on Blacks to prevent them from entering White areas at night, was also practised in municipalities across the colony. In the 1890s, with the rapid expansion of Cape Town, moves towards a more rigid system of segregation were accelerated. Large-scale African migration into the city from as far afield as Mozambique heightened fears among the White population of racial swamping and a deterioration in the standards of sanitation. Following the outbreak of bubonic plague in Cape Town in 1901, legal residential segregation was introduced for the first time with the establishment of the Blacks-only township of Ndabeni, located far away from the city centre.

Racial discrimination was also widely practised in the two Boer Republics in the interior, the Transvaal (officially known as the South African Republic) and the Orange Free State. The British recognized the independence of the republics in the Bloemfontein and Sand River Conventions, but the terms of these republics' treaties forbade them from reviving the institution of slavery. Nonetheless, slavery was still widely practised, and the constitutions of the republics were quite explicit in declaring the supremacy of White over Black. The discovery of gold on the Witwatersrand in 1886 led to the sudden and dramatic transformation of the Transvaal. Johannesburg soon emerged as the largest city in the region following a huge influx of mainly English-speaking White workers into the city. In addition, capital became concentrated in the hands of a small number of fabulously wealthy, mainly English-speaking, mining magnates who became known as the Randlords.

The dispute between the so-called *uitlander* population and the Randlords on the one hand, and the Afrikaner government of Paul Kruger on the other, over the issue of whether to extend the right to vote to all White people in the republic, was one of the main causes of the South African War of 1899–1902. However, one of the few things that all parties agreed upon was the need to ensure the perpetuation of White domination over Black in politics and in the wider economy. The Afrikaner farmers who supported the Kruger government required a ready supply of cheap and pliable African labour. It was also imperative that this workforce was rendered as immobile as possible so that Africans could not leave their farms in search of employment elsewhere. The Randlords obviously shared these objectives with regard to African labour working in their mines. The *uitlanders* sought labour protection against Black competition, an objective that could only be attained through the further erosion of the political rights of Africans. For all of these groups, the best means of securing these goals was through the entrenchment and extension of a system of racial segregation. While the economic effects of the South African War were devastating, the speed of the reconciliation between the British and the Afrikaners in the first decade of the 20th century was remarkable. One of the most important factors in this rapprochement was surely the recognition by all of the parties that the economic development of the region was ultimately dependent on a full political union between all four of South Africa's territories. The logic here was simple. Growth could only be promoted through economic and infrastructural planning on a national level and, crucially, through the rigorous and systematic implementation of a segregationist system. The concord between the recently warring White peoples of South Africa was thus achieved, but at a terrible cost to the non-White majority of the country.

The system of segregation

One of the main objectives of the new South African Party (SAP) government led by Louis Botha and Jan Smuts was to entrench in law a comprehensive system of racial segregation. The Act of Union, officially known as the South Africa Act, itself restricted all voting rights to the minority White population, with the exception of the very small number of Coloureds and Blacks who had previously met the narrow franchise qualification in the Cape Province and Natal. Elsewhere, all non-Whites were excluded from the voters' roll. More legislative measures soon followed. The Mines and Works Act of 1911 reserved all semi-skilled positions in the mining industry for Whites, meaning that Blacks had no option but to accept poorly paid unskilled jobs in the cities or on rural farms. The Natives Land Act of 1913 was a landmark piece of legislation. The forerunner of the homelands system of the apartheid era, the Natives Land Act prohibited Africans, who made up over two-thirds of the population, from owning or renting land anywhere outside certain parcels of territory that would be designated as native reserves. The native reserves made up roughly 7.5% of the total area of the country, and they were to be set aside for the exclusive use of Africans. The areas selected, which were economically marginal to begin with, soon became horribly overcrowded and even more impoverished. The act further stipulated that Africans could reside outside the reserves only on the condition they were employed by Whites. This brought an official end to the practice of rural sharecropping, where White farmers allowed Africans to cultivate some of the farmers' land independently in return for a share of the crop, and deprived many Africans of their livelihoods. In practice, the authorities turned a blind eye to an institution that clearly benefited White landowners, and it was to survive for decades until brought to an abrupt end by the apartheid system after 1948. The Natives (Urban Areas) Act of 1923 was another cornerstone of the segregationist system. It decreed that the cities were principally for the use of the White population, and that any Africans residing there would be required to carry passes. Any Black person found without a pass was liable to be arrested and expelled to the reserves. An Industrial Conciliation Act passed in 1924 allowed for the legal registration of Whites in a trade union, but not their Black counterparts. Blacks were therefore denied the opportunity to negotiate better pay and conditions.

In 1924, the SAP was swept from power and replaced by an NP-led coalition government under JBM Hertzog. Hertzog's approach to segregation, embodied in his "civilized labour" policy, was more strident and ambitious than that of his predecessors. His Wage Act of 1925 permitted the government to instruct private firms to grant preference to White workers in hiring, while the Mines and Works Amendment Act of 1926 further entrenched the colour bar in the mining industry. The economic devastation of the Great Depression led to the merger of Smuts' SAP and Hertzog's NP, and a new United Party (UP) government took office in 1934. The risk that the government might be outflanked by the more radical racialism of Malan's breakaway Gesuiwerde Nasionale Party (also known as the Purified National Party or GNP) led to a spate of further discriminatory legislation later in the decade. The Representation of Natives Act of 1936 removed Africans (but not Coloureds) from the electoral roll in the Cape. It also established an advisory Natives Representative Council, made up largely of traditional African leaders, which lacked any real power. The Native Trust and Land Act, also passed in 1936, extended the area of the native reserves to 13% of the total land area of the country (although this was never achieved in practice), but it also enhanced the power of the authorities to evict Africans who lived illegally in White areas. Finally, the 1937 Native Laws Amendment Act allowed for the stricter enforcement and tighter regulation of the existing pass laws.

The end of the 1930s saw a dramatic resurgence of the Afrikaner nationalist spirit. The semi-secret group the Afrikaner Broederbond, an extreme wing of populist Afrikaner nationalism, worked with the NP to organize centenary celebrations of the Great Trek and the Battle of Blood River. These events involved hundreds of thousands of participants.

By now, the GNP and the Afrikaner Broederbond were supported by the majority of poorer Afrikaners, who felt alienated by the perceived elitism of the UP and its inability to deliver a better standard of living for all Whites. They demanded an even more radical system of racial discrimination and segregation.

South Africa's entry into the Second World War on the side of the allied powers had a major impact on the country. Hertzog resigned from government over Smuts' support of the war, and his subsequent reconciliation with Malan led to the renaming of the nationalists, who now became known as the Herenigde Nasionale Party (Reunited National Party) or simply the National Party (NP). Many Akrikaners felt an affinity with Nazi Germany and this led to a surge in support for the Nationalists and a steady undermining of the Smuts government. Meanwhile, wartime economic demand led to a rapid expansion in manufacturing industry and a sharp increase in the number of urbanized Africans. Squatter camps mushroomed on the outskirts of the major cities as the Black labour force grew in confidence and militancy.

Trade unions were formed in defiance of the law. Foremost among these was the African Mine Workers' Union (AMWU), which organized a strike of nearly 100,000 gold miners in 1946. This was defeated when the police intervened and killed nine protesters. The 1946 miners' strike was a key event for many reasons, not least because it alerted the government to the urgency of the labour situation. Smuts's response was to set up the Fagan Commission. Fagan's report concluded that the tide of African urbanization was irreversible, and that it was in the best economic interest of the country for the government to bring about a partial normalization in the status of Blacks who lived in the cities. His recommendation included a relaxation of the pass laws. The Fagan Report formed the basis of the UP's policy manifesto going into the 1948 general election. This only served to heighten the racial anxieties of many White voters. The NP reacted by forming its own Sauer Commission. This body concluded that the survival of the White race in South Africa was dependent upon the preservation of the country's exclusively White identity. According to Sauer, this could only be achieved through policies designed to reverse the trend of Black urbanization and engineer the complete separation of the races.

The NP's ability to articulate a clear apartheid vision contrasted sharply with the uneasy complexity of the UP's position. It was a message which resonated with many Afrikaner voters in a fearful and embattled White electorate. The party's slogans of swart gevaar ("black peril") and rooi gevaar ("red peril") raised the twin spectres of White cities overwhelmed by migrant Black workers on the one hand, and the civilized Afrikaner way of life threatened by a godless, revolutionary communism on the other. This was enough to see Malan's NP triumph over its UP rival.

1.2 The nature and characteristics of discrimination

Conceptual understanding

Key concept
→ Consequence

Key questions
→ What were the nature and characteristics of discrimination in the apartheid system?

→ How did the apartheid system impact the lives of South Africans?

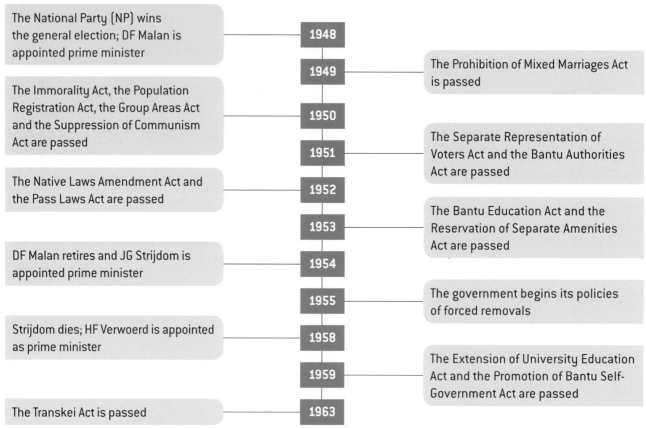

1948 — The National Party (NP) wins the general election; DF Malan is appointed prime minister

1949 — The Prohibition of Mixed Marriages Act is passed

1950 — The Immorality Act, the Population Registration Act, the Group Areas Act and the Suppression of Communism Act are passed

1951 — The Separate Representation of Voters Act and the Bantu Authorities Act are passed

1952 — The Native Laws Amendment Act and the Pass Laws Act are passed

1953 — The Bantu Education Act and the Reservation of Separate Amenities Act are passed

1954 — DF Malan retires and JG Strijdom is appointed prime minister

1955 — The government begins its policies of forced removals

1958 — Strijdom dies; HF Verwoerd is appointed as prime minister

1959 — The Extension of University Education Act and the Promotion of Bantu Self-Government Act are passed

1963 — The Transkei Act is passed

The nature and characteristics of discrimination under apartheid, 1948–64

Following the election in 1948, DF Malan's victorious National Party (NP) issued a spate of laws that became the basis of the system known as apartheid. By 1954, the essential components of the apartheid system had been put in place, and the pace of new legislation slowed somewhat thereafter. Nonetheless, some landmark apartheid laws, such as the Promotion of Bantu Self-Government Act of 1959, were introduced later.

In many ways, apartheid was an extension of the segregationist system that had been instituted by the Botha, Smuts and Hertzog governments before 1948. The segregationist and apartheid systems were similar in some very obvious respects, with their common goal of segregating the races and prioritizing White interests over those of the other groups. In other ways, apartheid was something altogether new. It was more profoundly ideological than its segregationist forerunner, and its laws were implemented with a rigour and enthusiasm that were unprecedented. Apartheid was more than just the passage of stricter racial laws and the closing of legislative loopholes, but it was also about more than these things. Its aim was to create a complete, all-encompassing system of institutionalized racism based on the complete superiority of South Africa's minority White population.

Apartheid developed in two stages. The first of these is commonly known as "petty apartheid", sometimes labelled *baasskap* (literally "boss rule") apartheid. This earlier period of apartheid is commonly associated with the first few years of NP rule when Malan and Strijdom served as prime ministers. The defining character of petty apartheid is often portrayed as negative. Its principal purpose was to ensure the complete domination, economic and political, of White over Black. The two labels most commonly used to describe this period of apartheid offer insights into its nature. The term *baasskap* connotes the brutal subjugation of the Black majority and the firm and decisive manner with which the government dealt with the anti-apartheid opposition. Similarly, the term *petty* is suggestive of the officious and unnecessarily fussy nature of many of the apartheid regulations.

The second and later phase of apartheid, known as "grand apartheid", was initiated by HF Verwoerd in the late 1950s. This version of apartheid was altogether more ideologically sophisticated. At least in theory, grand apartheid marked a departure from the more straightforward racial discrimination of the petty apartheid period. Its main objective was the complete territorial segregation of South Africa, leading ultimately to the full independence of each of its component parts. This would enable the completely separate development of the different peoples, each within their own national jurisdiction. By arguing that Africans would be allowed to achieve their full independence, grand apartheid aimed to establish a moral legitimacy for the apartheid system in the face of an increasingly hostile global community. These ambitions of grand apartheid are again reflected in its label: the word *grand* has connotations of loftiness and nobility.

▲ Apartheid prime ministers: DF Malan, JG Strijdom, HF Verwoerd

Apartheid prime ministers

Daniel Francois Malan was born in Riebeek West in the Western Cape in 1874. A minister in the Dutch Reformed Church, he became involved in politics after the founding of the NP in 1914 and edited the nationalist newspaper, *Die Burger*. He held a number of ministries in Hertzog's pact government, but broke with his mentor to found the GNP in 1934 following Herzog's decision to fuse his party with the SAP. He finally became prime minister in 1948. A divisive figure who was known for his moralising and unyielding approach, Malan finally retired from active politics in 1954.

Johanned Gerhardus Strijdom – although born in 1893 in the Cape – was known as the "Lion of the North" because of his domination of the NP in Transvaal. He was part of the Malanite split in 1934 and was appointed Minister for Agriculture in 1948. Regarded as radical and uncompromising even by the standards of the NP, he was elected leader after Malan's retirement and served as prime minister until his death in 1958.

Dr Hendrik Frensch Verwoerd was born in Holland in 1901 but moved to South Africa as a child. A brilliant young scholar, he studied psychology in Germany, Britain and the US before returning to lecture at the University of Stellenbosch. Verwoerd was an outspoken critic of the fusion government's decision to allow the immigration of German Jews fleeing Nazi persecution in the 1930s and he soon became active in nationalist politics, editing the pro-NP *Die Transvaler* newspaper. A hugely controversial Native Affairs Minister under Malan and Strijdom, he was chosen as prime minister in 1958 and became known as the "architect of apartheid". Highly charismatic, and more amiable than either of his predecessors, Verwoerd was stabbed to death by a mentally deranged parliamentary messenger, Dimitri Tsafendas, in Cape Town in 1966.

TOK connections

The problems with constructing historical categories

The tendency among historians is to neatly divide apartheid into the categories of petty apartheid and grand apartheid. Petty apartheid is assumed to be typical of the earlier period of NP rule, and it is often thought of as fussy and repressive. Typical petty apartheid laws include the Immorality Act and the Reservation of Separate Amenities Act. Grand apartheid is assumed to have been planned and implemented at a slightly later point in time. The classic grand apartheid law would be the Promotion of Bantu Self-Government Act. It can no doubt be useful to think in terms of petty apartheid and grand apartheid in order to better understand the dual nature of the system, in the sense that it was about racial oppression as well as racial separation, and how it evolved with different emphases in different periods. However, the problem with dividing apartheid into two distinct categories is that you run the risk of generalizing and oversimplifying a complex phenomenon. This can be an impediment to acquiring a more nuanced understanding of apartheid. In truth, all of the apartheid laws incorporated elements of both petty and grand apartheid. The long-term goal of fostering the separate development of the races was implicit in the "pettiest" of the petty apartheid laws. Similarly, the notion that separate development would lead ultimately to the equality of all of the independent "nations" of South Africa was clearly nothing more than an apartheid fiction. Each aspect of the system was obviously designed to perpetuate the political and economic domination of White over Black. Some laws very obviously straddled both of the categories. For instance, the Bantu Education Act qualifies as petty apartheid in the sense that it abandoned Black children to an education that was woefully substandard and inferior. At the same time, it can also be described as grand apartheid in that its purpose was, at least ostensibly, to allow Black people to evolve at their own pace and in their own communities so that they might, in the fullness of time, develop their own, self-governing political systems.

Source skills

A cartoon by Jack Leyden, published in the *Natal Daily News* in 1949.

'THERE'S NONE SO BLIND...' (1949)

▲ The figure on the right of the bench is DF Malan.

First question, part b – 2 marks

What is the message of the cartoon with regards to the introduction of apartheid by Malan's government?

ATL Research and communication skills

As you read through this chapter, identify the various ways in which the lives of ordinary non-White South Africans were affected by apartheid laws, and record this information under each of the five categories identified in the spider diagram below. You can also include the effects of some of the pre-apartheid segregationist laws, such as the colour bar which prevented Blacks from seeking skilled and semi-skilled jobs in the mining industry.

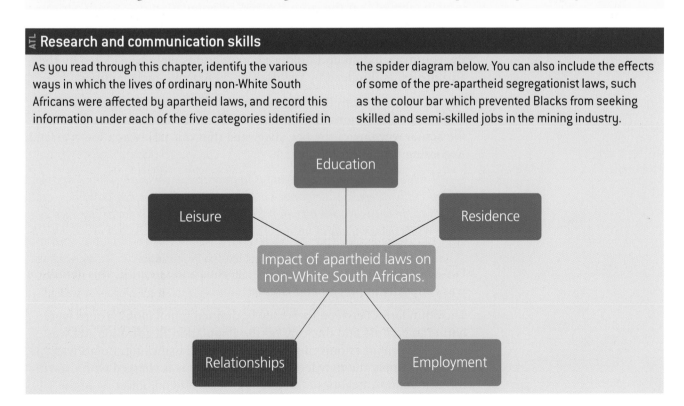

Division and classification of the population

The official division and classification of the different racial groups in South Africa was an essential prerequisite for the enforcement of other forms of apartheid legislation. It is therefore unsurprising that the Population Registration Act of 1950, which classified the entire population by race, was one of the first laws to be passed by the new NP government.

During the earlier segregation period, the way in which people identified their race was a relatively straightforward matter. A person born into a "White community" would simply be considered White, even if their skin was darker than average. Situations like this were fairly common in South Africa, a country with a long history of **miscegenation**. Generations previously, the light-skinned offspring of master-slave relationships would have often been accepted as part of the "White" family. Indeed, it was rumoured that Betsie Verwoerd, wife of the apartheid prime minister Verwoerd, was herself of mixed race ancestry. For the racially obsessed ideologues in the NP government, however, the obvious anomalies thrown up by this state of affairs, where, for instance, Whites were sometimes "darker" than Coloureds were simply unacceptable. New laws were required.

Miscegenation

Sexual relationships between persons from different racial groups.

The Population Registration Act provided for the creation of a national population register. Each citizen was defined according to the racial group to which he or she belonged. The classification was based on biological rather than cultural factors. Once an individual's race was determined, it was recorded in their official identity documents. A code representing the racial group to which they belonged was also included in their ID number. The act further decreed that South Africa's population was made up of three basic racial groups: White, Coloured and Bantu (apartheid parlance for "Black African"). The government initially denied that the country's Indian population was South African at all, and it was only in 1959 that this group was officially classified as an "Asian" component of the Coloured race. For the most part, however, the country's Indian and Coloured populations were considered by the authorities, and indeed by themselves, as separate racial entities.

The act set out to carefully define each of the country's racial groups according to common physical and intellectual characteristics. However the actual wording of the law suggested that this task was a fool's errand. According to the legislation:

> [A white person is someone who] is in appearance obviously white – and not generally accepted as Coloured – or who is generally accepted as White – and is not obviously Non-White, provided that a person shall not be classified as a White person if one of his natural parents has been classified as a Coloured person or a Bantu.

For a new law that was supposedly rigorous and scientific, this definition was comically imprecise and circular.

The boundaries between these newly-defined populations groups were bound to be fluid and unclear. Yet the Population Registration Act was enforced with an astonishing vigour. A Race Classification Board was created to apply the new legislation. This body was charged with drawing up further sub-categories of different groups, and adjudicating in the

many cases where an individual's racial category was disputed, either by the individual themselves or by the authorities. It embraced the former task with considerable gusto, creating a grand total of seven sub-categories of the Coloured race: Cape Coloured, Malay, Griqua, Chinese, Other Asiatic and Other Coloured.

Naturally, many people who had previously been considered Coloured now sought official reclassification as White. This was so that they could take advantage of the political rights and economic benefits that only the country's White minority could enjoy. In addition, members of the public would sometimes report individuals whose racial classification they believed to be suspect. In order to deal with such cases, the Race Classification Board introduced a number of bizarre and often humiliating measures that would act as indicators of a person's racial category. Some of these were tests of linguistic proficiency, but they also included such indignities as the taking of skull measurements, as well as the infamous "pencil test". This involved sticking a pencil into a person's hair; if the pencil dropped, the hair was deemed to be sufficiently straight for the person to be classified as White. However, final decisions were often taken on an altogether more subjective and arbitrary basis. Ayesha Hoorzook, a South African Indian woman whose interview is given as Source A on page 28, had two children: the first was classified as Indian, the second as Cape Malay. One unfortunate individual, Vic Wilkinson, was reclassified not once but twice: from Coloured to White and then from White back to Coloured.

The Population Classification Act had many tragic consequences for ordinary South Africans. Within the same family, certain genetic traits can skip generations only to resurface later. With the introduction of the act, members of the same mono-racial family could find themselves on different sides of the classification divide. A child born to two White parents but with a slightly darker skin could be classified as Coloured under the new law. The implications of this were profound, as later apartheid laws made it difficult, if not impossible, for people from different racial groups to live together. What is more, the social stigma attached to such cases became so strong that there were stories of Afrikaner families abandoning babies who were born with frizzy hair or dark complexions. For children with one parent classified as White and the other belonging to another racial group (miscegenation was still technically legal if a couple had managed to marry before the passage of the Prohibition of Mixed Marriages Act of 1949), there could only be one outcome. The government's obsession with preserving the purity of the White race meant that the child would invariably be classified as non-White.

As mentioned above, cases where a person would be compulsorily reclassified by the Race Classification Board were not at all uncommon. This would involve a person being downgraded from White to Coloured, or from Coloured to Black. Quite apart from the humiliation and indignity involved in this process, a person's prospects in the brave new world of apartheid were significantly harmed as a result of reclassification. The Race Classification Board was so powerful that a person's fate could hinge on a bureaucratic whim.

TOK connections

History and ethics: the moral responsibility of the individual

History students often ask themselves the question: what would I have done if I had been there at the time? If I had been a White South African, would I have been brave enough to speak out against the evils of the apartheid system, or would I have just gone along with or even been part of it? Apart from some notable exceptions such as the White communists, the women of the Black Sash organization, and Progressive Party leader Helen Suzman (see page 126), it seems that few White South Africans during the early apartheid era had the courage or conviction to stand up to the system. With this in mind, would it be fair to hold such a privileged community to account for not doing more to challenge apartheid? Why were so many Whites complicit in a system that oppressed and brutalized the majority of their compatriots? One answer may be found in the famous experiment conducted by Stanley Milgram at Yale University in 1963. Milgram found that when confronted with a choice between complying with the morally uncongenial instructions of a superior or standing on principle and refusing to comply with the order, most people will invariably reject the latter, more difficult course of action. The decision to go with the flow and not put oneself or one's family at risk was obviously made easier by the fact that Whites were the main material beneficiaries of the system.

Whatever the case, it can be argued that it is inappropriate for the historian to pass ethical judgment on the past. This is because we are all the product of the values of our own time, and the historian, from the point of view of the present, will find it difficult to understand or find sympathy with the moral climate of the past. Racial discrimination was a widely accepted norm in 1950s South Africa, and maybe it shouldn't come as a surprise that many Whites failed to see that there was anything intrinsically wrong with a system based upon the same racist assumptions.

The same logic also applies to the historian. The moral environment of today affects what we choose to research and how we interpret our findings. Does this mean that it is impossible for the historian to be truly objective?

Segregation of populations and amenities

Three of the most important apartheid laws governing the separation of populations and amenities were the Group Areas Act of 1950, the Bantu Authorities Act of 1951 and the Promotion of Bantu Self-Government Act of 1959. These laws were designed to achieve the complete residential separation of South Africa's different population groups. The Group Areas Act dealt with residential segregation in the cities, while the Bantu Authorities Act and the Promotion of Bantu Self-Government Act addressed the matter of the native reserves or the homelands, rural areas where Black people were allowed to reside permanently.

The three laws outlined in the box above are covered in more detail in the later sections of this chapter on forced removals, the creation of townships and the Bantustan system. This section covers other aspects of the segregation of South Africa's populations and amenities.

The Prohibition of Mixed Marriages Act and the Immorality Act

The Prohibition of Mixed Marriages Act and the Immorality Act were designed to promote the separation of the races by outlawing sexual relations and procreation between the different populations. To the apartheid mindset, miscegenation was closely associated with racial degeneration. It therefore had to be abolished. At the same time, one of the more peculiar features of the apartheid state was its obsession with public morality, a factor which disposed it to intruding into the private lives of its citizens. It was especially concerned with the field of human behaviour where contact between racial groups was at its most intimate: sexual relations.

The Prohibition of Mixed Marriages Act of 1949 was the first major law passed by the NP government. The act made it illegal for White South Africans to marry people of other races. The law was introduced despite the fact that the "problem" of mixed marriages was a tiny one: only 75 were recorded in the 3 years prior to the act's introduction. The Prohibition of Mixed Marriages Act was supplemented by the Immorality Act of 1950, which banned all extra-marital sexual relations between Whites and non-Whites. Under existing segregation-era laws, any extra-marital sexual relationships between Whites and Blacks were illegal, but this was now extended to cover sexual relations between Whites and other racial groups as well. Rather tellingly, the law failed to cover sexual relations between people of different non-White races. Clearly, the government only concerned itself with the purity of the White race.

The manner in which the authorities enforced the new laws was both intrusive and sordid. The police would react to a tip-off, typically from a neighbour, and stake out the home of the suspect. They would then burst into the house in the middle of the night, smashing down doors in the process, in the hope of catching the unfortunate couple together in bed, ideally *in flagrante*. The home would often be ransacked and items such as underwear seized for use as prosecution evidence. Brought before a court, the guilty couple would be handed down sizeable fines and prison terms. Even when it came to the punishments, the basic inequality of the apartheid system was still very much in evidence: Blacks convicted of having sexual relations with Whites would inevitably find themselves hit with far harsher punishments than their partners.

The Reservation of Separate Amenities Act

The Reservation of Separate Amenities Act, passed in 1953, is often seen as the epitome of the petty apartheid system. As its name implies, it provided for the strict segregation by race of all public amenities. Many public services, such as buses, trains, toilets and hospitals, had already been segregated to some extent before the advent of apartheid. This segregation was now taken much further. Separate entrances and service counters were made mandatory in buildings such as shops and post offices, and there were completely separate waiting rooms and stretches of platform for use by different races at train stations. Parks and other recreational facilities, including beaches and swimming pools, were designated for use by one race only. Hotels and restaurants that were located in city centres and other mainly White areas were instructed to refuse admittance to non-Whites. The separation was so thorough that it extended to such minor amenities as public benches and water fountains. Signs informing the public that a facility was reserved for "Whites only" were soon ubiquitous, and became a notorious feature of the civic landscape of apartheid South Africa.

Source skills

A photograph of a "White Persons Only" sign at a beach near Cape Town, taken during the apartheid era.

First question, part b – 2 marks

What conclusions can you draw about segregation and discrimination in apartheid South Africa from the evidence in the photograph?

Members of other racial groups risked arrest and imprisonment if they used Whites-only facilities. Naturally, the amenities reserved for Whites were the best available. This distinguished the new law from the segregation-era legislation, which allowed for the segregation of amenities as long as the amenities provided for the different races were equal in quality. The Group Areas Act of 1950 decreed that city centres were Whites-only for residence purposes. In these areas, where many Blacks nonetheless continued to work, the government could argue that there was no need to provide decent, or even any, public services for non-Whites, because they had no right to reside there permanently and could use their own amenities when they returned home to the townships. At the same time, the rapid growth of the townships, together with the fact that these areas were planned and constructed with little thought for the convenience and welfare of Africans, meant that amenities in these areas were extremely rudimentary.

It was obviously demeaning for non-White South Africans to have to use separate amenities, especially when those facilities were of a grossly inferior standard. In this sense, the Reservation of Amenities Act symbolized the dramatic decline in their status under apartheid. Yet it also influenced their lives in other, more subtle ways. It was no longer as easy for Whites and non-Whites to cultivate friendships, as they could no longer occupy the same civic spaces. Urban amenities to which Africans had been previously been given limited access, such as public libraries, theatres and concert halls, were now out of bounds. This had the effect of limiting the educational and cultural horizons of Africans.

Source skills

Source A

Interview with Ayesha Hoorzook, a South African of Indian ancestry who grew up during apartheid. She works as a history teacher and tour guide in the Apartheid Museum in Johannesburg.

I knew that as a child, we were not allowed to do many things, go to many places that other people could. But I thought that was normal, whatever [amenities] was available for us was meant for us – I never really questioned it …

I can recall an incident of going to the zoo – in those days, first of all, blacks were not allowed to go. Later on, the law was relaxed a little bit and certain days were allocated to blacks only … For non-whites, there would be public buses going to the zoo, but there would be five seats reserved at the back of the bus for non-white people, only five seats. The entire bus would be empty, but you could not use a seat anywhere else on the bus. Often by the time the bus comes to where we are, there are already [non-white people] on the bus and we'd let the bus go by … Then we'd get to [the zoo], and by this stage half the day is gone … my father starts looking at his clock, and he says we have to start having to go, there are so many non-whites at the zoo today and the chances are the buses are going to be very full.

http://overcomingapartheid.msu.edu/video.php?id=65-24F-D6

Source B

A cartoon by Abe Berry, published in *The Star* newspaper in Johannesburg, 1966.

First question, part a – 3 marks

According to Source A, in what ways were the lives of non-White South Africans affected by the separation of amenities?

First question, part b – 2 marks

What is the message of the cartoon in Source B?

Second question – 4 marks

With reference to its origin, purpose and content, assess the value and limitations of Source A for historians studying the impact of the separation of populations and amenities in apartheid South Africa.

The Pass Laws Act

Despite the misleading name of this key piece of apartheid legislation, the Pass Laws were yet another means of enforcing the segregation of populations. The Natives (Abolition of Passes and Co-ordination of Documents) Act of 1952, more commonly known as the Pass Laws Act, was a misnomer. Rather than abolishing passes, this new law replaced the existing passbooks with more comprehensive documents that Africans would be required to carry on their person at all times.

The new documents were 96-page booklets that were officially known as "reference books". These new passes were incredibly detailed, and contained such information as the person's employment record, tax payments, and reports of any encounters the person may have had with the police. It was made a criminal offence for a Black person not to present his or her new passbook on demand, at any time. A complicated system of special permits was built into this new system; these permits naturally had to be stamped in the reference book. For example, a permit was required if any Black person wished to travel to the city from a rural area. Once he or she arrived, a further permit had to be obtained from the police within a period of 72 hours. This would allow the person to remain in the city to look for work, but again only for a fixed period of time. If it proved impossible to find employment within this time limit, he or she would either have to return to the countryside or remain and break the law. Considering that these people had come to the city out of economic necessity in the first place, many had little choice but to remain. Police checks were so regular that it was rarely long before they were arrested and brought before a magistrate. Unable to pay the fine handed down by the court, many were imprisoned, typically for several months, before being sent back to their villages. As a result of this, significant numbers of South Africa's Black population, mainly the poorest and the most desperate, were criminalized by the system. Those who escaped arrest constantly had to run the gauntlet of police intimidation.

The reference books were a menace even for those Africans whose documentation was in order. The police would often stop and harass them on the pretext that they needed to inspect their passes. The system was also quite humiliating: any White person, even a child, was entitled to stop a Black person in a White area and demand to see the person's reference book.

The Pass Laws Act obviously permitted the authorities to enforce the segregation of the Black and White communities more effectively through the strict regulation of the movement of Blacks in the cities. However, they also served a secondary purpose, by allowing the government to extend its powers of surveillance over the Black population. The Pass Laws Act was a repressive instrument that could be used against African politicians. It permitted the police to intimidate ANC activists by conducting night-time raids on their residences, simply on the grounds that there may be someone staying there who did not have the right documents. The issue of reference books was also used as a weapon against the regime, however. Many of the most effective anti-government demonstrations used the Pass Laws Act as a means of channelling popular anger, and occasionally as a means of actual protest. The ANC's Defiance Campaign of 1952 was launched in the wake of the introduction of the new passes. This campaign frequently involved volunteers courting police arrest by attempting to enter a location without their reference books. The mass action called by the ANC and Pan Africanist Congress (PAC), which led to the Sharpeville massacre, required protesters to present themselves at police stations without their reference books. Following the massacre, ANC leader Chief Luthuli burned his reference book in a powerful act of protest at what had happened.

Other laws and policies governing the segregation of populations

The two laws described here were relatively minor pieces of apartheid legislation, but they also contributed to the separation of amenities and populations.

The Bantu Building Workers Act was passed in 1951 to clarify existing regulations pertaining to separation of the races in employment. Under existing laws, because of the colour bar, skilled and semi-skilled jobs were reserved for Whites, so the skilled labour required for the construction of homes in the Blacks-only townships would have to be performed by Whites. The new law confirmed that Africans were barred from skilled work in the building industry in general, but made an exception for skilled building work in residential areas from which Whites were excluded. Rather than a relaxation of existing labour laws, the 1951 act was therefore a means of reinforcing the residential segregation of the races.

The Prevention of Illegal Squatting Act of 1951 permitted the government forcibly to remove Africans who had formally settled in urban areas that were to be designated as Whites-only under the terms of the Group Areas Act (see below). However, it also allowed the authorities to extend further the separation of populations in the countryside by bringing a definitive end to the practice of sharecropping. This involved White farmers allowing Blacks to live, illegally, on their unused land and cultivate it in return for a share of the harvest. The 1913 Natives Land Act had made sharecropping illegal, but such were the benefits accruing to White landowners, especially in agriculturally marginal areas, that the authorities (for the most part at least) turned a blind eye to the practice. The 1951 act allowed the government to detain Africans residing in rural areas and resettle them in specially designated zones, typically in or around the townships, or simply to dump them in the native reserves. It obviously put an end to the problem of Blacks and Whites living in close proximity on farms in the countryside, but it removed the problem of rural squatting only by adding to urban squatting.

Apartheid governments also promoted the separation of populations in the cities by continuing the segregation-era practice of housing Black mining workers in compounds. The mineral revolution of the late 19th century had resulted in an influx into the cities of Black migrant labour from across the subcontinent. These mining workers were housed in enormous barracks-like fenced compounds, isolated from the outside world; hundreds of men would sleep in dormitories of simple concrete bunks. Their families were not allowed to come with them and had to remain in the native reserves or in neighbouring states such as Mozambique or Basutoland (Lesotho), leading to a profound gender imbalance in those areas. The mining compounds were segregated by ethnicity and tribal rivalries were encouraged by the authorities.

Forced removals and the creation of townships:
The Group Areas Act

The policies of forced removals and the creation and expansion of townships would not have been possible without the Group Areas Act of 1950. This single piece of legislation was so important that Malan called it "the essence of apartheid". It was designed to bring about the total residential segregation of the different racial groups in urban areas, specifically by removing non-Whites from inner city areas that would henceforth be designated as Whites-only areas.

The Group Areas Act was based on the racist premise that Africans were a rural people in their natural state, and that their permanent exposure to city life would lead to a breakdown in the social order. The assumption that Africans should have no place in the cities formed the basis of the NP's Sauer Report, commissioned in 1947. This report concluded that all Africans belonged in the native reserves, and that their presence in and around urban areas was to be tolerated only insofar as they remained economically useful to White people. City centres and the inner suburbs would now be the preserve of White residents, while Africans would be confined to vast townships on the far outskirts of the city, where they could live in a manner appropriate to their lowly status in the apartheid hierarchy. In theory, they would be permitted to reside in these sprawling settlements only temporarily, before being returned to the reserves once they ceased to be economically active.

Before 1955, the Group Areas Act was mainly used to target South Africa's Indian and Coloured populations. Many Indians, in particular, were traders who owned small businesses in the city centres. These were now forced to close. Their removal was welcomed by their White business competitors, many of whom had been enthusiastic supporters of the introduction of the legislation. Eventually, one in four Coloured people were forced to move under the terms of the act, as well one in six Indians, typically to outer suburbs that already had established Coloured or Indian communities. The situation regarding Africans was rather more complicated. It was illegal for Africans to own land or property outside of the native reserves. However, the government had no intention of sending them far away from the cities because their labour was needed for the urban economy. Rather, the plan was to relocate them to new or existing townships, far from the city centres and inner suburbs but still close enough for a daily commute to the workplace. However, the state would find it a challenge to uproot people to new areas where they had no legal right to own property.

It was inevitable, though, that the authorities would soon turn their attention to the matter. Many towns across South Africa had so-called *onderdorpe*, or mixed-population areas. Major cities also contained "Black spots", or mainly African enclaves, situated in the midst of White suburbs. To deal with the problem, the government passed the Natives Resettlement Act in 1954 and the Group Areas Development Act in 1955. These laws complemented the 1950 Groups Areas Act and armed the government with the bureaucratic machinery that would finally allow it to carry out its policies of the forced urban resettlement of Africans. The authorities were now permitted to remove Blacks forcibly from the magisterial district of Johannesburg. The creation of the Natives Resettlement Board, a body established to coordinate forced removals from the western inner suburbs of the city, meant that the authorities were now free to focus on the most celebrated of all the Black spots: Sophiatown.

The destruction of Sophiatown

Sophiatown was a predominantly Black neighbourhood located just to the west of the city of Johannesburg. It was surrounded by working class Afrikaner areas. Despite suffering from the typical inner-city problems of crime and violence, the suburb was an especially vibrant place. It was also an apartheid anomaly. Unusually, many Africans had acquired freeholds in the district prior to the Natives Land Act of 1913. In addition, the area was never brought directly under the control of the municipality of Johannesburg. These two factors meant that it was the one of the few remaining parts of the country where Africans could still legally own property.

▲ Forced removal from Sophiatown, 1955

Sophiatown was an obvious target for the government for other reasons too. The suburb was packed with illegal drinking establishments, called shebeens, and music halls. A creative and cultural hub, it produced such legendary figures of the South African jazz scene as Miriam Makeba and Hugh Masekela. It was also a centre of intellectual and political activity. The ANC frequently held meetings and rallies there, and many anti-apartheid activists were residents of the area. The destruction of Sophiatown would strike a blow against Black urban culture, and against the liberation movement.

In January 1955, the authorities initiated the Western Areas Removal Scheme and the forced removal of Sophiatown's residents began. Armed police were moved into the area in anticipation of the inevitable political backlash. One by one, residents were forced to load their belongings onto trucks before being transported to the Meadowlands area far to the south, part of what would become the vast township of Soweto. Even as the residents were evicted, bulldozers stood by to destroy their homes. Despite a valiant campaign to save Sophiatown, led by the Anglican priest Trevor Huddleston and involving leading anti-apartheid activists such as Nelson Mandela and Ruth First, the entire suburb was razed to the ground. By the end of the decade, 65,000 residents had been relocated. The entire area was replaced with a new Afrikaner suburb that the authorities christened *Triomf*, the Afrikaans word for "triumph".

▲ A child plays amidst the rubble in Sophiatown

The Sophiatown pattern of forced resettlement was repeated in countless other "Black spots" across the nation. After the removals had been carried out, those being resettled were made to report to a Native Resettlement Board in their new location. Here they would be given some basic provisions before being dumped outside their new homes. The speed with which the relocations were executed and the sheer numbers involved meant that the resettlement areas soon became hopelessly overcrowded. Homes were typically small and very cramped. Known as "matchboxes" because of their basic design, they were constructed in monotonous rows, one after the other, with no inside toilets and no running water. Anywhere between 7 and 14 people would be housed in a single dwelling.

Over a very short period of time, these resettlement areas were transformed into the sprawling townships that were to become the dominant feature of South Africa's Black urban landscape in the 1950s. The townships were not an entirely new phenomenon, however. Blacks had begun to cluster on the margins of the big cities following the advent of segregated municipal zoning at the turn of the century,

Rows of "matchbox" houses in Soweto. The Johannesburg skyline can be seen in the distance

Communication and thinking skills

Go to: overcomingapartheid.msu.edu/multimedia.php?id=65-259-6.

Watch the video clip of the interview with Mary Burton and Betty Davenport from 23 November 2005. Betty Davenport was a White anti-apartheid activist in the Eastern Cape and recalls the forced removals of Black people living in the rural Eastern Cape in the 1960s.

As you read on, try to think of the ways in which the experiences of the Black people of the Eastern Cape are similar to those of the residents of Sophiatown in Johannesburg.

and the growth of these settlements was accelerated after the Natives (Urban Areas) Act was passed in 1923. However, their populations exploded in the 1950s as a direct consequence of the forced removals, resulting in the huge townships that we know today. The largest and most famous of these is Soweto, with a population of nearly 2 million.

The policy of forced removals and the resulting creation and expansion of the townships had a major impact on the lives of millions of Black South Africans. The townships were located many miles away from city centres or the Whites-only suburbs where the majority of Black people were employed. Many were now faced with a long and expensive daily commute to work. Due to hasty construction and the absence of adequate planning, there was a lack of even the most basic of amenities in the townships. Sanitation was poor, as was infrastructure. There were few, if any, hospitals, clinics or police stations. Providing education for Africans was never a priority for the government, so schools were few in number and overcrowded. With police thin on the ground, criminal activity was rife as *tsotsis*, or urban gangsters, became a common sight on township streets. The disruption to traditional modes of behaviour brought about by relocation acted as a further stimulus to criminal behaviour. Old neighbourhoods had been obliterated, and so too had the established social norms and support networks that had been fostered in these communities. People suffered from a profound loss of identity. Compounding all of these problems was another new phenomenon: the presence of tens of thousands of squatters who, having been denied the right to formal resettlement under the government scheme, simply set up camp on the periphery of the townships, stretching scarce resources and services still further. All in all, about 3.5 million Black people across the nation were uprooted from their homes and forced to live miserably in these overcrowded, crime-infested townships.

The Group Areas Act did not quite confine all Africans to the townships. Even after the act was brought into effect, Black people who had been born and employed in the same city sometimes retained the right to live in municipal areas. However, the Native Laws Amendment Act, passed in 1952, imposed severe restrictions on the right of permanent residence in the cities. Black people could continue to live in a city only if they had been born there and employed there for more than 15 years,

or been in continuous employment for more 10 years. This had the obvious and immediate effect of excluding young Africans who were new to employment. Another exception was made for some Black women who were allowed to live in the homes of their White employers on the condition that they were engaged in full-time domestic service. However, the families of maids and nannies were prevented from living with them, exacerbating the problems of separation and dislocation that already beleaguered African families and communities. As with other apartheid legislation, exceptions were allowed to the Group Areas Act, but only as long as they benefited the White population. They served, once again, to highlight the hypocrisy of the system.

Segregation of education

The Bantu Education Act

The passage of the Bantu Education Act of 1953 was another landmark moment in the development of the apartheid system. This new law made it mandatory for schools to admit children from one racial group only, and brought the education of Africans under the direct control of the Native Affairs Department, headed by the apartheid hardliner HF Verwoerd. This new system was to be used instead of involving the Ministry of Education, which from now would be responsible only for the education of other races. As a result of this switch, the new system of education went much further than simply preventing children of different races from attending the same schools. It dispensed with the idea of a single educational model for all South African children and replaced this with a system of entirely separate school boards for each of the races. Each would now have its own distinct, and very different, curriculum. Curricular content would be tailored to what the authorities believed was appropriate to the intellectual capacity and practical requirements of each racial group in apartheid South Africa.

Under the Bantu Education Act, the education received by Black children would be grossly inferior to that enjoyed by Whites. The curriculum for Africans would have almost no academic content. Beyond equipping Black children with extremely basic levels of literacy and numeracy, it was designed to furnish Africans with the rudimentary technical skills that would allow them to perform domestic service for Whites or, alternatively, sell their unskilled labour to the mining and manufacturing industries. Under the new system, Black children would attend school in daily three-hour shifts. More often than not, books and other essential equipment were non-existent. Teachers and students would often write on the ground using sticks. The ratio of government spending on a White child compared with a Black child was about 7:1. With the enormous differential in the salaries paid to teachers in Black and White schools, many of the more talented Black teachers left the profession altogether. It is estimated that nearly 85% of all Black teachers had no professional qualification at all. Unsurprisingly, many parents simply took their children out of school. Attempts were made through Bantu education to foster a stronger sense of tribal identity. The medium of instruction was to be in mother tongue throughout primary school, with a gradual transition to Afrikaans and English thereafter. This stipulation further angered many Black parents, who believed that the hallmark of a decent education was instruction using English.

The brainchild of Verwoerd, the Bantu Education Act reconciled some of the basic philosophical imperatives of *baasskap* and grand apartheid. The new Bantu curriculum was designed to prepare Africans for a life of economic servitude to their White masters. It thus fulfilled the aim of promoting an institutional framework of White domination over Black. At the same time, the education received by Blacks would allow them to develop at their own, naturally slower, intellectual pace. It would be pitched to the ability levels of Africans, which the authorities believed to be innately low, as well as the sort of lowly professional status that Blacks could expect under the apartheid system. However, the very fact that Africans had now been given a separate model of education, and one that stressed the importance of their tribal identity, meant that each of the Black peoples of South Africa could now begin to evolve separately, apart both from one another and from the other races in the country. Bantu education was thus very much part of the policy of separate development, the core idea of the system of grand apartheid.

Despite the many forms of racial discrimination, some young Africans had enjoyed access to a quality education prior to 1953. This was courtesy of the many mission schools that were found right across the country, mainly in rural areas. These had been established by European missionary groups, mostly in the 19th century. All of them had been partially funded by the government. After 1953, they were informed that they should submit to the new system of Bantu education and come under the control of Verwoerd's ministry. If they resisted, their funding would end. Faced with this choice, many of these schools opted to close.

Source skills

Nelson Mandela, writing in his autobiography, *The Long Walk to Freedom* **(1995).**

> Under the [Bantu Education] Act … African teachers were not allowed to criticise the government or any school authority. It was "intellectual baasskap", a way of institutionalising inferiority. Dr Hendrik Verwoerd, the minister for Bantu education, explained that "education must teach and train people in accordance with their opportunities in life". His meaning was that Africans did not and would not have any opportunities, therefore, why educate them? "There is no place for the Bantu in the European community above the level of certain forms of labour," he said. In short, Africans should be trained to be menial workers, to be in a position of perpetual subordination to the white man.

First question, part a – 3 marks

According to the source, why did the apartheid government introduce the system of Bantu education?

The system of Bantu education now became the only one available to Africans. The philosophy that lay behind it was deeply paradoxical. It stressed the importance to African children of maintaining, or rediscovering, their traditional identities of village and tribe, which Afrikaner nationalists argued had been corrupted by the rootless cosmopolitanism of the city. This implied that traditional African cultures were of value. At the same time, Bantu education espoused a Christian nationalist message, one that stood in stark contrast to the liberal Christian philosophy of the mission schools. Christian nationalism was paternalistic and patronizing, and deeply demeaning of African culture. Bantu education taught young Black people that they and their communities were backward, and that they were incapable of making any progress in life outside the narrow confines of their tribal world. The best they could hope for was that they could be of service to their own people in the native reserves, or of temporary use to South Africa's White community.

▲ An overcrowded classroom in a government school for Africans under the "system" of Bantu education

In the short term, the introduction of the Bantu Education Act drew a fierce and determined response from African nationalists. Perhaps misguidedly, the ANC announced a permanent boycott of the new system, even though it lacked the resources required to provide any sort of a credible educational alternative for Black children. The boycott began in April 1955 and was only a partial success. Verwoerd had threatened to shut any school that supported the boycott, and permanently to exclude any children who did not attend school. The result was that many parents were frightened of taking part in the boycott. Nonetheless, Verwoerd was sufficiently rattled by the determination of the ANC's response. In a small victory for the liberation moment, he ordered the new syllabus to be redrafted in order to tone down the emphasis on tribalism. The ANC, faced with a choice of some education or none at all, chose to end the boycott.

One of the most powerful and influential critiques of Bantu education was elaborated by Steve Biko. Biko argued that Bantu education, and the apartheid system of which it was the cornerstone, was designed as a means of denigrating and dehumanizing Black people. His response was the Black Consciousness Movement, with its slogan "Black is beautiful", as a way of combatting the resulting psychological self-hatred. Despite Biko's efforts, the political and social fall-out of Bantu Education was immense. Across the country, young people lost hope and became desperate. Many turned to crime. Whole communities were condemned to permanent impoverishment, as any slim hopes of material advancement through education evaporated. Bantu education resulted in a lost generation.

Steve Biko

Born in the Eastern Cape in 1946, Steve Biko was attracted to the Africanism of the PAC from an early age. He became involved in its armed wing, Poqo, while still a teenager. After his expulsion from high school for political activity he studied medicine at the University of Natal and joined the multi-racial National Union of South African Students (NUSAS). Biko broke away from NUSAS in to found the Blacks-only South African Students Association (SASO), arguing that Africans needed to foster a spirit of self-reliance free from the influence and interference of other racial groups. SASO later formed the basis of Biko's Black Consciousness Movement (BCM). With the ANC and PAC crushed, Biko and the BCM took the fight to the apartheid authorities in the 1970s, leading the protests that climaxed in the Soweto Uprising in 1976. In 1977 Biko was beaten to death while in police custody. Minister of Justice Jimmy Kruger claimed that Biko had died while on hunger strike, and cynically remarked that his death had "left him cold".

The youth was only partially educated, if at all. The slogan "no education before liberation" became popular in the townships, and levels of absenteeism skyrocketed. Young people who did attend school were psychologically brutalized by the experience. It is possible to link Bantu education with the explosion of indiscriminate violence in the townships in the 1980s, when the anger of young people was directed against their own communities as well as against the authorities. The tribalism of Bantu education, which aimed where possible to segregate by ethnicity as well as by colour, denied young people the possibility of sharing a common African experience. The emergence of a single political consciousness among Black South Africans was stymied. In a way, this was the entire point of the exercise: Bantu education had been designed to inhibit the growth of a mass-based African nationalism. Here there was yet another malign long-term consequence. Driven by the Zulu tribalism of the Inkatha Freedom Party, violence once again erupted between different communities in the townships and elsewhere in the early 1990s. This descent into near-civil war between the ANC and Inkatha almost derailed the country's transition to a non-racial democracy.

▲ Children protest the introduction of the Bantu Education Act in 1953

TOK connections

The changing meaning of words over time

The word *Bantu* was originally used as a label for the large number of ethnicities belonging to the Bantu language group. In the first part of the 20th century, it was regarded as a neutral term that could be used to describe South Africa's Black populations. After 1948, it took on an altogether different meaning. Bantu became the official apartheid term for Africans and it began to carry some very negative connotations. In the 1950s, African nationalists rejected the term and instead referred to themselves as Blacks or Africans. Today the word (outside the contexts of history and the study of language and ethnicity) is regarded as pejorative and insulting.

The Extension of University Education Act

The Extension of University Education Act of 1959 was introduced to extend apartheid to tertiary education. It brought to an end the practice of allowing a small number of universities, most notably the Universities of Cape Town and the Witwatersrand, to register students of all races on their academic courses. All universities would now be required to admit students from just a single racial group, or in the case of African universities, a single tribe. The University of Fort Hare, which Nelson Mandela attended and which had previously been open to all African students, was forced to admit only Xhosa students. New universities were built for the Indian and Coloured students who had previously been allowed to attend White universities, in Durban and near Cape Town respectively. The policy was clearly part of Verwoerd's wider strategy of pursuing the entirely separate development of all population groups in South Africa. Each race and tribe would be endowed with its own set of educational facilities and institutions in an attempt to create completely self-contained political and economic units for each. The introduction of an act that removed one of the few areas that had managed partly to resist the apartheid onslaught – the university campus – led to an outcry in the academic community. Many senior academics, such as ANC stalwart Professor ZK Matthews, who lectured in anthropology and law at Fort Hare, resigned their positions in protest.

The Bantustan system

The Bantu Authorities Act and the Promotion of Bantu Self-Government Act

The Bantustan or homelands system was hailed by the NP as the flagship of grand apartheid. The plan was to give each of the Black peoples of South Africa their own self-governing homeland. This would be achieved by transforming the existing native reserves into a number of small, fully independent states. Over time, all Black South Africans would be required to reside in these homelands. They would become citizens of the various Bantustans rather than of the rest of South Africa, which would henceforth be an exclusively White country.

The first stage in this process was undertaken by the Malan government, which passed the Bantu Authorities Act in 1951. This created new regional authorities for Africans, which were based in the reserves, and dispensed with the old Natives Representative Council, an elected national body representing all Africans. The Promotion of Bantu Self-Government Act, the most important law in the creation of the homelands system, was passed by Verwoerd's government in 1959. This law divided the African population into eight distinct ethnic groups. This was later expanded to 10 groups. The members of each group were assigned a White commissioner-general, whose task it was to assist them in making the political transition to full self-government in their designated area. The government could now argue that Black South Africans were no longer its political responsibility, and it accordingly abolished the already extremely limited indirect representation of Africans in the South African parliament. In return, all Black South Africans, regardless of whether or not they were actually residents of a homeland, would be able to vote in homelands elections. In 1970, the government decreed that all Black South Africans were citizens of the homelands, and not of the Republic of South Africa. This in effect meant that millions of South Africans – Blacks who did not live in the homelands – immediately became foreigners in their own country, under constant threat of deportation and being dumped in the Bantustans.

Source skills

Source A

An extract from a speech by Prime Minister Verwoerd to the South African parliament, 14 April 1961.

The basis of our policy is to try to get away from [discrimination]. That is why we adopt the policy that the Bantu, wherever he may live in various areas of his own, must be given political control over his own areas and people. Just as the Italians in France retain their vote in Italy, so the Bantu, even when they are living temporarily in our urban areas, must be given a say in their homelands … We are also trying to solve the problem of the Coloured and of the Indian by accepting the principle of a state within a state so that … each will be given the fullest opportunity to control its own interests …

One has to choose between these three alternatives: the United Party's stand of perpetual discrimination and domination; absolute equality and Black domination; or apartheid …

We arrived at this clear standpoint that discrimination must be eliminated by carrying separation far enough … as I stated on the occasion of the dissolution of the Natives Representative Council , "Our policy of parallel development is aimed at domination for you in your areas, just as we want domination for ourselves in our areas". Therefore I indicated at a very early stage that our moral basis was that we were trying to give everyone full rights for his own people.

Source B

K. Shillington. *Encyclopedia of African History.* **Vol 1–3 (2005).**

The establishment of "homelands" for various African communities was a device to divert internal opposition to apartheid and a failed attempt to convince the international community that South Africa was addressing, on its own terms, the demands for emancipation of its majority population. It provided for the bogus fragmentation of the population into a collection of ethnically distinct "minorities". Only the white population had political rights in the Republic of South Africa. The indigenous peoples were deemed not to be South Africans at all, but "nationals" of self-governing "Bantustans". Africans living and working in "white South Africa" were regarded as "temporary sojourners" (migrant workers), always at risk of deportation to a "homeland" that many had never even seen.

Third question – 6 marks

Compare and contrast the views expressed in Sources A and B on the creation of the homelands system in South Africa.

Transkei: The creation of a Bantustan

The first of the former native reserves to be converted into a fully fledged Bantustan was Transkei, which had previously been part of the Eastern Cape. Due to the large amount of native reserve land in this area, it was an obvious choice as the homeland of the Xhosa. Following the 1959 Promotion of Bantu Self-Government Act, the Transkei Constitution Act was passed in 1963. This resulted in the creation of the Transkei Legislative Assembly based in the new capital of Umtata. Chief Kaiser Matanzima was appointed as the first chief minister. Personally selected by Pretoria, Matanzima was typical of all of the homeland leaders in that he was a tribal chief. The government believed that choosing a traditional ruler as chief minister would serve to legitimate the authority of the homeland in the eyes of the Xhosa. However, Matanzima was a relatively minor chief. Paramount Chief Dalindyebo had refused to collaborate with Pretoria, and the government had no option but to turn to the more junior leader. Verwoerd's response – hugely ironic considering his commitment to separate development – was to declare Matanzima "paramount chief" in his own right, on a par with Dalindyebo. No one was fooled by this sleight of hand. Even inside their homeland fiefdoms, "traditional leaders" such as Matanzima were deeply unpopular with their own people.

▲ The trappings of statehood: postage stamps issued to commemorate Transkeian "independence" in 1976

Revealingly, the government in Pretoria felt that there was little need to organize elections for the leaders of the new homelands. In their view, Africans were too childlike to be given responsibility for choosing their own leaders, and democracy was an institution that was alien and unsuited to African societies. Nonetheless, the "moral" dimension of separate development dictated that there would have to be some semblance of democracy, and the 1963 Transkei Act did provide for the election of some of the members of the Transkei Legislative Assembly. The first of these elections was won emphatically by the Democratic Party, which was anti-Matanzima and opposed to the whole idea of the homelands system. However, the assembly was constituted in such a way that it was dominated by hand-picked tribal leaders who were Matanzima allies. The opposition was either ignored or actively persecuted thereafter.

Matanzima headed a cabinet with five other ministerial portfolios. Crucially, Pretoria retained the responsibility for its internal security and foreign relations, as well as immigration and banking. Clearly, Transkei was not a sovereign state in a meaningful sense, as it had very little real independence. The homeland would become fully "independent" in 1976, but even then Pretoria insisted that it would remain in charge of its foreign relations and security.

The homelands only became fully "independent" in the 1970s: Transkei in 1976, Bophuthatswana in 1977, Venda in 1979 and Ciskei in 1981. Plans to offer full independence to the other homelands, namely KwaZulu, KwaNdebele, QwaQwa, Lebowa, KaNgwane and Gazankulu, were put on indefinite hold in the 1980s as the government took its first tentative steps towards dismantling the apartheid system. As in the Transkei, the other Bantustans were led by corrupt and brutal oligarchies which brooked no opposition or dissent. The South African government provided them with unconditional political backing as well as military assistance whenever it was required.

Transkei was always the most politically viable of the Bantustans, in that it was fairly large and had a single, continuous frontier with South Africa. Others were anything but politically viable. Bophuthatswana was an extreme

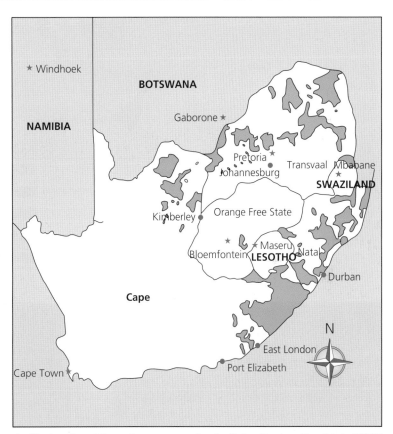

▲ The location of the native reserves after the Native Trust and Land Act of 1936

example of the fragmentation that typified the creation of many of the other homelands. It comprised dozens of tiny individual enclaves of territory, many of them divided by hundreds of kilometres, spanning three of the four provinces of the country. According to apartheid spokesmen, this was because these areas constituted the original "homelands" of the Tswana; they were being disingenuous. Dating back to the 1913 Natives Land Act, the land designated for the native reserves was some of the most agriculturally unproductive in the country. The Africans were given land that White farmers didn't want or, alternatively, land where there had been no historical White presence.

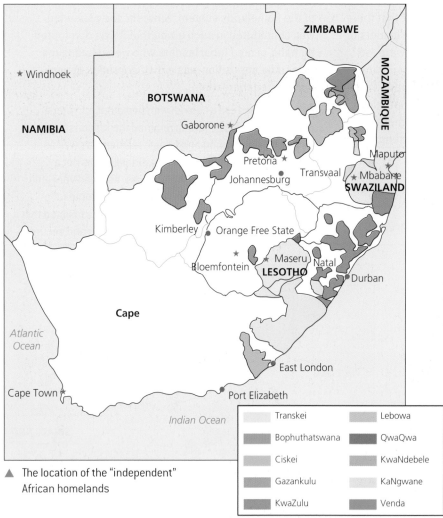

▲ The location of the "independent" African homelands

Transkei	Lebowa
Bophuthatswana	QwaQwa
Ciskei	KwaNdebele
Gazankulu	KaNgwane
KwaZulu	Venda

Most Black South Africans felt no political allegiance at all to their assigned homelands and regarded the Bantustan leaders as self-interested apartheid stooges. Nor did the international community acknowledge that the Bantustans were anything other than an attempt by the government to create a moral fig leaf for apartheid, by pretending that the system had delivered a modicum of genuine independence for Africans. With the partial exceptions of Israel and Taiwan, the Bantustans were never officially recognized by any country other than South Africa itself.

The apartheid authorities never thought of the homeland leaders as their political equals. As with the native reserves in previous decades, the government continued to use the Bantustans as a rural dumping ground for populations of Africans deemed surplus to employment requirements. At the same time, their very existence ensured a constant supply of extremely cheap labour for South African industry. Workers from the Bantustans were now citizens of foreign countries, and as such they had no employment rights under South African law.

Always close to bursting at the seams, the Bantustans became even more hopelessly overcrowded after their "independence". The homelands made up only 13% of the total land area of South Africa, and yet as much as 55% of the total population of the country would eventually reside in them. The squalor and deprivation of the rapidly constructed, semi-rural shanties of the Bantustans became notorious. The land,

▲ Overcrowding and environmental degradation in "rural" QwaQwa

Source skills

A cartoon by JH Jackson, published in 1959.

▲ Verwoerd is depicted as the painter and world opinion as the viewer.

First question, part b – 2 marks

What is the message of the cartoon with regard to the creation of the homelands system?

which had always been marginal, soon became over-grazed and its soil exhausted of nutrients. The result was severe environmental degradation. With populations comprising disproportionate numbers of the young and the elderly, the Bantustans were never economically productive. Men of working age would typically live and work far away in the cities or in the males-only mining compounds, leaving their families behind in the homelands.

The apartheid planners and Bantustan leaders had harboured some hopes that the homelands could be made economically viable, or at least partially self-supporting, by encouraging businesses and industries to relocate close to their borders in order to take advantage of the huge reservoir of cheap labour. This was officially encouraged through the Bantu Investment Corporation Act of 1959. However, these hopes failed to materialize. The Bantustans were to remain semi-rural backwaters, with few opportunities for Africans to work. A partial exception was to be found in the hotel and entertainment industry. The most famous example of this was the vast Sun City complex in Bophutatswana, with its casinos, cabarets and nude shows and performances. There is a deep irony here. The homelands system was designed to "rescue" traditional cultures from the moral cesspool of the African city. Instead, they became famous among white South Africans for their decadence and licentiousness, as places where strict moral sanction and apartheid law did not apply. Men in particular flocked to places like Sun City to experience some of the illicit pleasures which they could not get at home.

Other apartheid laws

The Separate Representation of Voters Act of 1951 was introduced in order to deal with one of the anomalies of the pre-1948 system of segregation. This was the presence of a small number of Coloureds who still remained on the voters' roll in the Cape Province. A legacy of the 1910 Act of Union, it was one of the so-called entrenched clauses of the constitution. The new law simply removed all Coloureds from the electorate. While it was quite predictable that the government would seek to disenfranchise the sole remaining non-White group that could still exercise the vote, it was the manner in which the law was forced through that aroused the ire of its critics. The 1951 act was overruled by the South African Supreme Court of Appeal, which argued that it violated the 1910 Constitution. This was because the government required a two-thirds majority of a joint sitting of the parliament if it wished to remove an entrenched clause from the Constitution. The government's response was to meddle in the affairs of the judiciary, itself an unconstitutional act, and increase the size of the Senate, packing it with new NP members. This ensured that the government was able to pass the original act in an amended form in a joint sitting in 1956. The episode illustrated the lengths to which the government would go in order to implement apartheid, and clearly demonstrated how it was prepared to ride roughshod over constitutional niceties in order to get its way.

Other apartheid legislation tended to fall into one of two categories as follows.

Repressive laws

These were laws designed to strengthen state security. The Suppression of Communism Act of 1950 was the most significant. This law made the Communist Party of South Africa (CPSA) illegal. However, it defined communism so broadly as to encompass all forms of opposition to the apartheid system. Anything that involved "the promotion of disturbances or disorder" would fall under the remit of the law, which was clearly designed to target the anti-government activists of the ANC as well as the country's small number of communists. Under the terms of the legislation, those involved in any political activities related to communism, as defined by the law, were liable to be prosecuted and subjected to banning orders, which prevented them from taking part in meetings and confined them to a particular location. These banning orders were a very effective weapon in the government's repression of the ANC. Senior leaders such as Chief Luthuli were effectively removed from day-to-day politics as a result of the successive orders issued against them. The Public Safety Act of 1953 gave the government the authority to suspend the Constitution and declare a state of emergency, something it was to do to great effect in the aftermath of the Sharpeville massacre. Meanwhile, the Criminal Law Amendment Act, passed in the same year, allowed the courts to impose severe penalties on those found guilty of committing acts of civil disobedience by breaking apartheid laws. It was used to bring an end to the Defiance Campaign. The Native Administration Act of 1956 permitted the state to "banish" Africans found guilty of persistent political offenses to remote rural areas. Two more repressive laws require a brief mention: the Unlawful Organisations Act of 1960 allows the government to ban the ANC and PAC after Sharpeville, and, following the launch of Umkhonto we Sizwe (the armed wing of the ANC), the General Laws Amendment (Sabotage) Act of 1962 made any act of sabotage a capital offense. Taken together, these laws constituted a formidable battery of repressive legislation that the government could deploy against the freedom struggle.

Censorship laws

Extreme censorship was another key feature of the apartheid system. The Customs and Excise Act of 1955 and the Official Secrets Act of 1956 were the most important laws in this area. They allowed the government to establish a Board of Censors that could rule on the restriction or banning of any media publication, book, film or other material, whether produced in South Africa or imported. It worked on the basis that anything that might upset the political, moral or religious sensibilities of the White public in general, and the values of Christian nationalism in particular, should be banned. Censorship would immunize White South Africans against the permissiveness found in other countries, which in the view of the apartheid government led to moral degeneration. Items liable to be banned included anything that was remotely uncongenial to the NP for racial reasons, or that might offend its stern Calvinist values. The popular children's novel *Black Beauty* was banned solely on the basis of its title. The authorities had a particularly priggish obsession with nudity, depictions of which were strictly prohibited. Even here, though, the double standards that typified the apartheid system were alive and well. Images of bare-breasted African tribal women were naturally permitted.

Source help and hints

(See page 27.)

A photograph of a "White Persons Only" sign at a beach near Cape Town, taken during the apartheid era.

First question, part b – 2 marks

What conclusions can you draw about segregation and discrimination in apartheid South Africa from the evidence in the photograph?

Examiner's hint: *Questions like this one carry 2 marks and they require you to mention at least two points in your answer. To be on the safe side it's a good idea to mention three points. These questions are often quite straightforward, so don't assume that there must be some tricky "hidden" meaning that you cannot see, and don't forget to state the obvious. Annotating a visual source can help you to pick out the key points. In the case of this photograph, there are some very obvious conclusions that you can draw.*

- Leisure facilities such as beaches were segregated by race.
- Apartheid signs were used to inform the public that facilities were reserved for use by one particular racial group.
- The facilities reserved for Whites were well maintained and of a very high standard.
- There was also ample space for the people who used the amenities.

Source A

Interview with Ayesha Hoorzook, a South African of Indian ancestry who grew up during apartheid.

I knew that as a child, we were not allowed to do many things, go to many places that other people could. But I thought that was normal, whatever [amenities] was available for us was meant for us – I never really questioned it … I can recall an incident of going to the zoo – in those days, first of all, blacks were not allowed to go. Later on, the law was relaxed a little bit and certain days were allocated to blacks only … For non-whites, there would be public buses going to the zoo, but there would be five seats reserved at the back of the bus for non-white people, only five seats. The entire bus would be empty, but you could not use a seat anywhere else on the bus.

Often by the time the bus comes to where we are, there are already [non-white people] on the bus and we'd let the bus go by … Then we'd get to [the zoo], and by this stage half the day is gone … my father starts looking at his clock, and he says we have to start having to go, there are so many non-whites at the zoo today and the chances are the buses are going to be very full.

First question, part a – 3 marks

According to the Source A, in what ways were the lives of non-White South Africans affected by the separation of amenities?

Examiner's hint: *You need to find three clear points in the source to answer the first question, part A on the document paper. It is a good idea to underline or highlight these points, when you first read the source. Once you have done this, it is an easy process to write out your answer. Here is a sample answer.*

Sample answer

The lives of non-White South Africans were affected by the segregation of amenities in a number of ways. First, their access to leisure facilities, such as zoos, was very limited, and on those days when they could use these amenities the facilities were often overcrowded. Second, public transport was also segregated, with only a limited number of seats provided for non-Whites. This meant that it was impossible to use buses if the non-White seats were taken, even when the seats reserved for Whites were empty. Third, non-White children growing up under apartheid were conditioned into thinking that the segregation of amenities was a normal thing, despite the fact that the facilities provided for them were inferior.

Second question – 4 marks

With reference to its origin, purpose and content, assess the value and limitations of Source A for historians studying the impact of the separation of populations and amenities in apartheid South Africa.

Examiner's hint: *The key to this question is to look at the introduction to the source. This will give you the origin of the source and thus clues about its purpose. The important point to pick up here is that the source is an interview with a person who is recalling events that happened many years previously, in her childhood. A sample answer follows.*

Sample answer

The source is an interview conducted with Ayesha Hoorzook, a South African Indian woman. In the interview, she recalls some of her experiences of growing up at a time when apartheid laws were being introduced. Her purpose in recording the interview is to help us understand the apartheid period better, and to contribute to the archive of testimonies of what it was like to grow up as a non-White person under apartheid. This is one aspect that makes the source valuable: as a personal, first-hand account it affords us an insight into how apartheid laws such as the Reservation of Amenities Act had an impact on the lives of non-White South Africans in a number of different ways. As well as this, Ayesha Hoorzook is a history teacher and guide at the Apartheid Museum. This means that she has a wealth of knowledge about different apartheid laws and is able to put her own experiences into the context of the discriminatory

system that was being put in place at the time. There are also some obvious limitations, however. One of these relates to the origin of the source: she is recalling events that happened many years previously in her childhood, and it is possible that there are certain aspects that she has forgotten or embellished in her recollections. One of the purposes of the interview (to highlight the wrongness of apartheid, having herself been a victim of its laws) could mean that she had exaggerated certain details. One line of the content – "by this stage half the day is gone" – suggests that this may indeed be the case.

Examiner's comment: *This answer makes clear and explicit reference to values and limitations, as well as to origin, purpose and content. It therefore deserves full marks.*

Examiner's hint: *If there is a general question on the separation of populations and amenities in a Paper 1 examination, don't forget to include in your answer an analysis of the laws outlined in this chapter.*

Source B

A cartoon by Abe Berry, published in *The Star* newspaper in Johannesburg, 1966.

First question, part b – 2 marks

What is the message of the cartoon in Source B?

Examiner's hint: *As mentioned above, when you have a visual source, annotate it to help you pick out the key points. Here is a possible answer.*

Sample answer

An obvious point of the cartoon is that South Africa has become a strictly segregated society. This is indicated by the Whites-only sign and by the fact that all of the people in the park are White with the exception of the Black maid, who is looking after a White baby in a pram. The second message is that the apartheid laws are fussy and even ridiculous. The Black woman is clearly in the Whites-only section of the park, but she has interpreted the sign to mean that only the grassy area where it has been placed has been segregated. She remains standing on the path, where she believes she is permitted to stand, while pushing the pram out onto the lawn, where she is not. None of the White people in the park seem perturbed by her presence. This may indicate that many White people do not really care too much for the strict apartheid laws.

> **Examiner's comment:** *The candidate has made three relevant points about the message of the source, each of which is supported by details from the cartoon. Since only two points are required in this question, the candidate has done more than enough to merit full marks. Note that it is always a good idea to use the phrase 'This may indicate that ...' if you are not entirely sure about a particular aspect of the source.*

Source

Nelson Mandela, in his autobiography, *The Long Walk to Freedom* (1995).

> Under the [Bantu Education] Act ... African teachers were not allowed to criticise the government or any school authority. It was "intellectual baasskap", a way of institutionalising inferiority. Dr Hendrik Verwoerd, the minister for Bantu education, explained that "education must teach and train people in accordance with their opportunities in life". His meaning was that Africans did not and would not have any opportunities, therefore, why educate them? "There is no place for the Bantu in the European community above the level of certain forms of labour," he said. In short, Africans should be trained to be menial workers, to be in a position of perpetual subordination to the white man.

First question, part a – 3 marks

According to the source, why did the apartheid government introduce the system of Bantu education?

> **Examiner's hint:** *Questions with 3 marks allocated to them are typically very straightforward. In order to gain 3 marks, you simply need to identify three relevant points in the source and write them in your answer. You can highlight or annotate the points as you read the source. Note that you do not need to quote directly from the source. It is better to paraphrase rather than using the same wording as the source because this indicates to the examiner that you have fully understood the source.*
>
> *Don't spend any more time on answering a 3-mark question than is absolutely necessary; you receive 1 mark for each point that you make, not for the style of your answer. For this question, the points you should have identified are as follows.*

Sample answer

The government wanted to stop African teachers from speaking out against apartheid.

Bantu education meant that the government would not have to waste time and effort in providing Africans with a good education, because they would have no opportunities anyway under the apartheid system.

Bantu education would train Africans to be of service to White South Africans.

Sources A and B

An extract from a speech by Prime Minister Verwoerd to the South African parliament, 14 April 1961.

The basis of our policy is to try to get away from [discrimination]. That is why we adopt the policy that the Bantu, wherever he may live in various areas of his own, must be given political control over his own areas and people. Just as the Italians in France retain their vote in Italy, so the Bantu, even when they are living temporarily in our urban areas, must be given a say in their homelands ... We are also trying to solve the problem of the Coloured and of the Indian by accepting the principle of a state within a state so that ... each will be given the fullest opportunity to control its own interests ... One has to choose between these three alternatives: the United Party's stand of perpetual discrimination and domination; absolute equality and Black domination; or apartheid ... We arrived at this clear standpoint that discrimination must be eliminated by carrying separation far enough ... as I stated on the occasion of the dissolution of the Natives Representative Council , "Our policy of parallel development is aimed at domination for you in your areas, just as we want domination for ourselves in our areas". Therefore I indicated at a very early stage that our moral basis was that we were trying to give everyone full rights for his own people.

Source B

K. Shillington. *Encyclopedia of African History* **(2005).**

The establishment of "homelands" for various African communities was a device to divert internal opposition to apartheid and a failed attempt to convince the international community that South Africa was addressing, on its own terms, the demands for emancipation of its majority population. It provided for the bogus fragmentation of the population into a collection of ethnically distinct "minorities". Only the white population had political rights in the Republic of South Africa. The indigenous peoples were deemed not to be South Africans at all, but "nationals" of selfgoverning "Bantustans". Africans living and working in "white South Africa" were regarded as "temporary sojourners" (migrant workers), always at risk of deportation to a "homeland" that many had never even seen.

Third question – 6 marks

Compare and contrast the views expressed in Sources A and B on the creation of the homelands system in South Africa.

Examiner's hint: *You should attempt to find at least six points of similarity and difference in your answer. Ideally there should be three of each in your answer but it isn't always possible to achieve this balance, so a breakdown of four comparisons to two contrasts, or vice versa, is acceptable. Try to keep up a clear running commentary between the two sources throughout your answer. An approach where each of the sources is described in turn before a short comparison is made at the end is far less effective. In this case, the quality of the answer is enhanced by the use of appropriate quotations from the sources. Note that even when sources appear to be quite different in their tone and content (as is the case here), it is still possible to identify a number of similarities.*

Comparisons

- The two sources agree that the homelands policy involved the fragmentation of South Africa into separate political components, where each group would exercise sovereignty in its own affairs.

- The two sources agree that under the policy many Africans would be "temporarily" resident in White urban areas. However, Source A argues that these migrant workers would enjoy political rights that they did not have before as they could now have a "say in their homelands". Source B, on the other hand, argues that their position was weakened because they were no longer considered to be citizens of the Republic of South Africa and were now constantly under the threat of deportation.

- Source A argues that the policy of separate development had a strong moral foundation because it allowed members of each group to develop in their own sphere without the risk of domination by other groups. Source B agrees with source A insofar as the government planned to use the homelands as means of establishing a moral basis for the apartheid system. This would allow the government to respond to its domestic critics and the international community. However, Source B argues that the government's attempts to do so were insincere and that it completely failed to achieve its objective.

Source B refers to the Bantustan system as "a device to divert internal opposition to apartheid". Source A, where Verwoerd contrasts his policies with the "perpetual discrimination and domination" of the opposition United Party, appears to confirm this.

Contrasts

- Source B argues that main purpose of the policy was to deny Africans their "political rights". In contrast, Source A argues that the purpose of the policy is to bring an end to "discrimination".

- Source A states that the government would attempt to "solve the problems" of the Coloured and Indian populations. Source B makes no mention of these communities apart from its reference to "minorities".

- Source A argues that the various units of the new South Africa would be political equals. In contrast, Source B implies that White South Africa totally dominated the Bantustans.

Source

A cartoon by JH Jackson published in 1959.

▲ Verwoerd is depicted as the painter and world opinion as the viewer.

First question, part b – 2 marks

What is the message of the cartoon with regard to the creation of the homelands system?

Sample answer

The cartoon depicts HF Verwoerd, the South African prime minister, showing the world his "painting" of the Bantustan system. Verwoerd is trying to fool the world by displaying a false picture of the homelands. He has represented them as beautiful "promised land" for Africans (who are presented as simple savages), a Garden of Eden where they can develop at their own pace and fulfil their dreams. However, world opinion seems unimpressed, as it can see the reality of the Bantustans through the window. The world can clearly see that they are desolate dumping grounds where Africans who oppose the apartheid regime are banished for their "crimes".

References

Mandela, N. 1995. *The Long Walk to Freedom*. London, UK. Little, Brown & Company.

Shillington, K. 2005. *Encyclopedia of African History*. Vol 1–3. New York, USA. Taylor and Francis.

1.3 Protests and action

Conceptual understanding

Key concepts

→ Change

→ Consequence

Key questions

→ What factors determined the various strategies adopted by the anti-apartheid movement between 1948 and 1964?

→ To what extent were the various protests and campaigns against apartheid successful?

→ Why did the ANC adopt the armed struggle?

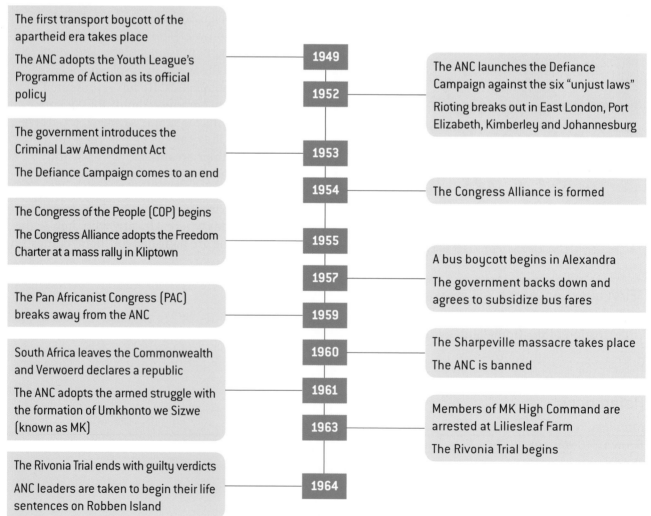

The first transport boycott of the apartheid era takes place

The ANC adopts the Youth League's Programme of Action as its official policy

1949

1952

The ANC launches the Defiance Campaign against the six "unjust laws"

Rioting breaks out in East London, Port Elizabeth, Kimberley and Johannesburg

The government introduces the Criminal Law Amendment Act

The Defiance Campaign comes to an end

1953

1954

The Congress Alliance is formed

The Congress of the People (COP) begins

The Congress Alliance adopts the Freedom Charter at a mass rally in Kliptown

1955

1957

A bus boycott begins in Alexandra

The government backs down and agrees to subsidize bus fares

The Pan Africanist Congress (PAC) breaks away from the ANC

1959

1960

The Sharpeville massacre takes place

The ANC is banned

South Africa leaves the Commonwealth and Verwoerd declares a republic

The ANC adopts the armed struggle with the formation of Umkhonto we Sizwe (known as MK)

1961

1963

Members of MK High Command are arrested at Liliesleaf Farm

The Rivonia Trial begins

The Rivonia Trial ends with guilty verdicts

ANC leaders are taken to begin their life sentences on Robben Island

1964

Non-violent protests

The Defiance Campaign

The Defiance Campaign was the first in a number of coordinated nationwide campaigns and protests organized by the ANC against the apartheid system. In many respects it was also the most significant, as it marked the opening of a new, more radical phase in the struggle against White minority rule. The campaign incorporated many of the more militant strategies that had been outlined in the ANC Youth League's Programme of Action, a platform which had been adopted as the official policy of the movement in 1949.

The Defiance Campaign was designed to apply concerted pressure on the government and force it into repealing apartheid legislation and negotiating with the ANC. These objectives would be achieved using the following methods:

- The political potential of the masses of ordinary Africans would be harnessed by involving them in a coordinated campaign of defiance against new apartheid laws. ANC leaders and other volunteers would deliberately break the law while crowds of onlookers would provide them with support and encouragement.

- The Defiance Campaign's philosophy of non-violent civil disobedience would be contrasted with the heavy-handed response of the authorities. The police would be given no choice but to arrest thousands of campaigners. As the campaign became the focus of global attention, apartheid would be put in the spotlight and the ANC would win a moral victory.

- South Africa's prisons would be filled until they were overflowing. The various institutions of state repression – the police, the courts and the prisons – would be stretched to breaking point.

- Other racial groups would be involved in the struggle against apartheid by coordinating the Defiance Campaign with the South African Indian Congress (SAIC) as well as activists from other communities.

Why did the ANC leadership decide to launch the Defiance Campaign in 1952?

The most obvious answer is that the ANC simply had to find a more effective response to the raft of apartheid laws being passed by the Malan government. By 1952, it was clear that apartheid was different from the old system of segregation. It was much more extreme and entailed the permanent political exclusion and oppression of non-Whites. Unless decisive action was taken, it would be too late to turn back the apartheid tide. The authorities had shown no inclination to engage the ANC in dialogue. Indeed, the government seemed utterly dismissive of African opinion and determined to repress any sort of opposition to its policies. The circumstances demanded a new strategy of resistance. Earlier demonstrations organized by the ANC, most notably a series of one-day strikes, had failed to provide sustained popular resistance to the regime. The old approach of *ad hoc* protests had to be replaced by a more cohesive and rigorous plan of action, one which would instil a sense of discipline in the people and inspire them to rally and persist in the face of the inevitable government backlash. Another reason for the launch of the Defiance

Campaign is that the ANC risked losing credibility among the masses unless it proved capable of providing a more effective response to government brutality. This was the argument used by the younger, more radical activists of the movement in their struggle against their more established leaders, who had favoured a cautious approach. The Defiance Campaign confirmed the ascendancy of the Youth Leaguers, who advocated a mass-based activism, over the conservative old guard of the ANC.

The immediate stimulus for the Defiance Campaign was an event organized by the National Party (NP). This event was the tercentenary of Jan van Riebeeck's landing at the Cape on 6 April 1652, the moment when a White presence was first established in South Africa. It was commemorated by Afrikaners across the nation in a spirit of unbridled triumphalism. The ANC responded by organizing mass rallies of its own in a number of major cities on the day of the tercentenary. These were so well attended that the leaders of the movement were encouraged to take further advantage of the rising popular anger against apartheid. Consultations between the ANC and anti-apartheid activists from the Indian, Coloured and White communities had already taken place in 1951. At the time, a joint action committee had recommended a national campaign with **civil disobedience** at its heart. Now, in June 1952, a National Action Committee (NAC) was created to organize this campaign. The NAC consisted of representatives of the ANC, the South African Indian Congress (SAIC) and the Franchise Action Council (FRAC), a Coloured organization created in order to protest the NP government's decision to remove Coloureds from the voters' roll. A National Volunteers Board (NVB) was created to coordinate the protests and Nelson Mandela was appointed national volunteer-in-chief, as well as chairman of both the NAC and NVB.

Civil disobedience

The strategy of protesting against unjust laws by deliberately breaking them, usually using nonviolent means. The approach was outlined by the American writer and philosopher Henry James Thoreau in the nineteenth century and was used, among others, by Mahatma Gandhi in his struggle against British rule in India, and by Martin Luther King during the civil rights struggle in America.

▲ Nelson Mandela confers with James Moroka and Yusuf Dadoo while awaiting trial during the Defiance Campaign, 1952

The official opening of the Defiance Campaign was set for 26 June. This was the second anniversary of the Day of Protest, a mass demonstration that had resulted in the fatal shooting of 19 protesters by the police. The official goal of the campaign was to force the government to repeal six "unjust laws" that had recently been introduced: the Pass Laws Act, the Group Areas Act, the Suppression of Communism Act, the Bantu Authorities Act, the Separate Representation of Voters Act and the Stock Limitation Act. This final law made it compulsory for Africans to cull their cattle and was hugely unpopular in rural areas; its inclusion was designed to broaden the base of the movement by drawing African peasants into the struggle.

However, civil disobedience leading to the repeal of apartheid laws were only part of the organizers' plans: at some later, as yet unspecified, time, a series of general strikes would be launched to coincide with the mounting acts of defiance. The hope was that this would bring the apartheid state to its knees and force its leaders to negotiate with the ANC.

The Defiance Campaign began with an ANC meeting in Johannesburg, which broke up after 11pm, even though the curfew time for Blacks in the city centre was 11pm. It soon developed a powerful momentum. Small groups of volunteers, including Nelson Mandela, Walter Sisulu, Yusuf Dadoo, Moses Kotane and JB Marks, deliberately defied apartheid laws in front of crowds of cheering onlookers and in full view of the police. The protests were typically good natured, with volunteers singing freedom songs, shouting political slogans (*Mayibuye!*, or "Let it return", to which the crowds responded *Afrika!*) and, following their arrest, giving their supporters the thumbs up sign that became a signature of the campaign. On being sentenced, they would chant "Hey Malan! Open the jail doors, we want to enter". Acts of defiance included burning or damaging passbooks, using segregated amenities and Whites-only entrances to railway stations, post offices and other buildings, illegally entering White suburbs without the required passes, and remaining in Whites-only areas after curfew. Since these infractions were minor ones, volunteers would be given short custodial sentences, typically a day or two in prison, as well a small fine before being released. They would then repeat the offences. Once the campaign was well underway, the volunteers who were most closely involved in its organization would often attend acts of defiance as onlookers in order to avoid rearrest and longer prison sentences.

While initially confined to Johannesburg and the traditional ANC strongholds of Port Elizabeth and East London, the campaign soon spread to other cities and smaller towns. The public response was very positive. Large numbers of Blacks and Indians were involved, both as volunteers and in supporting the defiers, with smaller representations from the Coloured and White communities. Membership of the ANC grew rapidly as a result, from under 20,000 members at the start of the Defiance Campaign to as many as 100,000 in 1953. A significant factor in this growth, and in the overall success of the campaign, was the involvement of women. Many of the protesters were female, and the ANC Women's League was at the forefront of organizing acts of defiance. The Black Sash, a group of White women opposed to apartheid, supported the campaign with great enthusiasm.

The Defiance Campaign peaked in July and August of 1952. By the end of the year, a total of more than 8,300 volunteers had been arrested. The campaign lost impetus in early 1953

ATL Communication and thinking skills

A South African policeman arresting volunteers during the 1952 Defiance Campaign.

What is the message of this photograph?

and never recovered. The main cause of the decline was the widespread rioting that broke out in the Eastern Cape in October 1952, and which then spread to Kimberley and Johannesburg. The risk that the ANC had been running now became apparent. Arousing popular anger against apartheid meant that peaceful protest could easily spill over into violence. This defeated the purpose of civil disobedience and provided the authorities with an excuse to use force to crush the campaign. With events now spiralling out of the ANC's control, the response of the government was typically swift and decisive. It introduced a Criminal Law Amendment Act in March 1953. This allowed the courts to hand down longer sentences and introduced whipping as a punishment for "offences committed by way of protest". The authorities also issued banning orders against individual organizers under the terms of the Suppression of Communism Act. This prevented ANC leaders from meeting and coordinating any further protests. Confronted with the prospect of draconian punishments, and struggling with the political fallout from the rioting, the ANC decided to wind down the Defiance Campaign.

Was the Defiance Campaign a success?

It can be argued that the Defiance Campaign was a failure in many crucial respects.

- The ANC failed to achieve any of its main political objectives.

- Not a single one of the six "unjust laws" was repealed.

- The government emerged with even stronger repressive powers with the passage of the Criminal Law Amendment Act and the Public Safety Act, which it also introduced during the campaign.

- With the exception of Ciskei, rural areas were hardly involved at all. Support was strongest in Johannesburg and especially in Port Elizabeth and East London, cities that were traditional ANC strongholds.

- The anticipated wave of general strikes that would herald the climax of the campaign and cripple the South African economy never materialized.

- Most of those who supported the campaign were middle-class Blacks from professional backgrounds. Poorer Africans from the working class and peasantry failed to play a significant part. Despite the impressive growth in its membership, the Defiance Campaign indicated that the ANC still had much work to do in expanding its support base before it could call itself a genuine mass movement.

- Very few members of the Coloured community joined in the campaign, a fact that helps to explain why it failed in Cape Town.

- Moreover, the campaign was viewed with hostility by many in the White community, who viewed it as a revolutionary challenge to their interests, particularly after the outbreak of rioting.

- The English language press was largely unsympathetic, as liberal Whites sought to distance themselves from a campaign they believed to be radical and confrontational.

A Whites-only general election held later in 1953 saw the NP returned to government with sweeping gains. The authorities were clearly far from weakened by the ANC's display of civil disobedience.

It may be argued, however, that the problems faced by the Defiance Campaign were to be expected if the ANC was to make the journey towards becoming a genuine mass movement, capable of challenging

apartheid. The government was always going to counter civil disobedience with the full force of state repression and the ANC, still in its infancy as a mass movement, was always likely to struggle in the face of this onslaught. Similarly, involving the masses in a struggle that had been dominated by Black elites was never likely to have been an easy task. It could be argued that the failures of the Defiance Campaign were necessary failures, and that the movement learned some very important lessons as a result.

Besides, few can argue that some of the achievements of the Defiance Campaign were extraordinary.

- For the first time in its history, the ANC had managed to coordinate an extended national campaign against apartheid. The leadership had proved itself capable of discipline and sacrifice.

- Thousands of ordinary South Africans had demonstrated their readiness to become involved in the struggle, as volunteers and as supporters. While popular involvement ebbed and flowed and the urban poor and the peasantry were largely uninvolved, the stage had been set for the development of a true mass movement.

- A broad coalition of interest groups was involved in the planning and execution of defiance, from communists and trade unions to members of the Indian community and the ANC Women's League.

- Hardly anyone in the party, including members of an emerging Africanist faction that objected in principle to working alongside groups that were not African, had openly opposed the campaign. Even the ultra-cautious former leader Alfred Xuma came out strongly in support.

- Finally, the national and global profile of the ANC grew enormously as a result of the Defiance Campaign.

The peaceful strategy of civil disobedience adopted by the resistance movement, together with the aggressive and disproportionate response of the government, revealed the brutality and moral bankruptcy of the apartheid system to the global community. In 1953, the United Nations established a Commission on the Racial Situation in the Union of South Africa. This marked the true beginning of the international campaign against apartheid.

Source skills

Source A

Defiance Campaign resister arrests by region in 1952, from Tom Lodge, *Black politics since 1945.*

Region	Defiance Campaign register arrests, 1952
East Cape	5,941
Transvaal	1,578
West Cape	490
Orange Free State	125
Natal	192
National total	8,326

Source B

Baruch Hirson, a White South African political activist and historian, "The Defiance Campaign, 1952: Social struggle or party stratagem?" in *Searchlight South Africa.* **Vol 1, number 1 (1988).**

As a prominent Marxist, Hirson was active in the African labour movement and in the South African Congress of Democrats in the 1950s. An early advocate of armed struggle, he became increasingly disillusioned by the ANC and other anti-apartheid groups, which he regarded as excessively cautious and, despite the

Defiance Campaign, out of touch with the masses of poorer South Africans.

> The repeal of the six laws in 1952 would have been a remarkable victory for the Congresses, but it did not envisage [foresee] any fundamental change in land holding, or in the country's economy … As the Campaign unfolded many of the original issues were seemingly forgotten. The Coloured votes ceased to be a factor in the Campaign – and the Bulletins of the Campaign were brought out in the names of the ANC and the SAIC, with no reference to the FrAC. There was little response from the Coloured community to the call for defiance, despite the claim that the Coloureds were ready for a fight … Finally, it was claimed that … the campaign marked a turning point in the history of South Africa, and provided the ANC with a mass base. The first contention is debatable and the second requires scrutiny [examination]. In comparison with the pre-1952 showing of the ANC, there was a decided change in the ANC presence, at least in the towns. However, it seems to have been much less than usually claimed.

First question, part a – 3 marks

According to Source B, why did the Defiance Campaign fail to achieve its political objectives?

First question, part b – 2 marks

What is the message of Source A?

Second question – 4 marks

With reference to origin, purpose and content, assess the values and limitations of Source B for historians studying the Defiance Campaign.

Historians and ideology

Baruch Hirson was a Marxist historian. Marxists argue that economic factors (as opposed to political, social or cultural factors) are crucial in determining the course of history. They contend that economic systems such as capitalism give rise to contradictions which the system cannot contain and from which revolution is the inevitable result. The preoccupation of Marxists with the economic causes of change raises a number of interesting questions about ideology and the production of history:

1   Is it possible for the historian to be objective in their selection and interpretation of sources (Marxists will naturally gravitate to economic evidence)? Can we speak of historical "facts" in a truly objective sense?

2   Are some historians more prone to bias than others? What other factors influence the bias of the historian? What, if anything, can historians do to mitigate this bias?

3   Marxist historians have been accused of economic reductionism (i.e. reducing complex historical events and processes to single-cause economic explanations)? Is this fair? Do we need to simplify history in order to make sense of it?

4   Marxists claim that they have identified a force which drives history forward, in the form of the changing modes and relations of economic production. Is it possible to see a pattern in history?

The Congress of the People (COP) and the Freedom Charter

The COP, convened in 1955, was an alliance of anti-apartheid congress movements, of which the ANC was by far the largest. The various congresses came together to create the COP in order to:

- forge a single popular front by uniting all of South Africa's racial groups in the fight against apartheid

- expand the membership and broaden the social base of the ANC through the direct involvement of poorer Africans in the COP and by doing so turn the freedom struggle into a truly mass movement

- draft a Freedom Charter for the COP, a document which would encapsulate the political goals of the congress movements as well as the democratic aspirations of all of the people of South Africa

- consolidate the ANC's strategy of working together with other parties and racial groups opposed to the apartheid system (like the SAIC) while also involving others, such as the Coloureds, whom had been largely excluded during the Defiance Campaign.

The idea of summoning a national convention of congress parties was first proposed by Professor ZK Matthews in 1953. In his discussions with ANC President-General Chief Luthuli, Matthews suggested that the convention should be known as the Congress of the People (COP). The plan was that the COP would, unlike the national parliament in Cape Town, represent South Africans of all races. It would draw up a Freedom Charter, a would-be constitution for a democratic, post-apartheid South Africa. Millions of ordinary South Africans would contribute to the drafting of this charter. Detailed

proposals were presented by Professor Matthews at the Cape provincial congress of the ANC in August 1953, and his plans were adopted to great acclaim at the annual conference in September. Following consultations with the ANC, the plan for the COP was then separately endorsed by:

- the SAIC
- the newly-formed South African Coloured People's Organization (later renamed the Coloured People's Congress)
- the South African Communist Party
- the South African Congress of Democrats, a group of left-wing activists from the White community.

▲ Delegates assemble at Kliptown for the mass rally of the COP, June 26, 1955

In 1954, these parties, along with the South African Congress of Trade Unions (SACTU), came together to establish, formally, the Congress Alliance, a popular front of congress parties. A meeting was held at Tongaat near Durban, where representatives agreed to establish a National Action Council (NAC) in order to organize the COP. The NAC would recruit thousands of "freedom volunteers", whose task it would be to bring the COP to the masses. From the very beginning, then, the objective of the COP was to involve as many ordinary South Africans as possible. It was hoped that this would transform the perception of the ANC as the party of narrow, middle class anti-apartheid elite.

The COP convened as a series of gatherings, conferences, campaigns and rallies. Many of the meetings were large and well attended, but most were on a much smaller scale. They were organized in factories, mining compounds, farms and homesteads across the nation. These took place during the first few months of 1955. The purpose of many of the smaller events was simply to raise awareness, with volunteers stressing that all Black South Africans should become involved in the struggle by registering as members of the ANC and joining in acts of protest and resistance. The volunteers also recorded the grievances of ordinary people and collected their signatures for the Million Signatures Campaign. Committees were established to incorporate the suggestions of millions of South Africans into the official draft of the Freedom Charter.

The COP reached a climax on 25 and 26 June at a mass meeting held at a football field in Kliptown, to the south of Johannesburg. It was attended by 2,844 delegates from all over South Africa. Chief Luthuli and ZK Matthews were prevented from leaving their rural homes by banning orders and were unable to be present. Nelson Mandela and Walter Sisulu, who were also banned, discreetly viewed the proceedings from the fringes of the crowd. A statement by Luthuli was read out to the delegates before the Freedom Charter was proclaimed.

Composed in ringing, declamatory tones, the Freedom Charter became the iconic document of the freedom struggle. It called for an end to the apartheid system, the election of a democratic, non-racial government, and the equitable distribution of the country's wealth and resources. The full document reads as follows.

The Freedom Charter

We, the People of South Africa, declare for all our country and the world to know:

- that South Africa belongs to all who live in it, black and white, and that no government can justly claim authority unless it is based on the will of all the people;

- that our people have been robbed of their birthright to land, liberty and peace by a form of government founded on injustice and inequality;

- that our country will never be prosperous or free until all our people live in brotherhood, enjoying equal rights and opportunities;

- that only a democratic state, based on the will of all the people, can secure to all their birthright without distinction of colour, race, sex or belief;

And therefore, we, the people of South Africa, black and white together equals, countrymen and brothers adopt this Freedom Charter;

And we pledge ourselves to strive together, sparing neither strength nor courage, until the democratic changes here set out have been won.

The People Shall Govern!

- Every man and woman shall have the right to vote for and to stand as a candidate for all bodies which make laws;

- All people shall be entitled to take part in the administration of the country;

- The rights of the people shall be the same, regardless of race, colour or sex;

- All bodies of minority rule, advisory boards, councils and authorities shall be replaced by democratic organs of self-government.

All National Groups Shall have Equal Rights!

- There shall be equal status in the bodies of state, in the courts and in the schools for all national groups and races;

- All people shall have equal right to use their own languages, and to develop their own folk culture and customs;

- All national groups shall be protected by law against insults to their race and national pride;

- The preaching and practice of national, race or colour discrimination and contempt shall be a punishable crime;

- All apartheid laws and practices shall be set aside.

The People Shall Share in the Country's Wealth!

- The national wealth of our country, the heritage of South Africans, shall be restored to the people;

- The mineral wealth beneath the soil, the Banks and monopoly industry shall be transferred to the ownership of the people as a whole;

- All other industry and trade shall be controlled to assist the wellbeing of the people;

- All people shall have equal rights to trade where they choose, to manufacture and to enter all trades, crafts and professions.

The Land Shall be Shared Amongst Those Who Work It!

- Restrictions of land ownership on a racial basis shall be ended, and all the land re-divided amongst those who work it to banish famine and land hunger;

- The state shall help the peasants with implements, seed, tractors and dams to save the soil and assist the tillers;

- Freedom of movement shall be guaranteed to all who work on the land;

- All shall have the right to occupy land wherever they choose;

- People shall not be robbed of their cattle, and forced labour and farm prisons shall be abolished.

All Shall be Equal Before the Law!

- No-one shall be imprisoned, deported or restricted without a fair trial; no-one shall be condemned by the order of any Government official;

- The courts shall be representative of all the people;

- Imprisonment shall be only for serious crimes against the people, and shall aim at re-education, not vengeance;

- The police force and army shall be open to all on an equal basis and shall be the helpers and protectors of the people;

- All laws which discriminate on grounds of race, colour or belief shall be repealed.

All Shall Enjoy Equal Human Rights!

- The law shall guarantee to all their right to speak, to organise, to meet together, to publish, to preach, to worship and to educate their children;

- The privacy of the house from police raids shall be protected by law;

- All shall be free to travel without restriction from countryside to town, from province to province, and from South Africa abroad;

- Pass Laws, permits and all other laws restricting these freedoms shall be abolished.

There Shall be Work and Security!

- All who work shall be free to form trade unions, to elect their officers and to make wage agreements with their employers;

- The state shall recognise the right and duty of all to work, and to draw full unemployment benefits;

- Men and women of all races shall receive equal pay for equal work;

- There shall be a forty-hour working week, a national minimum wage, paid annual leave, and sick leave for all workers, and maternity leave on full pay for all working mothers;

- Miners, domestic workers, farm workers and civil servants shall have the same rights as all others who work;

- Child labour, compound labour, the tot system and contract labour shall be abolished.

The Doors of Learning and Culture Shall be Opened!

- The government shall discover, develop and encourage national talent for the enhancement of our cultural life;

- All the cultural treasures of mankind shall be open to all, by free exchange of books, ideas and contact with other lands;

- The aim of education shall be to teach the youth to love their people and their culture, to honour human brotherhood, liberty and peace;

- Education shall be free, compulsory, universal and equal for all children; higher education and technical training shall be opened to all by means of state allowances and scholarships awarded on the basis of merit;

- Adult illiteracy shall be ended by a mass state education plan;

- Teachers shall have all the rights of other citizens;

- The colour bar in cultural life, in sport and in education shall be abolished.

There Shall be Houses, Security and Comfort!

- All people shall have the right to live where they choose, be decently housed, and to bring up their families in comfort and security;

- Unused housing space [shall] be made available to the people;

- Rent and prices shall be lowered, food plentiful and no-one shall go hungry;

- A preventive health scheme shall be run by the state;

- Free medical care and hospitalisation shall be provided for all, with special care for mothers and young children;

- Slums shall be demolished, and new suburbs built where all have transport, roads, lighting, playing fields, creches and social centres;

- The aged, the orphans, the disabled and the sick shall be cared for by the state;

- Rest, leisure and recreation shall be the right of all;

- Fenced locations and ghettoes shall be abolished, and laws which break up families shall be repealed.

There Shall be Peace and Friendship!

- South Africa shall be a fully independent state which respects the rights and sovereignty of all nations;

- South Africa shall strive to maintain world peace and the settlement of all international disputes by negotiation – not war;

- Peace and friendship amongst all our people shall be secured by upholding the equal rights, opportunities and status of all;

- The people of the protectorates Basutoland, Bechuanaland and Swaziland shall be free to decide for themselves their own future;

- The right of all peoples of Africa to independence and self-government shall be recognised, and shall be the basis of close co-operation.

Let all people who love their people and their country now say, as we say here:

THESE FREEDOMS WE WILL FIGHT FOR, SIDE BY SIDE, THROUGHOUT OUR LIVES, UNTIL WE HAVE WON OUR LIBERTY

ATL Thinking and social skills

The apartheid government argued that the Freedom Charter was a dangerous and revolutionary document. In pairs, use this document to prepare a case for the state that the COP aimed to overthrow the established order in South Africa through the Freedom Charter.

Source skills

A poster designed in the later apartheid era to commemorate the COP, and the Freedom Charter.

First question, part b – 2 marks

What is the message of this source?

Unsurprisingly, the Freedom Charter was unanimously adopted by the COP. The Kliptown rally ended in chaos, with armed police raiding the meeting and taking over the speaker's platform. The authorities arrested several of the delegates and many documents were seized. Rattled by the success of the COP, the government planned to use these documents as evidence against the ANC leaders in the next phase of its battle against the resistance movement. Beginning in 1956, the next few years of the freedom struggle were dominated by the marathon legal proceedings undertaken by the state against the accused in what was known as the Treason Trial. The government argued that the COP was designed to supplant the National Convention of 1908–1909. This was the body which had agreed the political union of the four White South African provinces in 1910 and had drafted the union constitution. The government could therefore argue that the Freedom Charter, an embryonic constitution for a new South Africa, amounted to nothing less than treason against the state. The Treason Trial took an enormous toll on the ANC. However, the charges laid against its leaders proved flimsy: all the accused were acquitted of treason in 1961.

ATL Research and thinking skills

An extract from Luli Callinicos's biography of senior ANC leader Oliver Tambo, *Oliver Tambo: Beyond the Engeli Mountains* (2004). Callinicos is a South African social historian who was herself a member of the Congress of Democrats in her youth.

The outcome of the COP, many have since agreed, was a turning point. Members of the Working Committee concurred. "For the first time, Congress activists had to learn to listen. From that process came a radical Freedom Charter, and the first outlines of a revolutionary new South Africa," observed [Lionel] Bernstein about the process of popular participation.

Of the Charter itself, Nelson Mandela wrote that "it is more than a list of demands for democratic reforms. It is revolutionary document precisely because the changes it envisages cannot be won without breaking up the economic and political set-up of present South Africa"; while Oliver Tambo… reported that the Freedom Charter has opened up a new chapter in the struggle of our people. "Hitherto we have struggled sometimes together, sometimes separately against pass laws, and Group Areas, against low wages, against Bantu education and removal schemes. With the adoption of the Charter, all struggles become one: the struggle for the aims of the Charter." …

[A] year later the Freedom Charter was adopted formally by the ANC without amendments... thousands of copies were reprinted over the next few years, and the document became a popular reference point – "our guide and organiser", to use Tambo's concept. …

[The] Freedom Charter was also to cause a major lurch towards an attempt by Africanists to challenge the ANC's direction and re-route it back to the Programme of Action and a "go-it-alone" policy. The dissident movement had been underground since the Defiance Campaign, when they supported the campaign in practice, but bided their time to see how the strategy would pan out.

Question

In pairs, identify the various arguments made in this extract to suggest that the decision of the COP to adopt the Freedom Charter was a "turning point" in the history of South Africa's freedom struggle. Using research and your own knowledge, identify some of the other consequences of the COP and the Freedom Charter.

Bus boycotts

Bus boycotts were a major form of Black protest against the South African authorities, even prior to 1948. The first major boycott was observed in 1940. Another took place in 1943, when a young Nelson Mandela marched the nine miles from Alexandra Township into the centre of Johannesburg in solidarity with tens of thousands of other protesters. Yet another boycott was held a year later. The causes of the boycotts tended to be economic rather than political. They were not a planned form of protest, but occurred as a popular reaction to the decisions of the various bus companies operating from the townships to raise their fares into the city. Boycotts were thus closely related to the extremely low wages paid to Africans and the high unemployment levels in the townships.

Once a boycott began, a committee was usually formed by activists or other community representatives on behalf of poor commuters who could not afford the fare increases. The committees negotiated with the bus companies and otherwise coordinated the boycotts. This was a major task as the boycotts were very well observed by commuters. At one point in 1944, up to 20,000 people were involved in boycotting buses. What was also remarkable about bus boycotts is that, unlike many other forms of demonstration against the authorities, they were often successful. The Johannesburg Chamber of Commerce, mindful of the impact of boycotts on businesses, would typically intervene in a dispute and persuade the bus companies to rescind the fare increases.

The success of these earlier boycotts had indicated the potential of organized popular action as an effective means of peaceful political protest. They influenced the various *ad hoc* protests and "stay-at-homes" organized by the ANC during the early years of apartheid, as well as the Defiance Campaign of 1952–53. However, boycotts had certain obvious limitations. They could not be initiated by the liberation movement, but were instead contingent upon the decisions of the bus companies. This meant that the ANC could not dictate the timing of any protests. Still, boycotts of buses and other transport were fairly frequent during the early years of the anti-apartheid struggle.

They included a tram boycott in the western suburbs of Johannesburg in 1949, as well as bus boycotts in Evaton in 1950, 1954 and 1955, and in the East Rand in 1954 and 1955.

The most important of all the boycotts was the famous Alexandra bus boycott, which began in January 1957. Predictably enough, it was triggered by the decision of the bus company, PUTCO, to raise fares from the township into the city from four to five pence. The resulting demonstrations were on a scale unlike anything seen before in the country, with hundreds of thousands involved in the boycott and, for the first time, widespread – and often sympathetic – coverage in the White media.

The sheer magnitude of the Alexandra boycott indicates that there was something more to the protests than a simple decision to increase bus fares. The political temperature, both in the township and nationally, had been steadily rising for some time. The forced evictions that had begun in Sophiatown in 1955 had been extended to "Black spots" across the nation by 1957. Tensions were understandably high in other Black urban areas, especially Alexandra. Minister of Native Affairs Verwoerd had made no secret of his determination to wipe Alexandra right off the map, and a series of removals, which had the effect of reducing the population of the township by the early 1960s, had already started. The government's 1956 decision to issue compulsory passes to women had led to an eruption of spontaneous protests. The imposition of native authorities in the reserves was another great source of anger among Black South Africans.

At the same time, there had been a significant lull in political activity since the COP, not least because many ANC leaders had been politically sidelined due to successive government banning orders and the Treason Trial. Still, the situation had become so tense that it would take little to trigger mass action. In early 1957, the stimulus duly arrived.

The announcement of the one penny rise in the bus fare provoked an immediate response from Alexandra's commuters. Their existing annual expenditure on bus fares, before the increase, amounted to more than a month's salary and they simply could not afford to pay the additional charge. On 7 January, thousands came out onto the streets in the morning and began the long trek into the city. From the outset, the mood of the protesters was festive, the air ringing with the sounds of freedom songs and cries of *Azikhwelwa!*, Zulu for "We will not ride!". The boycott immediately spread to Sophiatown and to the East Rand, as well as to a number of townships in Pretoria. Remarkably, by 15 January more than 20,000 workers from Moroka and Jabavu – squatter settlements on the outskirts of what is today Soweto – had joined in, even though their bus routes were not affected by the fare increases. Other cities, including Bloemfontein, Cape Town, Port Elizabeth and East London, initiated their own boycotts in a show of solidarity with the people of Alexandra. All in all, some 70,000 people walked daily for 12 weeks: from Alexandra, down Louis Botha Avenue, to the centre of Johannesburg. Tens of thousands were involved elsewhere. The sense of solidarity among the boycotters was palpable, with fitter marchers assisting the weak and the elderly. The police would regularly stop the marches and demand to see the participants' passes, and would often puncture bicycle tyres. Thunder showers were an additional hazard for the marchers, and yet the boycott continued.

On the very first day of the boycott, the Alexandra People's Transport Action Committee (APTAC) was created in order to coordinate the actions of the boycotters and to present their demands to PUTCO and the government. The ANC was well represented in APTAC, with Oliver Tambo and Alfred Nzo both prominent. Several civic organizations were also involved, and the dominant figure in APTAC seems to have been Dan Mokonyane of the Movement for a Democracy of Content. Initially non-political, the boycotters became increasingly confident and strident as the protests wore on and the influence of the ANC grew. Eventually, the Johannesburg Chamber of Commerce felt obliged to intervene. A deal was reached whereby the old fare structure was restored and PUTCO was effectively subsidized by the government to make up the difference. Celebrations erupted in the township as commuters won a rare victory against the authorities.

ATL Communication skills

Protesters make their way to work during the Alexandra bus boycott of 1957.

What is the message of the photograph?

The boycott was viewed as a major threat by the apartheid government. This was not a campaign that had been planned or initiated by the ANC or any other political party, and for that reason it seemed all the more dangerous. Tellingly, the government tried to argue that Africans had only boycotted the buses because of ANC intimidation, a charge that was patently untrue. For the authorities, spontaneous demonstrations involving hundreds of thousands of Africans, who felt that they had little to lose by protesting, could seriously threaten the basis of the apartheid regime. Previous protests that were orchestrated by the liberation movement, most notably the Defiance Campaign, had been quashed when the government clamped down on its organizers. The boycotts only came to an end only when the demands of the protesters had been met. Similar protests in future might result in the government having little choice but to make major political concessions.

The bus boycott also saw a sudden and unexpected outpouring of sympathy in the White community for the victims of apartheid. Liberal English language newspapers carried daily reports on the marches from the townships into the cities, as well as articles describing the penury of Africans. Large numbers of Whites from Johannesburg's wealthy northern suburbs drove their cars to Alexandra every morning to offer the marchers free lifts into the city. This strong display of White fraternity with Africans, which for the first time stretched beyond the narrow left-wing circle of the Congress of Democrats and the South African Communist Party (SACP), was viewed by the government as another dangerous development.

Source skills

E. Sisulu. *Walter and Albertina Sisulu: In Our Lifetime* **(2002).**

Local groups came together to form an Alexandra People's Transport Committee. Alfred Nzo, the ANC chairman for Alexandra, and Thomas Nkobi were part of the committee. Nzo and Nkobi regularly briefed the ANC leadership at Drill Hall about the progress of the boycott, which soon spread to Pretoria, Port Elizabeth, East London, Uitenhage and other centres. Beyond all expectations, the Alexandra Bus Boycott continued for over three months, and newspapers were filled with compelling images of people trudging their daily 20 miles, while sympathetic white motorists braved police intimidation to provide lifts to the weary walkers. The boycott finally ended in mid-April; six weeks later, the government introduced a new Bill in Parliament, the Native Services Levy Act of 1957, which provided a subsidy for bus fares. Anthony Sampson noted that "It was the first Act of Parliament in the 47 years of the Union to be passed directly as a result of African pressure."

First question, part a – 3 marks

According to the source, in what ways was the Alexandra bus boycott of 1957 a success?

For the ANC, the Alexandra bus boycott was a double-edged sword. It demonstrated that the government had little effective response to a demonstration that was genuinely popular. If mass public anger could be harnessed more effectively then there was no telling what might be achieved. The trouble was that the ANC might find it very difficult to control and direct a genuine mass movement that it had not itself initiated. This problem was amply illustrated in early 1960, when a breakaway party emerged in the shape of the Pan Africanist Congress (PAC). The ANC's Africanist foe correctly judged that it could take advantage of mounting public anger against the regime by launching its own rival campaign against the pass laws. The consequences, for the ANC and for the people of South Africa as a whole, were nothing short of disastrous.

Increasing violence

The Sharpeville massacre and the decision to adopt the armed struggle

The infamous Sharpeville massacre took place on 21 March 1960, when White policemen opened fire on a crowd of demonstrators outside a police station at a township on the outskirts of Vereeniging, some 60 kilometres south of Johannesburg. In total, 69 unarmed demonstrators were killed, including 8 women and 10 children, and 186 people were injured. It was an event that caused shock around the world as well as within South Africa. It also fundamentally altered the course of the liberation struggle. One of the main results of the massacre was the decision of the ANC to abandon its strategy of peaceful resistance to apartheid and instead embrace armed struggle.

The origins of Sharpeville can be traced to the split in the ANC in 1959. Africanists within the ANC, with their slogan of "Africa for the Africans", believed that best hope of liberation was through political self-reliance and a cultural focus that was rooted in African beliefs and traditions. In contrast to the non-racialism espoused by the mainstream of the movement, the Africanist believed that all of the land and wealth of South Africa be returned to its original, Black, owners. The first prominent Africanist in the organization was Anton Lembede, the first president of the ANC Youth

League, who died in 1947. His followers included Robert Sobukwe and Potlako Leballo. These men and their supporters became progressively disillusioned with the ANC's proximity to leading White communists and the movement's official embrace of other, non-African anti-apartheid groups through its involvement in the Congress Alliance. They argued that the ANC, with its continued insistence on peaceful protest, lacked dynamism and militancy. The Treason Trial, which began in 1956, had the effect of removing leaders such as Mandela and Sisulu from the day-to-day running of the organization. This allowed the Africanists, who until this point had been a relatively small group inside the ANC, the opportunity to mount a challenge from within. In 1958, the faction came out in open opposition to the ANC's national "stay-at-home". Rather ironically, this move won them the approval of the White press, who lauded Sobukwe and Leballo as the "respectable face" of Black political opinion. Matters came to a head in November 1958, when a group of Africanists attempted to break up a provincial conference chaired by Oliver Tambo in Orlando, Soweto. When they failed to achieve this objective, they announced their departure from the ANC. The break away Pan Africanist Congress (PAC), led by Sobukwe, was officially formed in early 1959.

The PAC's strategy was to hijack some of campaigns launched by the ANC. Hence, when the ANC announced in December 1959 that it planned to initiate a series of mass popular protests against the pass laws, a campaign that would culminate in a great bonfire of passes (also called reference books) in June 1960, the PAC responded by setting the date for its own anti-pass protest for 21 March. This was just days before the planned launch of the ANC protests. As the date of the demonstrations approached, the government became increasingly edgy in a political atmosphere that grew more combustible by the day. The PAC's plan for mass action involved thousands of protestors congregating without their reference books at police stations across the country and presenting themselves for arrest. The response of the authorities was to fortify police stations and put all police on armed alert. Despite this, the PAC was at pains to emphasize that the demonstrations would be non-violent, and Sobukwe urged the protesters not to provoke the police in any way.

On the morning of 21 March, as many as 5,000 demonstrators congregated in a field outside the main police station in Sharpeville. The mood was good-natured as the crowd sang freedom songs and chanted political slogans. Large numbers of people then moved towards the fenced compound, demanding that they be permitted to enter and surrender themselves for arrest. Exactly what happened next was to be hotly disputed. Police sources alleged there was a fracas involving an armed protester and a police officer. Whatever the nature of this incident, some in the crowd surged forward to get a better look. At this point, the same police sources alleged that many protesters began to throw stones at the officers. Eyewitnesses among the survivors argued that there was no such provocation. A jittery policeman, fearing that the station was about to be overwhelmed, then opened fire. This caused a chain reaction among his colleagues and a sustained volley of gunfire that lasted for two minutes. Dead bodies were strewn across the field in the aftermath. Almost all were found facing away from the station compound: they had clearly been shot in the back as they attempted to flee the carnage.

Source skills

Source A

A report published in the left-of-centre UK newspaper, *The Guardian*, 22 March 1960.

"I don't know how many we shot," said Colonel Pienaar, the local police commander at Sharpeville. "It all started when hordes of natives surrounded the police station. My car was struck by a stone. If they do these things they must learn their lesson the hard way."… The first African was shot dead after the police had been stoned. The Africans retaliated, causing casualties among the police. The police then opened fire with sub-machine guns, Sten guns, and rifles, and eye-witnesses said that the front ranks of the crowd fell like ninepins … Dr. Verwoerd, the South African Prime Minister, told the House of Assembly that last night about two thousand marched through Sharpeville, kicking open the doors of peace-loving people's homes, intimidating them and taking them on their march.

Source B

Protesters fleeing during the Sharpeville massacre, 21 March 1960.

Source C

An eyewitness account from Humphrey Tyler, assistant editor of *Drum* magazine, a popular weekly South African publication.

Drum magazine's readers were mainly middle-class Africans living in the townships. Tyler, who was White, was the only journalist present at the Sharpeville massacre.

Protestors were chanting "Izwe Lethu" which means "Our land" or gave the thumbs up freedom salute, and shouted "Afrika". Nobody was afraid, in actual fact they were in a cheerful mood. There were plenty of police and more ammunition than uniforms. A Pan Africanist leader approached us and said his organization and the marches were against violence and were demonstrating peacefully. Suddenly I heard chilling cries of "Izwe Lethu". It sounded mainly like the voices of women. Hands went up in the famous black power salute. That is when the shooting started. We heard the clatter of machine guns one after the other. The protesters thought they were firing blanks or warning shots. One woman was hit about 10 yards away from our car, as she fell to the ground her companion went back to assist, he thought she had stumbled. Then he tried to pick her up, as he turned her around he saw her chest had been blown away from the hail of bullets. He looked at the blood on his hand and screamed "God, she has been shot." Hundreds of kids were running like wild rabbits, some of them were

gunned down. Shooting only stopped when no living protester was in sight.

Source D

Brian Martin, a lecturer in Social Science at the University of Wollongong in Australia, *Justice Ignited: The Dynamics of Backfire,* **pages 8–9 (2007).**

The organizers of the rally had no well-developed plan of action, nor any system of crowd control. A few crowd members had weapons, mainly sticks and knobkerries, club-like weapons made from saplings with roots on their ends. There was some anatagonism towards the police, but at the same time there were elements of a carnival, "happy-go-lucky" atmosphere. There was no plan to attack the police station. The few weapons carried in the crowd served to boost morale rather than aid an attack …

At 1.30 pm, a drunk in the crowd named Geelbooi produced a small caliber pistol. A friend tried to stop him and two shots were fired into the air. At the same time, a key police officer named Spengler stumbled. Some in the crowd leaned forward. A constable helped Spengler to his feet. A few pebbles were thrown from the crowd and one hit the constable. The constable heard "shot" or "short" and fired. Spengler deflected the constable's shot but it was too late: the constable's shot triggered the police to fire 4000 rounds into the crowd, killing dozens of people and wounding many more.

First question, part a – 3 marks

According to Source A, why did the police take action against protesters at Sharpeville?

First question, part b – 2 marks

What is the message of the photograph in Source B?

Second question – 4 marks

With reference to its origin, purpose and content, assess the values and limitations of Source C for historians studying the Sharpeville massacre.

Third question – 6 marks

Compare and contrast the accounts of the Sharpeville massacre in Sources C and D.

Most non-White South Africans were outraged by what had happened. They were horrified not only by the massacre but also by the response of the government. Prime Minister Verwoerd seemed to embody the callousness and indifference of his government to the human suffering when he addressed a crowd of nationalist supporters shortly afterwards. He reassured them that the huge majority of Africans were peace-loving citizens who fully supported his policies of separate development, and that most of the protesters had been coerced into demonstrating by the ANC and the PAC. His opinion was wildly at odds with the violence and bloodshed that now threatened to engulf the country. Repeated clashes between police and protesters – at Langa near Cape Town on the same day as Sharpeville, and at Langa and elsewhere in the country in the following days and weeks – resulted in many more fatalities.

Verwoerd's response to the escalating crisis was typically bold and a state of emergency was declared on 30 March 1960. Thousands of ANC and PAC leaders were arrested and all political gatherings were outlawed. On 8 April, after passing the Unlawful Organizations Act, the government officially banned the two resistance movements. As an illegal organization, the ANC was now clearly running out of options if it wished to continue offering meaningful resistance to

TOK connections

Emotion, memory and the reliability (or otherwise) of eyewitness accounts

Eyewitness accounts are often regarded as an invaluable resource for historians. They add richness and colour to our study of important historical events and allow us to glimpse proceedings through the eyes of someone who was actually present as a witness to history. The problem is that eyewitness accounts are based on memory, which is notoriously unreliable . This is especially the case when we recall events that are particularly dramatic or laden with emotion and significance. Our recollection of what happened is often, at least partly, constructed. It is designed, unconsciously or otherwise, to fit with our general view of the world. We tend to exaggerate or embellish certain elements that suit our preferred narrative, and "reject" others that do not. Memory is subjective in that it is a mirror of our basic values and assumptions and, in the case of important historical events, our political sympathies.

apartheid. With the movement now completely at the mercy of the state, it seemed that only viable route was to go underground and begin armed struggle against the regime. Nelson Mandela, by now a fugitive on the run from the authorities and himself long convinced of the necessity of armed struggle, finally managed to persuade the ANC leadership at a secret party congress in July 1961. By the end of the year, the armed wing of the movement, Umkhonto we Sizwe (known as MK) had been created. MK immediately began its sabotage operations against the apartheid state.

Was the decision to adopt the armed struggle a direct result of the Sharpeville massacre?

On the one hand, it seems evident that the Sharpeville massacre and the decision to adopt the armed struggle were closely linked. Sharpeville marked a turning point in the history of the ANC, the moment at which more moderate figures in the leadership such as Chief Luthuli finally saw the apartheid state as incorrigibly vicious and unrepentant. Peaceful campaigns of civil disobedience had been scorned by the authorities, who had reacted with brutal repression. The old strategies had failed precisely because the government was prepared to use in its response all the considerable means at its disposal, and this now included the use of armed force against unarmed protesters. The ANC found itself banned and driven underground, and any lingering possibility of consultations and negotiation had now vanished. At the same time, the ANC now had a serious nationalist rival in the form of the PAC. The Pan Africanists had already created their own armed wing, Poqo, in the aftermath of the massacre. If the ANC failed to respond by launching its own armed struggle, it risked being outflanked by a rival party that had built a strong base of popular support in a very short space of time.

On the other hand, an internal debate about the desirability of armed struggle had been underway for many years before Sharpeville. A number of younger ANC leaders who had links with the SACP and were regarded as the "firebrands" of the movement – namely Nelson Mandela, Walter Sisulu, Oliver Tambo and Alfred Nzo – had been toying with the idea of creating an armed wing for some time. As early as 1953, Mandela had been asked to formulate a series of contingency measures that the movement could adopt in the event of a government ban. His "M Plan" had recommended that in such circumstances the ANC should dissolve its central organization and instead create a number of small clandestine cells, before launching a full-scale guerrilla insurgency against apartheid.

The wider significance of the Sharpeville massacre

One hugely important consequence of the Sharpeville massacre was the sea change that it brought about in global opinion. This turned decisively against South Africa after the incident. The historian Tom Lodge argues that, while the regime was strengthened in the short term by its crackdown on African nationalism, the Sharpeville massacre marked the true beginning of the international campaign against apartheid. Britain had already sounded a warning to South Africa with Harold MacMillan's "Wind of change" speech in Cape Town in February 1960, in which the British prime minister argued that the legitimate

nationalist aspirations of Africans would eventually have to be met. Now, after the Sharpeville massacre, the country's international isolation began in earnest. Economic sanctions were applied for the first time, despite the refusal of South Africa's major trading partners, Britain and the USA, to agree to a global trade embargo. Strong pressure from newly independent states led to South Africa being forced out of the British Commonwealth, its first major diplomatic setback, and becoming a republic in 1961.

The Rivonia Trial and the imprisonment of the ANC leadership

The Rivonia Trial of 1963–64 was named after the suburb in northern Johannesburg where the resistance movement's "safe house", Liliesleaf Farm, was located. This residence was used by senior leaders of the ANC and the SACP. Many of them had been on the run from the authorities since the resistance movement was driven underground in April 1960. When MK was established in December 1961, the house also became the operational headquarters of its high command. Following his arrest in August 1962, MK Chairman and "Black Pimpernel" Nelson Mandela could no longer play his key role in organizing acts of sabotage. Mandela had been stopped by police while returning to Johannesburg from Durban disguised as a chauffeur. After a brief trial, he was sentenced to five years' imprisonment for leaving the country without permission and inciting strike action. MK continued to operate in his absence, with Walter Sisulu and leading White communists taking the lead. However, Liliesleaf Farm was raided by special forces in July 1963 following a tip-off from a neighbour. The police found some of the remaining members of the MK high command – including Walter Sisulu, Govan Mbeki, Raymond Mhlaba, Lionel Bernstein, Ahmed Kathrada, Arthur Goldreich and Denis Goldberg – studying a document titled "Operation Mayibuye". This was a detailed plan for a revolutionary guerrilla war to be waged by MK from clandestine bases in rural parts of the country. Eleven defendants including Nelson Mandela, who was taken from his cell and put on trial once again, now faced charges of treason in a case that commanded the attention of the world.

The trial began in October 1963. The main law under which the defendants were charged was the Sabotage Act of 1962. This law defined sabotage as a capital offence and the chief prosecutor, Percy Yutar, called for the death penalty. The prosecution argued that the accused had carried out acts of sabotage that had endangered human life, and that they were planning to use violence to overthrow the state. From the outset, Mandela and his co-accused agreed that they would freely admit the charge of sabotage. However, they denied that any lives had been put at risk by their campaign. Their strategy was to politicize the trial by arguing that their struggle was morally legitimate, conducted on behalf of the people of South Africa for freedom and democracy and against racial domination and oppression. They contended that the harsh response of the government had given them little choice but to resort to armed struggle in the pursuit of their ideals. As Mandela asserted in his opening statement from the dock:

Above all, we want equal political rights, because without them our disabilities will be permanent. I know this sounds revolutionary to the whites in this country, because the majority of voters will be Africans. This makes the white man fear democracy. But this fear cannot be allowed to stand in the way of the only solution which will guarantee racial harmony and freedom for all. It is not true that the enfranchisement of all will result in racial domination. Political division, based on colour, is entirely artificial and, when it disappears, so will the domination of one colour group by another. The ANC has spent half a century fighting against racialism. When it triumphs it will not change that policy.

This then is what the ANC is fighting. Their struggle is a truly national one. It is a struggle of the African people, inspired by their own suffering and their own experience. It is a struggle for the right to live. During my lifetime I have dedicated myself to this struggle of the African people. I have fought against white domination, and I have fought against black domination. I have cherished the ideal of a democratic and free society in which all persons live together in harmony and with equal opportunities. It is an ideal which I hope to live for and to achieve. But if needs be, it is an ideal for which I am prepared to die.

— Mandela, 1963

The decision to politicize the trial was very risky and the accused showed great personal courage in pursuing this strategy. Mandela could have argued that he had been in prison since the introduction of the Sabotage Act in 1962 so he could not possibly be guilty under that law. Instead, he stood by his colleagues by confirming to the court that he had continued to act as MK leader while in jail and took personal responsibility for their acts of sabotage. Each of the accused agreed that since they considered their trial to be political, they would not appeal the death penalty if that was to be the sentence handed down by the judge.

As the trial drew to an end in June 1964, hundreds of journalists, photographers and diplomats from around the world descended on the court building in Pretoria. By this time, an international campaign against the trial had been underway for several months, spearheaded from London by veterans of the liberation movement who had managed to elude the authorities before escaping into exile. On 9 June, the UN Security Council passed a resolution calling on the government to end the trial and offer an amnesty to all of the accused. Just four countries – the USA, France, Britain and Brazil – abstained from the vote. On 11 June, Justice Quartus de Wet delivered his verdict: with the exception of Lionel Bernstein, all of the accused were found guilty of all of the charges. As the ANC leaders braced themselves for a sentence of death by hanging, the defence called the famous novelist Alan Paton, president of the Liberal Party (a parliamentary party that was strongly opposed to apartheid), to testify in an appeal for clemency. Despite his principled objection to the armed struggle, Paton argued that the judge should spare the guilty for the good of the country. To the surprise of everyone, the judge sentenced the men to life imprisonment. Apart from Denis Goldberg, who was sent to a Whites-only prison, the guilty were immediately taken to begin their sentences at the notorious maximum security prison of Robben Island.

Consequences of the Rivonia Trial

The Rivonia Trial marked the end of an era in the struggle against apartheid. The government had successfully broken the ANC and MK. With the exception of the still banned and physically frail Chief Luthuli,

all of the leaders were either imprisoned or in exile. For the most part, the townships would remain quiet, if defiant, for over a decade. There would be little to threaten the security of the apartheid state until the Soweto Uprising of 1976. In the meantime, unprecedented numbers of White South Africans would vote for the NP.

Yet the ANC was not quite dead, and nor was the freedom struggle. After the Rivonia Trial, Oliver Tambo became the effective leader of the ANC in exile, working from its principle base in Lusaka, Zambia. While its effectiveness in exile has been called into question (militarily, it failed to land a single telling blow until the 1980s), the ANC did at least manage to remain organizationally intact and was regarded by many around the world as the legitimate face of the anti-apartheid struggle. The ANC had been shattered in South Africa itself, but its imprisoned leaders were never forgotten. In particular, Nelson Mandela became an idol for the millions of South Africans who remained implacable opponents of the apartheid system. Meanwhile, new political movements were born and these provided renewed energy and focus for opposition: Steve Biko's South African Students' Organization (SASO) and the Black Consciousness Movement in the 1960s and 1970s, and the United Democratic Front (UDF) in the 1980s. In the first major act of Black opposition since the Rivonia Trial, hundreds of thousands of workers went on strike in Durban in 1973. The strike jolted the authorities and served as a reminder of the power of organized labour and the potency of mass-based political protest. The explosion of violence that accompanied the Soweto Uprising in 1976 marked the beginning of a dramatic new phase in the fight against apartheid. In the 1980s, with the townships in open revolt, and with international isolation and trade sanctions wreaking havoc with the South African economy, the NP finally took its first tentative steps towards bringing an end to the apartheid system.

Full document

Source A

An interview with Ahmed Kathrada, conducted in 2006, in which he remembers the Rivonia Trial and his early years on Robben Island.

Kathrada was tried alongside the other ANC leaders and sentenced to life imprisonment.

The very first night of our sentence they woke us up and handcuffed us. I was bound with leg irons to Govan Mbeki. They didn't even trust us on the airplane. Govan Mbeki got sick on the plane. They wouldn't even release the leg irons and I had to accompany him to the toilet. But that's the type of thing they were doing. They built up this fear until they started believing it themselves. I mean, what could we do on that plane?

Van Wyk [Captain Van Wyk, the police officer who carried out the arrests at Rivonia and was a witness at the trial] had told me, "You'll only serve five years." But on Robben Island, the head of prison security … said "In five years' time, nobody is going to know the name Mandela." And they tried to do that. Newspapers were not allowed to publish anything, photographs and articles about political prisoners were not allowed … They did everything possible to induce this amnesia among people – but they failed, of course.

Our leaders were absolutely exceptional – Mandela, Sisulu, Mbeki, Mhlaba. Right from the word go, they had said, "Chaps, we are now prisoners. We are not leaders. We don't make policy. We don't send instructions. The ANC exists outside, Oliver Tambo … and Chief Luthuli, those are our leaders, they make policy."

Source B

Yusuf Dadoo (chairman of the SAIC and SACP member) and Joe Slovo (a leading figure in the SACP) leading a demonstration against the Rivonia Trial, London, 1963.

Source C

T. Karis and G. Gerhart, professors of political science at the City University of New York and Columbia University respectively. *From Protest to Challenge: A documentary history of South African politics in South Africa, 1882–64.* **Vol 3.** *Challenge and Violence, 1953–64,* **page 684 (1977).**

The ending of the Rivonia trial did not appear to stir white public opinion. The press praised the police, the prosecutor, and the judge, and evidence of effective security contributed to growing white complacency and support for the government. Within a week of the sentencing, four incidents of sabotage were reported, probably the work of the mainly white African Resistance Movement. Within a month or so, the police had smashed this idealistic and heroic but ineffectual group. Most devastating, however, was the political blow to Alan Paton and the Liberal Party when it was discovered that Liberals were among the members of ARM. On July 24 whites reacted with horror to the news that a bomb had exploded in the white section of the Johannesburg railroad station, killing one old woman and injuring some two dozen others. John Harris, a Liberal who had joined ARM but had broken its basic rule against injuring human beings, was found guilty of the bombing. He became the first white man among some 45 persons hanged for politically inspired acts of violence since 1960.

Such violence was a last flickering of protest. White South Africa, confident that it faced no dangerous challenge from the United States or other Western states, was facing a period in which white strength was to be consolidated rather than undermined and white initiatives to enlist black collaboration and compliance were to be accelerated. Meanwhile, Luthuli's bitter verdict on Rivonia stood: sentencing "brave just men ... to be shut away for long years in the brutal and degrading prisons of South Africa ... will leave a vacuum in leadership," he said. "With them will be interred [buried] this country's hopes for racial co-operation."

Source D

D. Davis and M. Le Roux. *Precedent and Possibility: The (Ab)use of Law in South Africa,* **pages 56–57 (2009).**

The South African government's few foreign friends appeared to adopt a ... position of pragmatic support for the sentence. Anthony Sampson relates that the British ambassador to South Africa, Mr Hugh Stephenson, informed the British foreign secretary, Rab Butler: "We would be thankful that the judge did not give a death sentence because it means that a leader of the caliber of Nelson Mandela with his credentials enhanced by a term of imprisonment, should be available for the dialogue between black and white which must eventually take place in South Africa."

The evidence given by Paton and the comments of Stephenson indicated that there were many outside of the ANC camp who recognised how important ... Mandela, Sisulu and the other leaders ... would be to a future South Africa. But at the time, it was not how white South Africa saw the picture. The prevailing white attitude was well illustrated in an editorial in the *Sunday Times*:

"For the people of South Africa the prevailing lesson of Rivonia is that violence as a political weapon must be discarded once and for all ... Any reasonable assessment of the forces available leads to this conclusion. Meanwhile, the damage done in the hardening of white attitudes is incalculable ..."

The judgement in the Rivonia trial was used by politicians to bolster attitudes against the ANC for more than two decades …

As white attitudes hardened, so black leaders began to challenge, with growing intensity, the censure of their political struggle as violent, communist and criminal activity.

First question, part a – 3 marks

According to Source A, why were the leaders of the ANC put on trial and given life sentences in 1964?

First question, part b – 2 marks

What is the message of Source B?

Second question – 4 marks

With reference to its origin, purpose and content, assess the values and limitations of Source C for historians studying the impact of the Rivonia Trial.

Third question – 6 marks

Compare and contrast the views presented in Sources C and D concerning reactions to the Rivonia Trial.

Fourth question – 9 marks

Using the sources and your own knowledge, to what extent do you agree with the claim that the main consequence of the Rivonia Trial was *a period in which white strength was consolidated*?

ATL Communication, thinking, research and social skills

In small groups use the sources in this chapter, and/or other sources you find online, to draft your own version of a paper 1 examination.

- You will need four sources.
- One source will need to be a non-text source, such as a photograph, cartoon or statistics.
- You need to ensure that the total word count of your sources does not exceed 750 words.

You could use the following questions to help refine the "theme" of the paper.

1. Using the sources and your own knowledge, to what extent do you agree with the claim that the Defiance Campaign failed to achieve the objective of turning the ANC into a mass movement against apartheid?

2. Using the sources and your own knowledge, evaluate the impact of the COP and the Freedom Charter in the development of anti-apartheid resistance.

3. Using the sources and your own knowledge, assess the reasons why bus boycotts were such an effective means of protest against the apartheid system.

4. Using the sources and your own knowledge, to what extent do you agree with the claim that the ANC adopted the armed struggle as a direct result of the Sharpeville massacre?

5. Using the sources and your own knowledge, examine the reasons why the ANC leaders were not sentenced to death at the Rivonia Trial in 1964.

References

Callinicos, L. 2004. *Oliver Tambo: Beyond the Engeli Mountains*. Cape Town, South Africa. David Philip Publishers.

Davis, D and Le Roux, M. 2009. *Precedent and Possibility: The (Ab)use of Law in South Africa*. Johannesburg, South Africa. Double Story Publishers.

Hirson, B. 1988. "The Defiance Campaign, 1952: Social struggle or party stratagem?" *Searchlight South Africa*, Vol 1, number 1

Karis, T and Gerhart, G. 1977. *From Protest to Challenge: A Documentary History of South African Politics in South Africa, 1882–64*. Vol 3. *Challenge and Violence, 1953–64*. Stanford, CA, USA. Hoover Institution Press.

Lodge, T. 1983. *Black Politics in South Africa Since 1945*. London, UK. Longman.

Martin, B. 2007. *Justice Ignited: The Dynamics of Backfire*

Sisulu, E. 2002. *Walter and Albertina Sisulu: In Our Lifetime*. Cape Town, South Africa. David Philip Publishers.

Source help and hints

Source A

Defiance Campaign resister arrests by region in 1952.

Region	Defiance Campaign register arrests, 1952
East Cape	5,941
Transvaal	1,578
West Cape	490
Orange Free State	125
Natal	192
National total	8,326

First question, part b – 2 marks

What is the message of Source A?

> **Examiner's hint:** *To answer this question, you need to work out what you can from the table. In this case, you can find out the following information.*

- The Defiance Campaign involved "resisters" who courted arrest by the authorities.

- It was a nationwide campaign.

- Thousands of resisters were involved in the campaign and more than 8,000 people were arrested.

- The campaign was stronger in some areas (in the East Cape, for instance) than in others (Natal, the Orange Free State and West Cape).

> **Examiner's hint:** *Questions about statistical data require you simply to interpret the statistics. You should resist the temptation to read your own knowledge into your answers. For example, in answering the above question you should not conclude that the Defiance Campaign was more successful in the Eastern Cape because it was a traditional ANC stronghold, or in the Transvaal because Johannesburg was the operational headquarters of the organization.*

Source B

Baruch Hirson, a White South African political activist and historian, "The Defiance Campaign, 1952: Social struggle or party strategem?" in *Searchlight South Africa.* **Vol 1, number 1 (1988).**

> The repeal of the six laws in 1952 would have been a remarkable victory for the Congresses, but it did not envisage [foresee] any fundamental change in land holding, or in the country's economy …
> As the Campaign unfolded many of the original issues were seemingly forgotten. The Coloured votes ceased to be a factor in the Campaign – and the Bulletins of the Campaign were brought out in the names of the ANC and the SAIC, with no reference to the FrAC. There was little response from the Coloured community to the call for defiance, despite the claim that the Coloureds were ready for a fight … Finally, it was claimed that … the campaign marked a turning point in the history of South Africa, and provided the ANC with a mass base. The first contention is debatable and the second requires scrutiny [examination].
> In comparison with the pre-1952 showing of the ANC, there was a decided change in the ANC presence, at least in the towns. However, it seems to have been much less than usually claimed.

First question, part a – 3 marks

According to Source B, why did the Defiance Campaign fail to achieve its political objectives?

> **Examiner's hint:** *You need to find three clear points in the source to answer the First question, part a on the document paper. It is a good idea to underline or highlight these points, when you first read the source, before writing them out.*

- The Defiance Campaign never became a mass movement because it was too superficial, focusing only on the six "unjust laws". It failed to address the real concerns of poor Black South Africans, such as land ownership and White domination of the economy.

- The campaign failed to exploit Coloured resentment of apartheid and instead focused on issues concerning the Black and Indian populations. The role of the mainly Coloured FrAC was ignored.

- The campaign failed to establish a significant presence for the ANC outside of the main cities, despite claims to the contrary.

Second question – 4 marks

With reference to its origin, purpose and content, assess the values and limitations of Source B for historians studying the Defiance Campaign.

> **Examiner's hint:** *The question is asking you to evaluate the author's work. It is important that you look carefully at the title of the work and its date of publication, as well as any clues about the author from the information provided.*

Values

- Written by a professional historian, the source is a scholarly article focusing exclusively on the Defiance Campaign. Unlike many of the secondary sources available, it is not a general survey of the apartheid period, or of Black politics as a whole during the liberation struggle.

- It was written in 1988, towards the end of the apartheid era. It therefore has the benefit of hindsight. The author was also able to make use of the ground-breaking research on Black politics (such as the books by Peter Walshe and Tom Lodge) produced in the 1970s and 1980s.

- The author was active in the anti-apartheid movement during the period. He would have known many of those who were involved in the Defiance Campaign personally, and may well have interviewed some of them for his article.

- The author presents a critical view of the Defiance Campaign and examines its failings, unlike many historians who simply proclaim it as a landmark moment in the history of the struggle.

- The source seems incredibly detailed, with a reference to the bulletins published by the Defiance Campaign. This suggests that it was meticulously researched.

Limitations

- As a Marxist, Hirson may be too focused on economic factors in history. In the first part of the extract he refers to land ownership and other economic factors, and he berates the ANC for its lack of radicalism in not basing its campaign on these issue. He fails to acknowledge the many other ways in which the Defiance Campaign was radical and ambitious.

- As someone who became disillusioned with the strategies of the liberation movement in the 1950s, Hirson may well have been preoccupied with the failings of the campaign. This may have stood in the way of a more balanced analysis. The content of the source, which is on the whole negative and pessimistic, would seem to confirm this.

Source skills

(See page 64.)

First question, part a – 3 marks

According to the source, in what ways was the Alexandra bus boycott of 1957 a success?

> **Examiner's hint:** *Remember that you need to find three clear points in the source to answer the First question, part a on the document paper. Any three of the following points would be acceptable.*

- The boycott spread from Alexandra to other centres and became a nationwide protest.

- The boycott confounded expectations by continuing for over three months.

- Newspapers published for Whites carried sympathetic articles about the protesters and White motorists assisted the marchers.

- The government eventually responded to the pressure of the boycott by providing subsidies for bus fares. Cancelling the fare increases is precisely what the protesters had demanded.

Source A

(See page 67.)

First question, part a – 3 marks

According to Source A, why did the police take action against protesters at Sharpeville?

> **Examiner's hint:** *Don't spend any more time on answering a 3-mark question than is absolutely necessary; you receive 1 mark for each point that you make, not for the style of your answer. Here are three reasons you might give.*

- The crowd threw stones at the police and the police responded with gunfire, to "teach them a lesson".

- After the initial shot was fired, the crowd retaliated by attacking the police. The police then responded in order to defend themselves.

- According to Verwoerd, the protesters at Sharpeville had behaved aggressively towards "peace-loving people". The implication is that strong police action was required in order to contain the situation.

Source B

Protesters fleeing during the Sharpeville massacre, 21 March 1960.

First question part b – 2 marks

What is the message of the photograph in Source B?

> **Examiner's hint:** *When you have a visual source, annotate it to help you pick out the key points. Here are some points you might make about the message of this photograph.*

- The crowd at Sharpeville was fired upon by the police, some of whom appear to have taken up elevated positions.

- The majority of the protesters were clearly attempting to flee the scene after the shooting started.

- The crowd, which contains many women, appears to be well dressed and respectable.

- There is no indication that any of the protesters are armed.

Source C

(See page 67.)

Second question – 4 marks

With reference to its origin, purpose and content, assess the values and limitations of Source C for historians studying the Sharpeville massacre.

> **Examiner's hint:** *The following values and limitations would be relevant in your answer.*

Values

- Humphrey Tyler was the only reporter present at the massacre. This means that his testimony is of immense value to historians. His account is especially important because it represents an alternative account to the official version of what happened. It also went some way towards moulding the public perception of the Sharpeville massacre at the time.

- As a journalist, Tyler offers a dramatic and colourful account of the events of the massacre. He also provides a wealth of detail for the historian, as he is someone with journalistic training and experience.

- Tyler manages to convey the sheer horror of the massacre. This factor is often missing from more sober scholarly accounts of important historical events.

Limitations

- The events witnessed by Tyler were traumatic and distressing. For instance, he describes a woman whose chest was "blown away by a hail of bullets". This may well have influenced his ability to recollect the exact nature and sequence of what happened.

- There is no mention of Tyler's location in the crowd during the protest. It is unlikely that he was anywhere near the front. As a result, he may not have witnessed any altercation between the police and protesters, and the result is that this aspect of the massacre is missing from his account.

- Tyler was the assistant editor of *Drum* magazine, a publication that was strongly opposed to the apartheid system. His impartiality as an eyewitness to the massacre might therefore be called into question. Some of the heavily emotive language used in his report, such as "kids running round like wild rabbits", would suggest that this may be the case.

Source D

(See page 67.)

Third question – 6 marks

Compare and contrast the accounts of the Sharpeville massacre in Sources C and D.

> **Examiner's hint:** *You should attempt to find at least six points of similarity and difference in your answer. Ideally there should be three of each in your answer but it isn't always possible to achieve this balance, so a breakdown of four comparisons to two contrasts, or vice versa, is acceptable. Try to keep up a clear running commentary between the two sources throughout your answer.*

Comparisons

- Both sources stress that there was no plan to attack the police station.

- Both sources stress the festive atmosphere in the crowd.

- Both sources indicate that there were many fatalities. Source C mentions that the police stopped firing when "no living protester was in sight". Source D mentions the "dozens of people" who were killed.

Contrasts

- Source C stresses a political element in the protests (political chanting, Black power salutes) but maintains that the demonstrations were peaceful. There is no mention of a political dimension in Source D.

- Source D argues that there was no organization or crowd control. Indeed, the author stresses that there was "no well-developed plan of action". Source C describes the presence of a Pan Africanist (obviously present as an organizer) who informs the journalist that the protest was entirely peaceful.

- Source C indicates that the protesters were unarmed. Source D mentions knobkerries and a pistol.

- Source C suggests that the gunfire from the police was unprovoked, or that it was in response to political slogans from the protesters. Source D mentions a drunk who fired a pistol shot and pebbles thrown from the crowd, as well as "some antagonism towards the police". It also suggests that the police may have opened fire because they panicked.

Source A

(See page 73.)

First question, part a – 3 marks

According to Source A, why were the leaders of the ANC put on trial and given life sentences in 1964?

> **Examiner's hint:** *You need to make three clear points. Here are some examples.*

- The apartheid authorities had started to believe their own propaganda. They feared the ANC leaders, seeing them as dangerous criminals who had to be imprisoned for the rest of their lives.

- Imprisoning the ANC leaders would mean that they would soon be forgotten by the outside world.

- Having been imprisoned, the "exceptional" leaders of the ANC were no longer in a position to dictate policy or otherwise contribute to the party.

Source B

Yusuf Dadoo (chairman of the SAIC and SACP member) and Joe Slovo (a leading figure in the SACP) leading a demonstration against the Rivonia Trial, London, 1963

First question, part b – 2 marks

What is the message of Source B?

> **Examiner's hint:** *Remember that annotating a visual source can help you to identify key points about its message.*

- The lives of the 11 accused at the Rivonia Trial are in danger.

- An international campaign against the Rivonia Trial in particular, and against apartheid in general, was already underway in 1963.

- Senior leaders such as Yusuf Dadoo and Joe Slovo have managed to escape into exile and are now leading this campaign.

Third question – 6 marks

(See page 73.)

Compare and contrast the views presented in Sources C and D concerning reactions to the Rivonia Trial.

> **Examiner's hint:** *You should attempt to find at least six points of similarity and difference in your answer. If it isn't possible to achieve three of each in your answer, a breakdown of four comparisons to two contrasts, or vice versa, is acceptable. Try to keep up a clear running commentary between the two sources throughout your answer.*

Comparisons

- Both sources indicate that, on the whole, the Rivonia Trial resulted in a hardening of White attitudes and increasing levels of support for the NP government from the White community.

- Both sources indicate that there were reservations about the government's hardline approach from some in the White community. Source D mentions Alan Paton and quotes the comments of the South African ambassador to Britain, who hoped that the imprisoned ANC leadership could be used for the purposes of political reconciliation in the future. Source C also refers to Paton and mentions that some members of his party were part of the ARM.

- Both sources suggest that the authorities had little to fear from the reaction of the international community. Source C mentions that it faced "no dangerous challenge", while Source D makes reference to the "pragmatic support" of the British. However, Source D does concede that South Africa now has "few foreign friends".

Contrasts

- Source C describes a fatal bombing carried out by the ARM and the response of the authorities to this attack. Despite the mention of Alan Paton, Source D does not go into the detail of these events.

- Source D mentions that Black leaders eventually rose to challenge the official censure of their struggle in the aftermath of the Rivonia Trial. Source C quotes Chief Luthuli, but only in the context of his despair at the sentencing.

- Source D holds out the prospect of inter-racial cooperation in the future. Source C is altogether more pessimistic about South Africa's prospects after the Rivonia Trial.

Second question – 4 marks

(See page 73.)

With reference to its origin, purpose and content, assess the values and limitations of Source C for historians studying the impact of the Rivonia Trial.

> **Examiner's hint:** *Here are some examples of the values and limitations of the source that could be used to answer this question.*

Values

- Source C comes from a three-volume survey of the political history of South Africa. Its purpose is to provide a comprehensive record and analysis of the history of the country from a political perspective, for use by students as well as historians. It is written by renowned academics and the likelihood is that has been very well researched using an abundance of supporting historical detail.

- The fact that Source C is a documentary history means that the historians will have a wealth of primary source materials to study.

Limitations

- The chronological cut-off for the study is 1964. It is unlikely that there will be a thorough assessment of the impact of the Rivonia Trial in the longer term.

- The source was written in 1977. At this point, the apartheid system still appeared to be alive and well, despite the start of the Soweto Uprising a year earlier, and some of the longer-term ramifications of the trial and imprisonment of the ANC leaders had not yet become evident. The pessimistic tone of the extract may have been very different had it been written a decade or so later, when the apartheid system was unravelling.

- As a related point, the source focuses entirely on the negative consequences of the Rivonia Trial for the resistance movement. It suggests that South Africa was entering into a long period of political darkness from which it has yet to emerge. There is no mention of growing international opposition to apartheid, the full impact of which only became evident after 1977.

Fourth question – 9 marks

(See page 73.)

Using the sources and your own knowledge, to what extent do you agree with the claim that the main consequence of the Rivonia Trial was *"a period in which white strength was consolidated"*?

> **Examiner's hint:** *Here are some of the points made in the sources that would help you answer the question.*

- Source A: The attempts of the authorities to "induce amnesia" about the imprisoned ANC leaders were a failure. This meant that the government's efforts to erase the struggle from the minds of Black South Africans would ultimately prove futile. The ANC leaders were in prison and could not make policy, which obviously strengthened White minority rule. However, the ANC continued to function despite the imprisonment of its leaders, through Albert Lithuli in South Africa and Oliver Tambo, in exile, in Zambia.

- Source B: An international campaign has been launched against apartheid South Africa. This obviously put pressure on the government. Senior leaders of the struggle were directing this campaign and they continued to be thorns in the side of the authorities, even in exile.

- Source C: White South Africans did not turn against the government as a result of the trial. The few Whites who had opposed the trial were compromised as a result of the association of the Liberal Party with the ARM. International opposition was muted, especially in the USA and other Western countries. The ANC had been left devoid of senior leaders.

- Source D: White South Africans were opposed to the violence of armed struggle and so sympathized with the government. Despite the apparent hardening of attitudes, some influential White South Africans held out the prospect of a reconciliation between the government and the imprisoned ANC leaders in the not-so-distant future. South Africa had become diplomatically isolated as a result of the trial and Blacks were increasingly angry at the government's depiction of their struggle as violent. This would have significant repercussions for White minority rule in the future.

Examiner's hint: *The following are some points you could include from your own knowledge.*

- The organizational structure of the ANC had been effectively destroyed as a result of the trial, and this obviously strengthened White power. While the resistance movement continued to operate in exile, its impact was very limited and it failed to make any significant dents in minority rule.

- The Rivonia Trial and the imprisonment of the ANC leaders created a great deal of anger and resentment in the townships. This simmered for several years before exploding in the Soweto Uprising in 1976. This marked the beginning of a new stage of acute crisis for the apartheid system, which would eventually result in its unravelling.

- The ANC leaders became legendary figures as a result of their imprisonment, and remembered and revered by the huge majority of Black South Africans.

- New resistance movements such as Steve Biko's SASO and the Black Consciousness Movement emerged to replace the ANC.

- A huge international campaign against apartheid was launched during the Rivonia Trial. This continued afterwards and intensified in the 1970s and 1980s. The plight of the imprisoned leaders became a major focus of this global attention. The campaign resulted in trade sanctions and these led to major economic problems which ultimately undermined the basis of White rule in South Africa.

1.4 The role and significance of key individuals and groups

Conceptual understanding

Key concepts

→ Causation

→ Significance

Key questions

→ What was the impact of key groups such as the African National Congress (ANC), the South African Communist Party (SACP) and Unkhonto we Sizwe (known as MK) between 1948 and 1964?

→ To what extent were the key groups successful in their opposition to the apartheid system?

→ How important was the role of key individuals such as Albert Luthuli and Nelson Mandela?

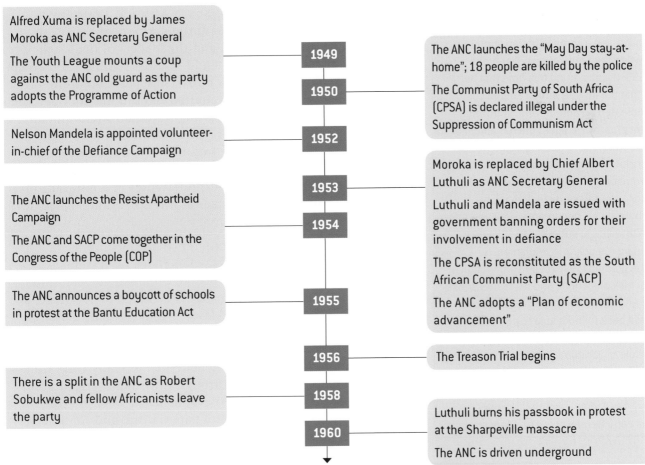

Alfred Xuma is replaced by James Moroka as ANC Secretary General

The Youth League mounts a coup against the ANC old guard as the party adopts the Programme of Action

1949

The ANC launches the "May Day stay-at-home"; 18 people are killed by the police

1950

The Communist Party of South Africa (CPSA) is declared illegal under the Suppression of Communism Act

Nelson Mandela is appointed volunteer-in-chief of the Defiance Campaign

1952

1953

Moroka is replaced by Chief Albert Luthuli as ANC Secretary General

Luthuli and Mandela are issued with government banning orders for their involvement in defiance

The ANC launches the Resist Apartheid Campaign

The ANC and SACP come together in the Congress of the People (COP)

1954

The CPSA is reconstituted as the South African Communist Party (SACP)

The ANC adopts a "Plan of economic advancement"

The ANC announces a boycott of schools in protest at the Bantu Education Act

1955

1956

The Treason Trial begins

There is a split in the ANC as Robert Sobukwe and fellow Africanists leave the party

1958

1960

Luthuli burns his passbook in protest at the Sharpeville massacre

The ANC is driven underground

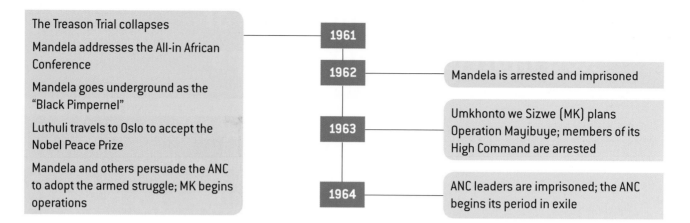

The Treason Trial collapses

Mandela addresses the All-in African Conference

Mandela goes underground as the "Black Pimpernel"

Luthuli travels to Oslo to accept the Nobel Peace Prize

Mandela and others persuade the ANC to adopt the armed struggle; MK begins operations

1961

1962 — Mandela is arrested and imprisoned

1963 — Umkhonto we Sizwe (MK) plans Operation Mayibuye; members of its High Command are arrested

1964 — ANC leaders are imprisoned; the ANC begins its period in exile

---

Mahatma Gandhi in South Africa.

Gandhi arrived in South Africa in 1893 at the age of 24, to act as a legal representative to the Indian trading community in Pretoria. However, he soon experienced racial discrimination first-hand (most famously, he was forcibly ejected from a train because he refused to move from a segregated first-class compartment) and became an increasingly outspoken critic of the authorities, founding the Natal Indian Congress in 1894. Nonetheless, he volunteered for the British and raised a corps of Indian stretcher-bearers when the South African War broke out in 1899. It was around this time that he realized that the mighty British Empire could only be defeated by *Satyagraha*, or truthful, nonviolent protest. He spent the remainder of his time in South Africa refining *Satyagraha*, both as a philosophy and as a political strategy. He led protests against the introduction of compulsory identity cards for Indians by publicly burning his documents, and urged his followers to willingly submit to the violence meted out by the police in retaliation. He earned the grudging respect and admiration of Smuts for his convictions and his fearlessness. His fame and reputation grew, and in 1915 he was invited back to India to take part in that country's independence movement against the British. While his attitude towards Africans was complex (he argued that Indians should not be subjected to the same discriminatory policies as Blacks), he is today regarded by many as one of the early heroes of the freedom struggle.

The African National Congress (ANC)

Formation and early history

The African National Congress (ANC) was the dominant force in the African nationalist opposition to the apartheid system in the period between 1948 and 1964. The party was founded as the South African Native National Congress (SANNC) at a conference in Bloemfontein in 1912. Prominent members of the Black community had recognized the need for a nationwide party that could effectively represent the interests of Africans after the creation of a Union of South Africa in 1910. It was by now obvious that union meant the permanent exclusion and subordination of Africans, and the leaders of the Black community realized that they could not just stand by and accept this fate. The idea of creating a non-White party opposing racial discrimination was not new. Mahatma Gandhi had founded the Natal Indian Congress in 1894, while Abdullah Abdurahman created the African People's Organization (a Coloured party) in 1902. As the South African National Convention negotiated union in 1908 and 1909, both of these parties, having recognized the consequences for non-Whites of a new national government dominated by Afrikaner interests, campaigned strongly against it.

Delegates at the first SANNC conference in Bloemfontein were part of a tiny elite of middle-class Black professionals. The first president, John Dube, was an ordained minister and schoolteacher. Other leading members included Pixley Seme, a Columbia and Oxford-educated lawyer, and Solomon T Plaatje, a court translator and newspaper editor. From the outset, the SANNC was a politically moderate organization. It worked on the assumption that Africans had benefited in many ways from British colonial rule, not least through Christian evangelization and education. It appealed to what it believed were the true British traditions of liberalism and paternalism, and contended that the best hope for Africans was to persuade White opinion

that Black people were civilized and respectable, and therefore worthy of greater political inclusion. The strategy of the SANNC was to work with liberal White politicians in attempting to reverse the tide of segregation, and to petition politicians in London (South Africa was still formally part of the British Empire even after 1910) by arguing that the actions of the union government were a betrayal of Britain's colonial traditions of promoting the welfare of Africans and its values of decency and fair play.

This strategy did not work out as planned. A delegation was sent to London in 1914 to protest the Natives Land Act of 1913, but was informed by the colonial secretary that he was powerless to act. Another deputation was sent all the way back to London in 1919, only to be told by Prime Minister David Lloyd George that the SANNC should return home and negotiate directly with the Smuts government in Pretoria. This response should not have come as a surprise. Smuts was by now a statesman of considerable international standing: he was a leading delegate at the peace conferences in Paris and would soon play a key role in the creation of the League of Nations.

▲ The SANNC delegation to London in 1914. John Dube is seated in the centre with Solomon T Plaatje on the right

Following these setbacks, the SANNC fell into a state of abeyance. Its leadership was dominated by traditional and conservative figures. The initiative in African politics passed to a more radical and energetic organization in the form of Clements Kadalie's Industrial and Commercial Workers' Union (ICU). The ANC (it changed its name from the SACCP to the ANC in 1922) enjoyed a brief revival in the late 1920s under the more assertive left-wing leadership of Josiah Gumede, but this was followed by another long period of dormancy in the 1930s, as many Africans suffered severe economic hardship due to the effects of the Great Depression and politics took a back seat. The ANC was viewed, by poor urban Africans in particular, as elitist and out of touch, and its membership shrank to just a few thousand. This perception of elitism continued to be a problem for the ANC well into the 1950s.

The Second World War brought about a dramatic revival in the ANC's fortunes. The South African manufacturing industry boomed and large numbers of Africans flooded into the cities. New trade unions such as the African Mine Workers' Union (AMWU) were created, many under the tutelage of the Communist Party of South Africa (CPSA). A number of these were also affiliated to the ANC, as the organization finally began to acknowledge the potential of the Black working class as a political force. An ANC Youth League was formed in 1944 with Anton Lembede as its first president. Leading members included Walter Sisulu, Oliver Tambo and Nelson Mandela. The emergence of this new generation of leaders marked a break in the strategy as well as the composition of the movement. The Youth League rejected the cautious, constitutional approach of the old guard, and instead embraced a more assertive, thrusting political stance. Gone forever was the tried and failed strategy of lobbying and attempting to negotiate with the authorities from a position of weakness. In its place, finally, was the acknowledgment that Africans could not depend on goodwill from the architects of the very system that discriminated against them, but could only look to themselves for their liberation. As Nelson Mandela put it, *"the ANC was not going to rely on a change of heart. It was going to exert pressure to compel the authorities to grant its demands."*

In line with its new strategy of reaching out to ordinary South Africans, the party began to forge links with squatters' groups and community organizations, with trade unions and other centres of opposition to the government. The Youth League drew up a radical Programme of Action, which included proposals for mass strike action and other acts in defiance of the authorities. By the time of the apartheid election of 1948, the ANC was a movement transformed. With members of the Youth League at the fore, it was a party that had placed itself in a much stronger position to challenge the imposition of a new, altogether harsher racial order.

After 1948

The ANC acted quickly in the wake of the nationalist victory. The ineffectual president-general, Alfred Xuma, was replaced by the more dynamic James Moroka in 1949, as the Youth League mounted a successful coup against the old guard. This move was accompanied by the ANC's official adoption of the Programme of Action. The party was galvanized as a result, as it enjoyed a spike in membership. It was obvious that increasing numbers of Africans, though by no means all, regarded the movement as the legitimate voice of the people. Buoyed by these events, the party announced a series of one-day general strikes in response to the quick succession of new apartheid laws. A "May Day stay-at-home" in 1950, organized in conjunction with the South African Communist Party (SACP) in response to the Suppression of Communism Act, was particularly successful. About half of the Black workers of Johannesburg refused to go to work. However, the strike also offered an early indication of the sort of response that the ANC would come to expect from the apartheid government: armed police were used to fire on protesters and 18 people were killed. Flash one-day strikes, called at short notice and in response to breaking political developments, would be a weapon that the liberation movement would use time and again in the years to come.

Source skills

Source A

E. Sisulu, a Zimbabwean writer and human rights activist. She is the daughter-in-law of former ANC leader Walter Sisulu, and his biographer. *Walter and Albertina Sisulu: In Our Lifetime,* **pages 125–26 (2002).**

Mandela was one of those who opposed the May Day strike and argued with Walter [Sisulu] that the ANC should concentrate on its own campaign …

There was indeed substantial support for the strike, and it is estimated that half the African workforce on the Witwatersrand heeded the call to stay at home on 1 May, 1950 … A heavy police contingent was deployed and meetings and gatherings were banned for the day. On the evening of the strike, 19 people were killed and over 30 injured in clashes with the police. Walter and Mandela almost found themselves on the casualty list. They were watching protestors marching in Orlando West when a group of policemen fired in their direction. They flung themselves to the ground as mounted police galloped into the crowd, lashing out with batons …

Walter's personal experience of the May Day strikes demonstrated to him the value of thinking carefully about strategy and tactics before embarking on militant action.

Source B

B. Bunting, a South African journalist, political activist and a member of the SACP. *Moses Kotane: South African Revolutionary* **(1998).**

Meanwhile, preparations went ahead for May 1st to be celebrated as a People's Holiday – being a Monday this meant a one-day strike. Not all the elements in the ANC were happy about this …

The May 1st demonstration was a huge success, and the Rand's industries came to a standstill when about 80 per cent of the black workers remained at home in response to the Convention's call. But the police resorted to brutal reprisals, breaking up every gathering of more than 12 people and towards evening the repeated provocations and terrorism of the police inevitably culminated in violence, at least 18 people being killed and an unknown number injured by police bullets.

[In the aftermath of the massacre] the ANC executive decided to launch a campaign for a national day of protest.

Third question – 6 marks

Compare and contrast the accounts presented in Sources A and B of the "May Day stay-at-home" strike in 1950.

By 1952, however, it had become obvious to the ANC leadership that irregular strike action was no longer generating the desired political traction. The circumstances demanded a new, more coordinated strategy of continuous resistance. The result was the Defiance Campaign, the details and results of which are described on pages 51–55.

One unforeseen consequence of the Defiance Campaign was another change in the leadership of the party. Having taken part in an act of defiance of the apartheid laws, Moroka inexplicably pleaded not guilty to the charges brought against him. His actions compromised the integrity of the campaign, the purpose of which was to offer guilty pleas and fill apartheid prisons with protesters. Moroka's position was untenable and he was forced to resign. He was replaced as president-general by Chief Albert Luthuli. This change was important for the ANC, as Luthuli, a man with impeccable moral credentials, was to prove himself a redoubtable opponent of the apartheid regime. As he was a committed Christian and a traditional leader, it would be harder for the government to portray the ANC under Luthuli as a communist-dominated revolutionary group with no legitimacy among ordinary Africans.

Building a mass base: the Women's League was one of the ways in which the ANC sought to extend its support among ordinary Africans in the 1950s

Under Luthuli, the ANC continued to move in the direction that had been set by the Youth League. Despite the rapid growth in its membership, part of its challenge after the Defiance Campaign was to find a way of successfully tapping into the grievances of the masses. Too many Blacks still regarded the ANC as an elite party that had little concern for the hardships of their daily lives. It was perceived as too narrowly political and seemed more concerned with apartheid laws that directly affected the interests of the Black middle classes than with addressing the more pressing issues of extreme poverty and homelessness. In response, the ANC adopted a "Programme of Economic Advancement" in 1953 in an attempt to highlight its commitment to fighting against the extreme economic marginalization of poor Africans under apartheid. The ANC was also determined to reach out to women. The Women's League was immensely successful in attracting women to the party and its president,

Lilian Ngoyi, was elected to the ANC National Executive Committee in 1956. The party strove to work with other anti-apartheid groups in building a common front against apartheid. The result was the creation of the Congress Alliance, which in turn organized the Congress of the People (COP). This important development, and the hugely symbolic Freedom Charter that stemmed from it, is described on pages 56–60.

As seen on page 37, another campaign in which the ANC was involved at this time (1953–55) was the campaign against the introduction of Verwoerd's notorious Bantu Education Act. This was, in the main, a failure. Instead of sending their children to schools that offered the new,

Senior leaders of the ANC in the 1950s: Walter Sisulu, Govan Mbeki, Oliver Tambo, Robert Sobukwe

inferior curriculum, the ANC urged parents to observe a boycott of these government schools and instead enroll their children in community-run "cultural centres". It quickly became evident that the ANC lacked the resources necessary to make this a viable educational alternative, and the boycott soon lost momentum as the campaign spluttered to a halt.

Another notable development during this period was the initiation of the ANC's Resist Apartheid Campaign. At the heart of this was the strident opposition of the ANC to the forced evictions from Sophiatown that were planned as part of the government's Western Areas Removal Scheme (see also pages 22–23). The campaign was launched at a meeting in Johannesburg in July 1954. This was due to be addressed by Luthuli, whose first two-year banning order was due to expire on that day. Unfortunately, Luthuli was arrested at the airport and issued with a second ban, which prevented him from making his speech. Nonetheless, the speech, which referred to the scheme as the "legalized robbery" of African property, was read out at the meeting.

Once the evictions began in January 1955, the ANC swung into action with its campaign of resistance to the removals, which rallied people behind the slogan "We shall not move". This resistance involved a coalition of other anti-apartheid organizations and community groups, led by Sophiatown's charismatic Anglican parish priest, the Englishman Trevor Huddleston. Despite an international outcry and the steadfastness of the opposition to the scheme, the campaign failed to achieve its objective of saving Sophiatown. The suburb was completely razed by the end of the decade. The campaign also exposed a still-present chink in the armour of the ANC. Bizarrely, many poor Black tenants appeared to be visibly elated during their forced removals from Sophiatown. They knew that the new housing provided by the state would free them from exorbitant rents charged by their (mainly Black) landlords, and their failure to resist the resettlement had the effect of undermining opposition to the scheme. As the leading ANC and SACP activist JB Marks noted, the party still had much work to do in overcoming class divisions in Black society and winning the unwavering support of the poorest South Africans.

Two more events are worth mentioning in this section: the Treason Trial of 1956–61, and the split in the movement which resulted from the Africanist breakaway and formation of the Pan Africanist Congress (PAC) in January 1959. As mentioned on page 60, the former was a prolonged legal case mounted by the government against hundreds of the organizers of the Congress of the People (COP), including all of the leaders of the ANC. The authorities argued that they were guilty of planning to overthrow the state. The charges were clearly spurious, but the trial did have the effect of temporarily removing from the scene, at a crucial juncture in the history of the movement, senior

▲ The 156 defendants at the Drill Hall in Johannesburg at the start of the Treason Trial

leaders such as Luthuli, Mandela and Sisulu. Their absence allowed the emergence of a major Africanist challenge from within the ranks of the party. The final split came in late 1958, when Robert Sobukwe and his followers failed to prevent Oliver Tambo from formally rewriting the ANC's constitution to incorporate the ideals and goals of the Freedom Charter. The result was the creation of the PAC in early 1959.

The major campaigns and protests in which the ANC was involved for the remainder of the period have also been described at length in earlier sections of the book. They included the bus boycotts, the "stay-at-home" strike and passbook protests, which contributed to the Sharpeville massacre. This was followed by the banning of the movement, the decision to create Umkhonto we Sizwe (MK), then finally the defence mounted at the Rivonia Trial.

One of the major failures of the ANC in the 1950s – its inability to achieve its objective of creating a true mass movement against apartheid, one which included poor Africans as well as the middle classes – has already been alluded to earlier in this section. However, by the early 1960s, with the harshly repressive measures of the government and the high national profile it enjoyed following the creation of MK and the publicity of the Rivonia Trial, it came close to achieving this aim. It is enormously ironic that the resistance movement reached the height of its popularity at precisely the time that it was being brought to its knees by the might of the apartheid state, first by its prohibition and then by the arrest, trial and life imprisonment of its leaders.

How successful was the ANC between 1948 and 1964?

It can be argued that the ANC's successes were many. It completed its transformation from a moribund and largely inactive organization into a radical, more mass-based movement that represented the aspirations of the majority of South Africans in the face of massive injustice and repression. Despite its many setbacks at the hands of overwhelming state power, it time and again carried the fight to the apartheid authorities, first with the Defiance Campaign, then with the COP and the bus boycotts, and finally with the decision to embrace armed struggle. It brought the injustices of the apartheid regime to the attention of the world and gained the moral high ground through its early strategy of non-violent resistance.

The ANC was also successful in forging alliances with a range of other anti-apartheid groups, including the South African Indian Congress (SAIC), the South African Coloured Peoples' Organization and the South African Congress of Democrats, through the Congress of the People (COP) in 1955. The Freedom Charter became one of the iconic documents of 20th-century struggle. Despite the government's success in crushing the ANC and MK in 1964, the movement was without question the political voice of the huge majority of Black South Africans by the end of the period from 1948 and 1964.

At the same time, the ANC was found wanting on a number of important counts. Its failures include the following:
- The movement failed in its ultimate objective of bringing down the apartheid system. Indeed, it found it impossible to win even simplest concessions from the government. The Defiance Campaign and

the bus boycotts were of symbolic importance but they had no real impact in weakening the NP.

- Attempts to maintain party unity failed with the Africanist breakaway to form the PAC in 1959.

- Close relations with the SACP contributed to this breakaway, and also alienated White liberals who may otherwise have supported the movement.

- The decision to adopt the armed struggle confirmed the suspicion of many Whites that the ANC was at heart a terrorist organization. This played into the hands of the government and emboldened it to extend the apartheid system still further.

- The ANC had no effective answer when the government launched its crackdown in the aftermath of the Sharpeville massacre.

- The jailing of senior ANC leaders in 1964 was followed by a lengthy period of relative quiet. While the townships seethed with resentment, the authorities managed to keep a lid on tensions until the sudden eruption of violence in Soweto in 1976. Clearly, the authorities had succeeded in destroying anti-apartheid resistance by the end of the period.

The South African Communist Party (SACP)

The Communist Party of South Africa (CPSA) was founded in Cape Town in 1921. Two major events were crucial in shaping the early history of the party. The first was the Bolshevik Revolution in Russia in 1917, an event that inspired revolutionaries across the globe and prompted many of them to found Marxist parties of their own. The second was the dramatic growth of the South African labour movement in the years after the First World War. This growth took place against the backdrop of the fierce struggle between White workers and the mining houses. Due to a fall in the price of gold, the mining magnates, with the full support of the Smuts government, proposed to cut costs by lowering the wages of White workers and suspending the so-called colour bar by allowing Blacks to be employed in some semi-skilled and supervisory positions. This prompted a furious reaction from the White proletariat, and a series of strikes that brought production to a virtual standstill by the end of 1921. Considering the revolutionary potential in this situation, the newly formed CPSA decided to throw its lot in with the White protesters. One of the leading agitators in the struggle was CPSA leader WH Andrews, popularly known as "Comrade Bill". Ironically, this meant that the communists found themselves allied to an avowedly racist labour movement. One of the main goals of the White workers was the reinstatement of the colour bar, and their protests frequently involved random assaults on innocent Black passers-by. The struggle climaxed in the Rand Revolt (also known as the Rand Rebellion) of March 1922, an armed uprising of 22,000 White workers against the state. Smuts sent in the army and the revolt was bloodily suppressed, with 200 workers killed in the fighting.

Smuts was punished by White voters for his role in putting down the rebellion and his South African Party (SAP) lost power in the general election in 1924. It was replaced by a coalition "Pact Government" of Hertzog's nationalists and the mainly anglophone South African Labour Party. The Labour Party had competed with the CPSA for influence over White miners during the 1922 revolt. As a revolutionary communist organization, the CPSA was obviously far more radical (and less racist) than the Labour Party – a party that was now willing to join a coalition with Afrikaner nationalists in order to secure the interests of its White workers at the expense of the Black majority. The formation of the coalition was followed by a flurry of new racist legislation.

With its rival, racist White workers' party now in government, the CPSA performed a dramatic about-turn. Under orders from the Comintern (the global organization of communist parties dominated by Moscow), the party shifted its focus from White labour to the African proletariat. By the end of 1925, the majority of party members were Black. In 1928, it called for Black majority rule in the country. Nonetheless, the CPSA was still a party in which White intellectuals remained very prominent. Many leading figures, including Solly Sachs and Bram Fischer, were also Jewish. Blacks, as well as Indians, were also represented in the upper echelons of the party: JB Marks, Johannes Nkosi and Moses Kotane were all important leaders during its early history.

The CPSA first began to forge close links with the ANC in the late 1920s. The radical Josiah Gumede became the leader of the congress in 1928 and the party veered sharply to the left under his stewardship. A number of Black communists joined the ANC during this period. They remained influential members of both parties for years to come. However, the close relationship faded in the 1930s, as the ANC swung back to the right under the conservative leadership of Pixley Seme. The CPSA struggled at this time, with dwindling membership and the attempts of some of its leaders forcibly to Stalinize the party. Despite its troubles, the CPSA worked assiduously to develop the labour movement, and its influence over workers grew once again in the late 1930s. While the principal focus was on the African proletariat, the party was scrupulously non-racial in its approach, always seeking to build a broad coalition of workers. It formed the South African Trades and Labour Council, a federation that affiliated many unions, some of which were Afrikaner. The party was also instrumental in establishing the AMWU in 1941, whose first president was the leading Black communist JB Marks.

In the early post-war years, the CPSU was so successful in influencing workers across the racial divide that the NP began to view it as a major threat to its own strategy of creating an Afrikaner nationalist movement that united all social classes. The NP argued that the country was now threatened by a global communist conspiracy. NP members paradoxically contended that communism sought to undermine the unity of the "*volk*" (Afrikaner people) by exposing the White working class to ideas of non-racialism, while simultaneously turning Black against White and

fomenting civil war. Anti-communist fervour reached a peak in the build-up to the 1948 election, when the twin fears of "red peril" (communism) and "black peril" (Africans) were fused in the Afrikaner nationalist mindset. Anti-red paranoia played a significant role in DF Malan's election victory. The historian and political scientist Philip Nel (1990) argues that this period marks the beginning of the NP's long-running obsession with communism. He suggests that this stemmed from a need to explain the growth of internal opposition to racial policies in terms of the pernicious influence of an outside actor, in this case the Soviet Union.

The official crackdown on communism and African labour was already well underway before the NP took power in 1948. The AMWU-organized miners' strike of 1946 was crushed by police action. The strike failed to achieve any of its objectives and workers were forced back into the mines a few days later. However, the strike brought about a profound change in political consciousness in the country, with workers and government officials becoming more aware of the potential of communist-inspired, mass-based protest against the regime.

▲ The mine workers' strike of 1946

The new government took action against the CPSU as soon as Malan assumed office in 1948. Clearly signalling its intent, the NP immediately closed down the Soviet consular offices in Johannesburg and Cape Town (diplomatic ties had been established in 1942 when South Africa and the Soviet Union unexpectedly found themselves allies in the Second World War). The CPSA was an obvious target of the government's Suppression of Communism Act, which was passed in 1950. However the legislation was designed as a weapon that could be used not only against communists, but against the anti-apartheid movement more generally. The conflation of the ANC with communism was part of a deliberate government strategy. This was the time of McCarthyist anti-communist witch hunts in the USA, and the South African authorities believed they could stigmatize the ANC by associating the party with communism.

The upshot of the new law was that that the CPSA was declared illegal and driven underground. Many of its leaders were issued with banning orders, which they defied by continuing to speak in public, resulting in their imprisonment. Others, including JB Marks, Moses Kotane and Solly Sachs, organized the Defiance Campaign along with the ANC and the SAIC. The party was reconstituted, still illegally, as the South African Communist Party (SACP) in 1953. SAIC leader Yusuf Dadoo was elected chairman and Moses Kotane party secretary. The party's change of name was significant. It emphasized that the party, while still part of a wider communist movement, was now primarily South African rather than internationalist in its orientation. Its principal goal was to work with other groups to bring an end to apartheid. The emancipation of the global proletariat could come later.

In other important respects, however, the party remained much the same as it had been before. Ideologically, it remained true to its revolutionary heritage of seeking the overthrow of a capitalist economic order. It argued that it was capitalism that had given rise to the system of exploitation and racial oppression in the first place, and that apartheid could be defeated only with a simultaneous assault on the economic system that provided its sustenance. The SACP was also a highly disciplined vanguard party, in the sense that it was headed by a small group of professional revolutionaries whose role was to lead the masses from the front. It was also intensely secretive: it was only confirmed after his death in 2013 that Mandela had served on the central committee of the party shortly before his arrest in 1962.

As the struggle against apartheid developed, the SACP and the ANC drew ever closer. The party was a key player in moves to further integrate anti-apartheid groups through the COP. The White-dominated Congress of Democrats, an organization at the heart of the Congress Alliance, was essentially a front for the communists. The influence of the SACP was obvious in some of the strongly socialist principles enshrined in the Freedom Charter. For example, the Freedom Charter stated that *"The mineral wealth beneath the soil, the banks and monopoly industry shall be transferred to the ownership of the people as a whole"*, and that *"the land [shall be] re-divided amongst those who work it"* (see pages 58–59). Ruth First, the leading SACP activist and wife of another leading figure in the SACP, Joe Slovo, played an important role in founding the Congress of Democrats and drafting the Freedom Charter.

▲ Leading members of the SACP: Moses Kotane (pictured with Nelson Mandela), JB Marks, Ruth First, Lionel Bernstein

The government used the Freedom Charter as evidence in its case against ANC leaders in the famous Treason Trial, which began in 1956. It alleged that the movement had been thoroughly infiltrated by the SACP and that both organizations were guilty of treason by conspiring socialist revolution. SACP member Bram Fischer led the defence of the accused. The state managed to drag the trial on until 1961, but it failed to prove its case and all the defendants were acquitted.

ATL Communication and research skills

Choose to research the background and career of either Ruth First or Oliver Tambo. Find a partner who has chosen to research the same leader. As a pair, find information about that leader on the internet, then prepare a 10-minute presentation. Make your presentation to a pair of students who have chosen the other leader. The other pair then make their presentation to you and your partner.

The Treason Trial was important because it helped persuade the new generation of ANC leaders that the government was determined to increase its repression of peaceful protest and destroy the resistance movement come what may, and that the time for non-violent opposition had perhaps passed. Following Sharpeville and the government's prohibition of the ANC, Umkhonto we Sizwe (MK) was finally formed in 1961. Its creation was strongly influenced by SACP leaders who were also members of the ANC. An initial decision to launch the armed struggle had been taken at a secret Communist Party conference held in Johannesburg in December 1960, with Nelson Mandela and Walter Sisulu both present on behalf of the ANC. Interestingly, the main dissenting voice at this meeting was that of SACP Secretary-General Moses Kotane, who warned that the movement was not yet ready for military action and would surely be crushed by its formidable opponent. After the creation of MK, a SACP delegation was sent to Moscow in early 1962. It managed to secure funding, training and other support for MK. SACP funds paid for MK's "safe house", Liliesleaf Farm in Rivonia, which was owned by leading party member Arthur Goldreich. Denis Goldberg, Joe Slovo, Lionel Bernstein and Goldreich were all members of the MK High Command.

At the Rivonia Trial, the defendants, who included Goldberg and Bernstein (the latter being the only one to be acquitted), were represented once again by communist lawyer Bram Fischer. During the trial Mandela, falsely, denied being a communist, although he did admit that the relationship between the ANC and the SACP was a very close one. Following the guilty verdicts, Fischer was himself tried for treason in a separate trial in 1965–66. He died of illness while on compassionate release from his life sentence in 1975. After life sentences had been handed down to the accused, the mantle of leading the liberation struggle fell to the ANC in exile, headed by Oliver Tambo.

▲ Bram Fischer addresses a secret CPSA meeting in the early 1950s. The portraits on the left and right of the stage are of Moses Kotane and "Comrade Bill" Andrews

At this point, the role of the SACP became even more important, as the movement had little option but to rely on friendly communist governments to provide the necessary funding and logistical support and training for the establishment of its frontline military camps and bases. Tambo, Kotane and Slovo all travelled to the Soviet Union to receive guerrilla training in 1964. The intimate connection between the ANC and Moscow, and the strong influence of the SACP over the ANC, were to continue thereafter.

Assessment

It is evident that the SACP had a hugely important influence on development of the liberation movement between 1948 and 1964. This was due in large part to its close ties with the ANC. The party helped orient the ANC towards non-racialism and in a more militant direction, to such an extent that the ANC was eventually persuaded to embrace armed struggle against the apartheid regime. However, the SACP's importance goes beyond its links with the ANC. The party played a key role in organizing strike action through its union affiliations, most notably during the miners' strike of 1946. While this strike obviously falls outside the time frame of the period being examined, it was of major significance in terms of its impact on the politics that followed. Indeed, some historians have argued that the strike marked the true beginning of the struggle against segregation and apartheid.

There are other perspectives on the degree of SACP influence during this period. One is that it is all too easy to exaggerate its role because of the incessant anti-communist propaganda of the government. The authorities were never slow to identify the malign hand of global communism behind every development in the anti-apartheid movement, and to argue that all opposition was the work of Moscow's handmaiden in South Africa, the SACP. In reality, the ANC was always by far the larger and more influential of the two organizations. Several of its leading members, including Anton Lembede, Alfred Xuma, James Moroka and Albert Luthuli, were never communists. Some of them were actively hostile to communism. If one organization was at all dominate over the other, it was more probable that it was the ANC over the SACP. Indeed, the SACP was unique among communist parties in that it prioritized, at least in the short term, domestic factors (the struggle against apartheid) over proletarian revolution.

Another perspective is that the role of the SACP was indeed profound, but that its influence was very much to the detriment of the liberation movement. The association with communism offered the government a convenient stick with which to beat the ANC. The ANC may also have won more sympathy and support from the White population had it not been for its ties with the SACP. Similarly, the ANC's proximity to the SACP alienated its Africanist wing, which broke away to form the PAC, thus splitting the liberation movement.

The historian Stephen Ellis (2012) has argued that the SACP's sway over the ANC was so great that the ANC effectively allowed itself to be taken over by the communists after the Rivonia Trial and the exile of its remaining leaders. SACP leader Joe Slovo became the head of MK, as the movement focused on building relations with communist states instead of taking the fight directly to the apartheid regime by carrying out combat operations on South African soil.

Source skills

Source A

An extract from Nelson Mandela's autobiography, *The Long Walk to Freedom* (1994).

Marxism's call for revolutionary action was music to the ears of the freedom fighter. The idea that history progresses through struggle and that change occurs in revolutionary jumps was similarly appealing … I was prepared to use whatever means necessary to speed up the erasure of human prejudice and the end of chauvinistic and violent nationalism. I did not need to become a communist in order to work with them. I found that African nationalists and African communists generally had far more to unite them than to divide them … The cynical have always suggested that the communists where using us. But who is to say that we were not using them?

Second question – 4 marks

With reference to its origin, purpose and content, assess the values and limitations of Source A for historians studying the role of the SACP and its influence on Nelson Mandela and the ANC during the 1950s and early 1960s.

Source B

A letter written by Rian Malan, a well-known South African writer, journalist and songwriter, to the editors of the *New York Review of Books*, 21 March 2013. Malan was at the time embroiled in the controversy surrounding Stephen Ellis' book, *External Mission: The ANC in Exile*.

[We] are only just beginning to understand the extent of [the SACP's] influence historically. New research by historian Stephen Ellis shows, for instance, that SACP militants found themselves in an awkward position in 1960, when their secret plans for armed struggle encountered resistance from South Africa's two most important black politicians – ANC president Albert Luthuli and SACP general secretary Moses Kotane. Rather than back down, these militants co-opted Nelson Mandela onto the Communist Party's Central Committee and tasked him to "bounce" the mighty ANC into agreement with their position. The result, said veteran Communist Roley Arenstein, was tantamount to "a hijacking" of the mighty ANC by a tiny clique of mostly white and Indian intellectuals.

Third question – 6 marks

Compare and contrast the views expressed in Sources A and B regarding the influence of the SACP on the ANC.

Umkhonto we Sizwe (MK)

Unkhonto we Sizwe (MK), which means "spear of the nation" in Zulu and Xhosa, was the armed wing of the ANC. It was created on 16 December 1961, on the anniversary of the famous Boer victory over Zulu armies at the Battle of Blood River in 1838, and commenced operations on the same day, carrying out a series of explosions targeting government buildings and electrical installations across the nation.

The decision to create MK

The ANC's decision to embrace armed struggle by creating MK was both complex and contentious. It was by no means clear to all in the party that non-violent resistance, which had served the party for over a decade and become part of its moral fabric, should be abandoned. The non-violent approach was embodied in the person of the leader of the ANC, Chief Albert Luthuli. His formidable authority within the party would have to be overcome if armed struggle were to be adopted. Opponents of armed struggle argued that abandoning the path of civil disobedience in favour of armed confrontation would gift the regime with the opportunity to

History and ethics

Modern history is filled with examples of moments when key individuals or groups were confronted with decisions that had profound moral implications. One of these was the dilemma facing the ANC when it had to decide between continuing its strategy of non-violent resistance or creating MK and taking up armed struggle against apartheid. The example illuminates many of the issues which arise in the field of ethics as an area of knowledge. These include the following:

1 Can the circumstances justify the use of violence? How does whether an action is considered right or wrong depend on the context?

2 Which is the surer guide to moral action: individual conscience or universal ethical principle?

3 How can we use different ethical systems (for example, deontological and consequentialist ethics) as a guide to our moral decision making? Is it possible to resolve the contradictions between these systems? How might these positions apply to the ANC's debate about the armed struggle?

4 Does the example of the anti-apartheid struggle prove that it is possible for people to act against their own interests? Does altruism define what is good?

5 Should moral considerations matter in politics? Does the end always justify the means?

depict the ANC as a terrorist body and then completely destroy it. This organization lacked any experience of armed struggle and its members had no military training. It was faced with the might of one of the most powerful armed forces in the world. In addition, by embracing violence, the ANC risked surrendering the moral high ground and alienating many of its moderate allies in the anti-apartheid struggle. Global opinion was now increasingly on its side, and it risked squandering some of this international goodwill if it came to be perceived as a movement committed to violence.

At the same time, the arguments in favour of armed struggle were compelling. By the early 1960s, the ANC risked being outflanked by the PAC, which had already launched its own armed wing, Poqo. The ANC stood to lose even more popular ground to its Africanist rival if its response to Sharpeville and the other brutal events of 1960 was seen by the masses as ineffectual. There was already a concern at the ease with which the PAC had been able to hijack the ANC's anti-pass laws campaign.

The party seemed at risk of being overtaken by the pace of events in other ways too. Rural revolts were an increasingly regular feature of the struggle in the 1950s. These culminated in peasants taking up arms against alleged government collaborators in Zeerust, Pondoland and Sekhukhuneland in the late 1950s and early 1960s. Amid a general atmosphere of violence, the ANC's principled stance of peaceful protest was beginning to look idealistic and untenable. The argument that the government would use the establishment of an armed wing as an ideal excuse to prohibit the movement was rendered moot with its decision to ban the ANC anyway in April 1960. The party was driven underground and the scope for legal protest had dramatically narrowed. For many, the logical next step was armed struggle.

The most powerful of all of the arguments in favour of armed resistance, though, was the sheer implacability of the NP government and its willingness to resort to extreme force to quash any form of protest. Apartheid's planners had proven themselves resistant to any attempts at moral persuasion or peaceful protest, whether from the Black resistance movement inside the country or from the global community that had turned decisively against South Africa. The government had grown steadily more brutal, answering non-violence with the overwhelming force of the state security apparatus. It had also embarked on an extending and deepening of the country's racist laws with the advent of Verwoerd's grand apartheid. In spite of the peaceful resistance of the ANC, the predicament of Africans had steadily worsened.

The idea of an armed wing had been gestating in the minds of leading ANC members for some time. Mandela had spoken publicly of armed struggle as early as 1953 when he addressed a meeting in Sophiatown, and subsequent developments were to lead to a gradual hardening of his position. His "M Plan" envisioned the government's prohibition of the ANC, and the creation of an armed wing as a necessary precondition for the guerrilla war that would constitute the next stage of the anti-apartheid struggle. Mandela was not the only member of the party to consider more radical measures. The left-wing youth of the movement, the trade unions and radical Africanists alike grew restive at what they perceived to be the unduly cautious approach of the leaders. Luthuli's calls for patience could only be heeded for so long, and he was seen as increasingly out of step with the rank and file of the party.

The events of 1960 proved decisive in swinging the argument in favour of moving the struggle on to a new phase. The scale of the violence unleashed by the police at Sharpeville shocked even the veterans of the movement. The government's response to further protests was to declare a state of emergency that made all political protests illegal. Both the ANC and the PAC were banned when the authorities passed the Unlawful Organizations Act in April. Leading ANC and SACP members were arrested and were not released until August. While they were in prison, Walter Sisulu and Nelson Mandela, along with SACP leaders Joe Slovo and Lionel Bernstein, held discussions about an imminent move to armed struggle. At a secret SACP meeting at the end of the year, the party, with Mandela and Sisulu in attendance, resolved to create its own armed wing, ideally with the involvement of the ANC but if necessary without it.

In March 1961, the defendants in the marathon Treason Trial were finally acquitted. Fearing rearrest, Nelson Mandela finally decided to go on the run from the authorities, beginning the period during which he became known as the "Black Pimpernel". With Mandela's decision to go underground, the prospect that the movement as a whole would adopt a more radical strategy moved closer. In May, a planned three-day strike was called to protest against the government's decision to leave the British Commonwealth. The resulting government crackdown on the "stay-at-home" was emphatic. All police leave was cancelled and tanks were sent into the townships. Predictably, the strike was a failure. This remarkable show of force left the ANC

▲ Veterans of the MK High Command meet at Liliesleaf Farm in 2001: Lionel Bernstein, Andrew Mlangeni, Denis Goldberg, Raymond Mhlaba and Arthur Goldreich

to question the viability of further peaceful demonstrations. According to Slovo, both the ANC and the SACP were now moving together towards recognising the necessity of armed struggle. In June 1961, Mandela presented his proposal for an official MK to senior party leaders at an ANC working committee. A decision was finally taken at a Durban ANC Party Congress in July when, crucially, Luthuli was persuaded that his party had simply run out of other options.

MK operations

MK was hastily constituted on 16 December 1961 (ironically, this was the anniversary of the famous Boer victory over the Zulu at Blood River in 1838), and it began operations on the same day. A National

High Command included Nelson Mandela, Walter Sisulu, Joe Slovo and Raymond Mhlaba. This body liaised with the political leadership of the movement and directed smaller MK regional commands. These regional commands in turn organized small cells of MK cadres, which planned and executed acts of sabotage. Many of the regional members were White communists, selected for their technical expertise and knowledge of explosives.

The first phase of the armed struggle involved a series of sabotage operations. The purpose was to register symbolic strikes against the apartheid state while also hitting the regime financially by destroying high-value installations such as power stations and electricity pylons. Other infrastructural targets such as post offices and telephone exchanges were selected, as well as more obvious symbols of the state, such as police stations and tax offices. Every effort was made to avoid loss of life during these operations. A second phase of the armed struggle envisaged a series of guerrilla campaigns conducted by MK in rural areas. Continued acts of sabotage were to be combined with mass political agitation and strike action in the cities. Unfortunately for the movement, this phase was never reached.

The first phase of the armed struggle gradually petered out towards the end of 1963 as daring attacks on government installations became less frequent. The reason lies not with any diminishing appetite for armed struggle, but in the typically forceful response of the Verwoerd government. The General Laws Amendment Act of 1962 (better known as the Sabotage Act) made it a criminal offence to plan or execute even the most minor act of sabotage, which was vaguely defined as "wrongful or willful acts". Sentences ranged from a minimum of five years' imprisonment to the death penalty. The police spared no effort in hunting down underground leaders of the movement. Mandela, the "Black Pimpernel", was eventually captured, tried and imprisoned, and then subsequently brought before a court once again to face new charges along with the other MK leaders at the famous Rivonia Trial of 1963–64. Following the guilty sentences, attempts were made to reconstitute the MK High Command but these efforts met with little success. The authorities had the movement well and truly on the run. Regional commands were in disarray: with all of the major leaders either arrested or in exile there was no direction from the centre. The "spear of the nation trial" of MK cadres in Natal in 1964 extinguished the armed wing in the province where it had been most effective. By the end of the year, all armed activity in South Africa had ceased. The next phase of the armed struggle, conducted from exile and on an altogether more limited scale, had begun. With the ANC and MK destroyed on the ground, the anti-apartheid struggle seemed to be at the lowest of ebbs. It would be over a decade before it would rise again.

▲ MK sabotage of an electricity pylon, 1962

Assessment

By any objective reckoning, MK was in many ways a failure. Its creation gave the government the green light to launch an all-out assault on the liberation movement. The result is that the first phase of the armed struggle lasted only a couple of years. By 1964, MK had been hunted down and its organizational structure in South Africa dismantled. Its most important leaders were arrested and imprisoned by the authorities, and the others forced into exile. Moreover, its operations were largely limited to acts of sabotage. Not once did MK directly engage in combat with the South African security forces, nor did it ever land a really decisive blow against the apartheid state. The "M Plan" failed to get off the ground, with MK failing to spark its planned rural insurgency. Once the first phase of MK operations had ended, a lengthy period of almost complete inaction ensued, during which time the ANC and MK were organizationally moribund in South Africa.

Yet these criticisms of MK tell only half the story. The South African government was determined to crush the ANC come what may. It can be argued, then, that the outcome of 1964 was nearly inevitable after Sharpeville, and the creation of MK had little bearing on this result. Indeed, the ANC had already been banned and driven underground before MK was even founded.

MK was successful in other ways:

- It showed that Africans were not afraid to take up arms against the might of the government. The courageous acts of sabotage carried out by MK operatives added lustre to the ANC legend. Its cadres struck at the apartheid goliath at great risk to themselves, and in so doing became heroes to many South Africans.

- The fact that MK even existed helped to keep the spirit of resistance alive during the dark days of the late 1960s and early 1970s. Indeed, it can be argued the first stage of the armed struggle served as an important precedent and a source of inspiration for the dramatic surge in resistance in the townships during and after the Soweto Uprising of 1976.

Source skills

Source A

An extract from Govan Mbeki, senior leader of the ANC and SACP, and a member of the MK High Command, *The Stuggle for Liberation in South Africa: A Short History* **(1992).**

In its manifesto, Umkhonto pointed out that it would include in its ranks "South Africans of all races" in carrying out a struggle into which it was forced by government policies. "The time comes in the life of any nation when there remain only two choices: submit or fight. That time has now come to South Africa. We shall not submit and we have no choice but to hit back by all means within our power in defence of our people, our future and our freedom ..."

The manifesto further emphasised the point that, by taking the action which it did, MK was seeking to avoid a civil war in the country: "We of Umkhonto we Sizwe have always sought as the liberation movement to achieve liberation without bloodshed and civil clash. We do still. We hope even at this late hour that our first actions will awaken everyone to a realisation of the disastrous situation to which the Nationalist policy is leading."

The manifesto ended by assuring the people of South Africa that there could be no happiness or peace in the country until the Nationalist government had been overthrown. "In these actions, we are working in the best interest of all the people of this country – black, brown and white – whose future happiness and well-being cannot be attained without the overthrow of the Nationalist government, the abolition of white supremacy and the winning of liberty, democracy and full national rights and equality for all the people of this country."

First question, part a – 3 marks

According to Source A, why did the ANC resort to armed struggle in 1961?

First question, part b – 2 marks

What is the message of the cartoon in Source B?

Source B

A cartoon by Norman Mansbridge, published by *Punch* magazine in 1960.

DRAGON'S TEETH

Albert Luthuli

The revered figure of Chief Albert Luthuli (often spelled "Lutuli") was president-general of the ANC from 1952 until his death in 1967.

Albert Luthuli was born near Bulawayo in Southern Rhodesia in 1898. His father was a Seventh-day Adventist minister and Albert was educated in a mission school in his ancestral home of Groutville in Natal, before training as a teacher. Luthuli's religious background was to be hugely important in influencing his later career. His abiding commitment to the use of non-violence and moral example as a means of opposing the apartheid system was a product of his Christian upbringing. His background as an educator was also significant. Luthuli constantly stressed the value of education as a means of advancement for Africans. From the early 1920s, he worked on the staff of Adams College near Durban.

However, Luthuli's standing in his Zulu community, together with his growing indignation at the policies of the Hertzog government, meant that he was drawn towards a career in politics. He joined the Natal Native Teachers' Union and was involved in the organization of school boycotts. In 1935, he was elected by tribal elders to the chieftaincy of Groutville, which had been designated as a native reserve area under the Natives Land Act of 1913. In 1936, the decision of the Hertzog government to introduce the Representation of Natives Act, a law that finally removed Blacks from the common voters' roll in the Cape, contributed to the growing radicalism of Luthuli's outlook. He joined the

ANC in 1944 and was elected to the Native Representative Council, an advisory body established under the 1936 act, a year later. He used his position on the council to lead opposition to the government's bloody suppression of the 1946 miners' strike, and this resistance influenced the decision of the authorities to disband the council shortly afterwards. Luthuli was able to devote more time to his activities in the ANC thereafter, and he became provincial president in Natal in 1951.

Luthuli's increasing prominence as a leader of the resistance movement meant that he was one of the key organizers of the Defiance Campaign. His firm Christian principles and noble bearing made him an ideal figurehead for a series of protests that were designed to highlight the moral injustice of the apartheid system. The government reacted to his involvement in the campaign by insisting that he either resign his membership of the ANC or face the prospect of surrendering his chieftaincy. He refused to comply and was duly dismissed as chief of Groutville reserve. His growing reputation in the ANC was further enhanced when he wrote "The Road to Freedom is via the Cross", a public statement in response to this decision. In this statement, Luthuli argued that principled non-violence was the only viable strategy in opposing apartheid, and that the system would eventually collapse when the peaceful resistance of Africans finally convinced Whites of the fundamental injustice of a racist system.

Luthuli was elected president-general of the ANC in December 1952, after the embarrassing episode involving incumbent president James Moroka (see page 85). His election was important in restoring dignity to the office, especially at a time when the authorities were using the widespread rioting that was threatening to engulf the Eastern Cape and other parts of the country to portray the movement as violent and revolutionary. However, Luthuli's effectiveness as ANC leader was curtailed by the government almost as soon as he assumed the office. He was immediately slapped with a two-year banning order under the Suppression of Communism Act. This was the first in a series of banning orders that were to dog the remainder of his political career. The bans prevented him from holding large meetings or speaking in public, and confined him to his home in rural Groutville. Following the expiry of an existing ban in July 1954, his attempt to travel to Johannesburg and address a rally marking the launch of the ANC's Resist Apartheid Campaign resulted in his arrest and re-banning as soon as he arrived at the airport.

Despite these repeated bans, Luthuli still played a role in formulating the overall strategy of the movement. Other ANC leaders would visit to consult with him in Groutville before any important decisions were made. He wrote speeches and could attend the occasional ANC conference. It was around this time, in the mid-1950s, that Luthuli attempted to mediate between the two factions that emerged in the ANC: the Africanists, and the "Charterists", left-wingers who favoured non-racialism and collaboration with the SACP. Initially wary of committing the ANC to a full alliance with leftist parties, he was eventually accused by the Africanists of openly siding with their opponents. This was a factor in the decision of Robert Sobukwe and his supporters to break away and form the PAC.

Luthuli was arrested in 1956 and was held for over a year as one of the defendants in the Treason Trial, before being released due to a lack of evidence. Despite enjoying a period of relative freedom in the late 1950s, he had little direct involvement in major protests such as the Alexandra bus boycott. Instead, younger, more energetic figures were increasingly taking the lead, men such as Mandela, Sisulu, Tambo, Mbeki and Sobukwe.

▲ Albert Luthuli accepts the Nobel Peace Prize in Oslo, December 1961

Luthuli symbolically burned his passbook following the Sharpeville massacre, and was briefly prominent in the ANC's campaign of strikes, protests and "stay-at-homes" that followed. He was arrested once again and charged under the government's new emergency powers. Found guilty by the court, he escaped a prison sentence due to ill health. However, he was now subject to almost constant banning orders by the government. He had little option but to retire to semi-obscurity in Groutville and allow the younger generation to seize effective control of the movement. The ease with which he capitulated to Mandela and Sisulu in the debate over the adoption of armed struggle, a move which he had passionately opposed for much of the previous decade, illustrated the degree to which his political influence was waning. Recent studies suggest that he may not even have been consulted when the final decision to create MK was made. Nonetheless, with the ANC now banned and operating underground, Luthuli remained a figure of enormous symbolic value to the movement. He was allowed to travel to Oslo in December 1961 so that he could accept the Nobel Peace Prize he had been awarded in the previous year, and in 1963 he published his celebrated autobiography, *Let My People Go*. By now his health was sharply deteriorating. He had a minor stroke and suffered from poor hearing and eyesight. These factors probably contributed to his death in 1967, when he was run over at a railway crossing near his Groutville home.

Assessment

Albert Luthuli's contribution to the anti-apartheid struggle in the 1950s and early 1960s was prodigious. While his organizational involvement was often limited due to the repeated government banning orders, he remained the symbolic colossus of the liberation movement throughout. His moral authority stood in stark contrast to the government's approach of brutal repression and this contributed to

the international isolation of Pretoria. Luthuli was the first global icon of the South African liberation movement. His acceptance of the Nobel Peace Prize brought the cause of the ANC to international prominence and provided succour during some of the darkest days of the anti-apartheid struggle. His commitment to peaceful methods of protest also won the ANC the sympathy and support of many White South African liberals.

Some have played down Luthuli's achievements by stressing his limited personal involvement in the various ANC campaigns after 1952. However, this stance overlooks the formidable power of the apartheid system that opposed him, a factor which made a more hands-on role impossible. Luthuli was arrested whenever he attempted to defy his banning orders, and typically re-banned as soon as an existing order expired. Another related criticism concerns the way in which he was increasingly sidelined by the end of the 1950s and his capitulation to more junior members of the party in the debate on the armed struggle. However, it can be argued that the main causes of this defeat were unrelated to his diminished personal standing or weaknesses in his moral argument. Rather the case of continued non-violence had been fatally undermined by the vigour with which the government banned and repressed the ANC after the Sharpeville massacre.

In a recent biography, *Albert Luthuli: Bound by Faith* (2010), Scott Couper argues that the very characteristics that made Luthuli such a redoubtable opponent of apartheid in the early 1950s – his upstanding Christian morality and principled opposition to any form of violence – can also be used to explain his increasing irrelevance to the movement later on in that decade and in the early 1960s, when the new circumstances demanded a more strident response. Couper points out that the "official" ANC accounts of the period attempt to rewrite history by making Luthuli fit into a more mainstream nationalist narrative. This account, propagated among others by Luthuli's early biography, Mary Benson, held that he was eventually and reluctantly persuaded that armed struggle was the only way forward. The result is that Luthuli's opposition to the decision to embrace armed struggle is downplayed or even ignored. Couper argues that this is a move that Luthuli steadfastly refused to authorize.

Source skills

Source A

An extract from "The Road to Freedom is via the Cross", a public statement issued by Albert Luthuli on 1 November 1952 in response to a government order to revoke his chieftaincy.

What have been the fruits of my many years of moderation? Has there been a reciprocal tolerance or moderation from the government? No! On the contrary, the past thirty years have seen the greatest number of laws restricting our rights and progress until today we have reached a stage where we have almost no rights at all: no adequate land for our occupation, our only asset, cattle, dwindling, no security of homes, no decent and remunerative employment, more restriction to freedom of movement through passes … in short we have witnessed … an intensification of our subjugation to ensure and protect white supremacy.

It is with this background … [that] I have joined my people in the new spirit that moves them today, the spirit that revolts openly and boldly against injustice and expresses itself in a determined and non-violent manner.

Source B

The Black Christ, a painting by the White South African artist Ronnie Harrison, 1961. It depicts Chief Luthuli being crucified by Prime Minister HF Verwoerd and Minister of Justice John Vorster.

Source C

A speech by President of South Africa Jacob Zuma, who delivered the Chief Albert Luthuli Centenary Lecture in Kimberley on 7 September 2012.

The membership saw outstanding qualities in [Luthuli] and was convinced that he would take the ANC to greater heights. He did not disappoint them …

While Inkosi [the Zulu word for "chief"] Luthuli was under his severe ban, he was

informed that he had been awarded the 1960 Nobel Prize for Peace award … His acceptance speech helped focus world attention on apartheid and its evil atrocities against Africans. He also emphasized reconciliation and unity. He made the fundamental point that it would have been easy for the feelings of resentment at white domination to have been turned into feelings of hatred and a desire for revenge against the white community. He praised the ANC leadership which had preached non-racialism and restraint in the face of extreme provocation … Inkosi Luthuli obtained a long standing ovation after his moving acceptance speech. He rose to sing the National Anthem, locating himself in Oslo as a proud African. He made every African, in the continent and the diaspora, extremely proud of themselves …

We have noted some works doubting President General Luthuli's commitment to the armed struggle. Dominant records indicate that he was a pacifist whose hand was "twisted" to accept the armed struggle even though he did not believe in it. When he took over as President the policy of the ANC had not changed from petition politics. However, when conditions changed and radicalism set in, he was ready to embrace the new approach. Inkosi Luthuli was a man of peace, but he was also a militant leader. Like all ANC leaders, he detested violence. The armed struggle was adopted as a last resort, in the face of an intransigent, aggressive state that was hell-bent on perpetually riding roughshod over the rights of the black majority.

Source D

S. Couper, a Christian minister from the USA who worked at the Groutville Congregational Church (Luthuli's former parish). He is a senior honorary lecturer in the school of religion at the University of KwaZulu-Nalal. "My People Let Go". *International Congregational Journal.* **Vol 5, issue 1 (2005).**

Luthuli's keen intellect and powerful personality held together in solidarity against incredible

odds Indians, Whites, Blacks, Communists, Liberals, Christians, Muslims, modernists and traditionalists within the ANC thus enabling the survival and future growth of the anti-Apartheid struggle and the creation of the present day democratic South Africa. In 1960 the Nobel Committee selected Luthuli from the midst of obscurity to proclaim to the world the height to which humankind ought to strive …

As President-General of the ANC for seventeen years, [he] was a secular politician, yet he argued that he was first and foremost a Christian … Perhaps the greatest paradox of Luthuli's life is his consistent advocacy of non-violence previous to and during his last seven years of ANC leadership and the ANC's sanctioned and sponsored use of violence … Clearly, the decision to resort to violence led his followers to turn away from Luthuli as the leader of the ANC despite his retention of the titular position as General-President. Luthuli's people had let him go.

First question, part a – 3 marks

According to Source A, what were the results of Luthuli's *"many years of moderation"*?

First question, part b – 2 marks

What is the message of Source B?

Second question – 4 marks

With reference to its origin, purpose and content, assess the values and limitations of Source D for historians studying Chief Luthuli's involvement in the freedom struggle.

Third question – 6 marks

Compare and contrast the views of Chief Luthuli expressed in Sources C and D.

Fourth question – 9 marks

Using the sources and your own knowledge, to what extent do you agree with the claim that Chief Luthuli took the ANC *"to greater heights"*?

Nelson Mandela

An icon of the freedom struggle, Nelson Mandela was, along with Albert Luthuli, the dominant figure in the liberation movement between 1948 and 1964.

Born in 1918, Mandela was the scion of minor African royalty. His father was the chief counsellor to the king of the Thembu, a branch of the Xhosa. He studied at the Africans-only University of Fort Hare, a college that had a well-deserved reputation as a hotbed of political activism. Rebellious since his early childhood, Mandela was expelled for taking part in a student protest. After fleeing his home in Qunu at the prospect of an arranged marriage in 1941, he met Walter Sisulu on his arrival in Johannesburg. Sisulu introduced Mandela to a firm of attorneys where he began work while studying to obtain his legal articles. He was involved in cases where he helped to defend Black people who had fallen foul of the country's segregation laws. Mandela became ever more politicized.

Mandela joined the ANC in 1944, the same year as Luthuli. He formed the ANC Youth League along with Sisulu and his early political mentor, the Africanist Anton Lembede. Mandela was soon noted for his organizational capacity and dynamism, as well as for his strong opposition to the old guard of the movement. He found the

ANC Youth League activists and partners in law: Nelson Mandela and Oliver Tambo

constitutional approach, with its strategy of politely petitioning the authorities, to be dangerously passive and increasingly obsolete in a more repressive post-war political environment. He argued that the authorities' suppression of the 1946 miners' strike, and the menacing emergence of a radical Afrikaner nationalism, justified a more assertive strategy of non-cooperation and mass action. Following the NP election victory in 1948, Mandela was a key figure in persuading the party's leaders to adopt the Youth League's radical Programme of Action, a document which he had helped to draft. Capping a heady rise through the ranks of the party, Mandela was elected to the National Executive Committee of the ANC in late 1949, and appointed president of the Youth League in 1950. He helped turn the Programme of Action into a political reality through his role in the Defiance Campaign in 1952. Nominated as national volunteer-in-chief, he was perhaps the single most important member of the party in organizing civil disobedience across the country. It was around this time that Mandela rose to national prominence, with newspapers frequently reporting his involvement in acts of defiance.

The Defiance Campaign was significant in Mandela's career in other ways too. First, his arrest and subsequent six-month banning order meant that he had the time to sit his attorney admission examinations and open South Africa's first Black law firm in Johannesburg, in partnership with Oliver Tambo. Needless to say, the company soon gained a reputation for its fearless representation of the victims of apartheid laws (incidentally, the firm was itself an early victim of the 1950 Group Areas Act and had to move its offices from the city centre to a distant outlying suburb). Second, Mandela's experience of working with other groups during the Defiance Campaign convinced him of the value of creating a common front against apartheid. Heavily influenced by Lembede, he was known as an Africanist prior to 1952. Despite a close friendship with SACP Secretary-General Moses Kotane, he had also been a vocal opponent of communism within the ANC. Indeed, Mandela had opposed the "May Day stay-at-home" strike of 1950 on the grounds that the ANC should be organizing its own protests rather than working together with the communists. Now, through his involvement with leading communists such as Kotane, Yusuf Dadoo and JB Marks, Mandela became a firm believer in a non-racial approach as his politics swung to the left.

Mandela drew closer to the SACP following the secret relaunch of the party in 1953. He was an influential force behind the decision to create an alliance with other anti-apartheid groups through the Congress Alliance. He defied banning orders to take part in planning the COP, and helped compose the Freedom Charter. Mandela, along with Sisulu, watched silently from the sidelines while the Charter was proclaimed at the Kliptown rally, lest he be rearrested for violating the terms of his ban.

In 1953, Mandela drafted the "M Plan", a series of contingency measures that the movement would have to adopt in the event that it was banned and driven underground by the government. He was also very active in the angry but ineffectual ANC response to Verwoerd's Bantu Education Act in 1953–54, and in the Resist Apartheid Campaign, the fierce but ultimately futile opposition to the forced removals of Africans living in the Johannesburg suburb of Sophiatown during the government's Western Areas Removal Scheme.

Mandela was one of the principal defendants in the long-running Treason Trial, which began in 1956 and lasted for five years before his eventual acquittal in 1961. Although held in custody for lengthy periods, it was during this time that he became a dominant figure in the ANC, with Albert Luthuli invariably removed from the political action due to the banning orders confining him to rural Stanger. Following the Sharpeville massacre and the government's decision to ban the ANC, Mandela was the main driving force in persuading the party to accept the inevitability of the armed struggle, a possibility that he had outlined earlier in the "M Plan".

Following the collapse of the Treason Trial in March 1961, Mandela knew that the government would seek to rearrest him immediately. He had time for one final act of public defiance when he addressed a huge crowd of delegates at the All-in African Conference, a gathering that had been organized by the ANC in Pietermaritzburg. In an audacious speech, Mandela urged the government to admit the error of its ways and establish a democratic convention representing all South Africans, or else face a general strike which would paralyze the country. Ironically, the NP would accede to precisely these demands. However, South Africa would have to wait another three decades for this development, following consultations between President FW de Klerk and a newly released Mandela in 1990. De Klerk agreed to convene the Convention for a Democratic South Africa (CODESA), a body representing South Africans of all parties and races. This convention finally agreed a new constitution for a non-racial South Africa, leading to the end of the apartheid system in 1994.

Following his Pietermaritzburg speech Mandela knew that he would have to go on the run from the authorities. He went undercover at the ANC's safe house at Liliesleaf Farm and travelled across the country organizing resistance, often disguised as a house boy, gardener or driver. His ability to evade the police became legendary and earned him the nickname the "Black Pimpernel". From December 1961, he was deeply involved in constituting Umkhonto we Sizwe (MK) as its new commander-in-chief, and in organizing its regional command structures. He escaped the country in early 1962 and travelled extensively across Africa, where he met national leaders and received guerrilla training in Algeria. He also arranged for exiled MK recruits to train in Ethiopia. After returning to South Africa, he was finally arrested by the police while returning to Johannesburg from a trip to Durban. He was sentenced to five years in jail for leaving the country without permission and for inciting strike action. While serving this sentence, the police

A cartoon, "The Trial", that appeared in Punch magazine after the Rivonia Trial.

THE TRIAL

Under the "Sabotage Act" there is no need for South Africa to bring accused persons to trial. They may be kept in prison for an indefinite series of ninety-day periods merely on suspicion, even when — as last week — indictments are quashed.

Using your own knowledge, as well as the information about the Rivonia Trial found elsewhere in this book, answer the following questions about this cartoon.

1 Whose is the ubiquitous White face in the cartoon?

2 What is the message of the cartoon? Note that you will have to do your own research in order to understand the meaning of "indictments are quashed" in the caption.

TOK links

Is it appropriate to place "icons" of the liberation movement, such as Mandela and Luthuli, on historical pedestals? What are the dangers of elevating historical figures to hero status? Is it correct to portray the fight against apartheid as a simple matter of "good against evil"?

Was Thomas Carlyle right when he argued that "the history of the world is but the biography of great men"? Do "great men", such as Mandela and Luthuli in South Africa, really change the course of history, or are social and economic forces equally, if not more, important?

arrested the remaining members of the MK High Command following a raid of Liliesleaf Farm. They found documents relating to explosives manufacture and a draft of Operation Mayibuye, MK's plan for a guerrilla struggle to be waged against the government. Between 1963 and 1964, Mandela was brought before a court once again, in the famous Rivonia Trial (see pages 69–71).

Following the trial, all but one of the defendants were found guilty and, contrary to expectations, sentenced to life imprisonment instead of death by hanging. They were immediately transferred in secret to their prison on Robben Island. Mandela and his comrades were to disappear from the political scene for the next 27 years. A defining era in South African politics, the period when the government implemented the apartheid system and the ANC responded, first with non-violent resistance and then with armed struggle, came dramatically to a close.

Assessment

Mandela's contribution to the ANC in particular, and to the anti-apartheid movement in general, was immense. He revitalized the party in the late 1940s through his activism in the Youth League and was a leading light of the Defiance Campaign in 1952, the point at which the party really began to make its mark as the vanguard of African resistance to the apartheid system. He was instrumental in uniting South Africans of all races in the struggle against apartheid through his advocacy of the COP. A principal target of the apartheid regime, his defence in the drawn-out Treason Trial epitomized the resilience of those struggling against an unjust racial system. The armed campaign of MK, which he led, together with his exploits as the "Black Pimpernel" and the drama of the Rivonia Trial, where he was once again cast as the principal defendant, all ensured that the focus of the world remained on the iniquities of apartheid South Africa in the years following the Sharpeville massacre.

Why Mandela became such an icon of the struggle is a question that has long interested historians. His first biographer, Mary Benson (1986), argues that he came to embody the freedom struggle through his leadership of the Defiance Campaign. The courage and fortitude he demonstrated in inviting arrest and then in persevering with his opposition to apartheid was a source of inspiration for many, both inside and outside the ANC. The historian Tom Lodge acknowledges that Mandela was a rising star of the ANC in the 1950s, but argues that this was a time when he was still struggling to forge his own political identity, free from the influence of Luthuli on the one hand and his comrades in the SACP on the other. According to Lodge, the Mandela legend was born after Sharpeville, when he came to be viewed by many Africans as the saviour of the liberation struggle. He cut a romantic, Che Guevara-like figure as the "Black Pimpernel" and commander of MK. His reputation as a fearless and principled opponent of apartheid was confirmed with his famous speech from the dock at the Rivonia Trial, when he announced that the ideal of democracy was one for which he was prepared to die.

ATL Communication skills ▶

Go to: https://www.youtube.com/watch?v=-Qj4e_q7_z4.

Watch this video clip to hear another of Mandela's famous and passionate speeches, the one he made on the day of his release after 27 years in prison.

In what ways has Mandela's political attitude remained unchanged since he was sent to prison in 1964?

Details of Mandela's speech from the dock at the Rivonia Trial can be found on page 70, and the audio can be listened to here:

https://www.youtube.com/watch?v=g50J205MdKI.

Full document

Source A

Tom Lodge, a South African historian who is professor of peace and conflict studies at the University of Limerick in Ireland. *Mandela: A Critical Life* **(2006).**

Certainly, Mandela himself [in the early 1950s] was highly conscious of his authority; apparently both Sisulu and his wife Albertina were concerned that he could be rather too domineering [controlling], although as Albertina conceded later: "it didn't matter because people liked to look up to a leader who was regal and maybe a bit distant". Matthews remembers him disconcerting [unsettling] a gathering of ANC notables in Port Elizabeth in April 1952, mainly his elders, by informing them in the middle of his after-dinner speech that "he was looking forward to becoming the first president of a free republic of South Africa". Anthony Sampson's "authorised" biography reflects the ANC's preferred projection of the younger Mandela at the time it was written, the early 1990s, as a pioneering militant, one of the more radical ANC leaders, a "maverick" [unorthodox or independent-minded person], increasingly impatient with non-violent methods.

Source B

Volunteer-in-chief Nelson Mandela prepares to burn his passbook in the back garden of his home in Orlando West during the Defiance Campaign, 1952.

Source C

M. Maharaj and A. Kathrada, eds, senior ANC politicians who were imprisoned with Mandela on Robben Island. Kathrada worked as political adviser to Mandela while Mandela served as president. Maharaj was minister for transport from 1994 to 1999 and was appointed as spokesperson for President Jacob Zuma in 2011. *Mandela: The Authorized Portrait,* **page 62 (2006).**

During a brief lifting of his ban and before fresh and more stringent bans were served on him, and galled by the recently instituted Bantu Education Act which further downgraded black education and placed it firmly under the government's authority, Mandela addressed a large gathering in Soweto. He spoke for ninety minutes, every word inaccurately recorded by a policeman, and, although the tone was militant, evoking warrior memories of Shaka, he suffered no repercussions …

In the new year Mandela spent time behind the scenes organizing protests in Sophiatown, and time in court defending people who were about to lose their houses. Both efforts proved hopeless. Early in February, the removal trucks and two thousand police and army troops entered the township. The houses were razed; the people dumped in a designated area of Soweto known as Meadowlands. Again Mandela realised how tame were their efforts at nonviolent protest when the state simply lashed out its iron fist.

Source D

M. Meredith, a British historian and journalist who has written several books on Africa. *Nelson Mandela: A Biography,* **pages 114–15, 119–21 (1999).**

The ANC, stirring itself for the first time since the Defiance Campaign, decided … to launch a joint protest [against forced removals] at the Odin cinema. Among the speakers invited were Huddleston, Yusuf Cachalia and Mandela, whose six-month banning order had just expired … Shortly after Huddleston had finished his speech, a group of armed police strode in, marched to the stage and arrested the next speaker, Yusuf Cachalia, dragging him towards the exit. Mandela, fearing an ugly turn of events, jumped on stage and began singing a well-known protest song … "I had seen and felt, in those moments, the terrifying spectre of the police state," Huddleston wrote in his book *Naught for Your Comfort*. "There was the fiery breath of police totalitarianism in every movement." …

Opposition to the Bantu Education Act was widespread, both among churches and in the African community. Some churchmen decided to shut their schools than submit to the government. The response of the ANC was more confused … Despite his reputation as a firebrand, Mandela favoured a more pragmatic approach. At the end of a heated session, the national executive committee recommended a week's boycott starting on 1 April 1955 … The campaign soon collapsed in bitterness and recrimination. Only a small fraction of parents and schoolchildren were ever involved in the boycott.

First question, part a – 3 marks

According to Source A, in what ways did a young Nelson Mandela stand out as a politician in the early 1950s?

First question, part b – 2 marks

What does Source B reveal about Nelson Mandela's role in the ANC in 1952?

Second question – 4 marks

With reference to its origin, purpose and content, assess the values and limitations of Source C for historians studying Mandela's involvement in ANC protests and campaigns in the 1950s.

Third question – 6 marks

Compare and contrast the views expressed in Sources C and D about anti-government protests and Nelson Mandela's role in these demonstrations.

Fourth question – 9 marks

Using the sources and your own knowledge, evaluate Nelson Mandela's contribution to the struggle against apartheid in the years 1948–55.

Source help and hints

Sources A and B

(See page 85.)

Third question – 6 marks

Compare and contrast the accounts presented in Sources A and B of the "May Day stay-at-home" strike in 1950.

Comparisons

- Both sources indicate that that there was resistance, from within the ANC, to working with the communists in organizing the strike.

- Both sources emphasize the success of the strike, with a large proportion of the African workforce choosing to stay at home.

- Both sources mention that gatherings were banned on the day of the strike.

- Both sources describe brutal police action.

Contrasts

- The sources disagree about some of the details of the strike. Source A claims that 50% of the workers observed the strike, while Source B gives a figure of 80%. Source A mentions 19 dead, while Source B puts the number at 18.

- Source A describes the involvement of Mandela and Sisulu in observing strike action and indicates that they almost became casualties. Source B refers to the role of the ANC's executive (of which the two were members) but does not describe their role during the strike.

- Source A mentions that Sisulu had reservations about using militant action in the future. Source B mentions no such reservations, and states that the ANC executive announced another protest immediately afterwards.

Sources A and B

Third question – 6 marks

(See page 95.)

Compare and contrast the views expressed in Sources A and B regarding the influence of the SACP on the ANC.

Comparisons

- The sources agree that the influence of the SACP on the ANC was very great. Source A suggests that the Marxist ideas of the SACP were "music to the ears" of the ANC, and that the two organizations had much in common. Source B goes even further by arguing that the ANC was "hijacked" by the SACP.

- Both sources indicate that Nelson Mandela had a key role to play in the developing relations between the ANC and the SACP.

- Both sources indicate that Mandela was very sympathetic to the aims of communism. In Source A he makes a case for cooperation between the ANC and SACP based on their common ideals and goals. Source B argues that he "bounced" the ANC into following the SACP.

Contrasts

- Source B refers explicity to the debate about the armed struggle. Source A describes relations between the ANC and the SACP more generally.

- Source B suggests that Mandela had to overcome significant resistance from within the ANC, not least from Luthuli, to the idea of armed struggle. However, Source A argues that "revolutionary action" was "music to [the ANC's] ears".

- Source B states that Nelson Mandela joined the central committee of the SACP. In Source A Mandela argues that he had no need to join the communists.

- Source B argues that the ANC was used by the SACP. Source A suggests that the opposite was true.

Second question – 4 marks

With reference to its origin, purpose and content, assess the values and limitations of Source A for historians studying the role of the SACP and its influence on Nelson Mandela and the ANC during the 1950s and early 1960s.

Values

- The source is Mandela's autobiography, published more than three decades after the events he is describing. His reflections have the benefit of hindsight, and his views are not mediated by a biographer. Mandela's influence was crucial to the ANC drawing increasingly closer to the SACP during this period, so his reflections on the matter are invaluable to the historian's understanding.

- The source gives us a valuable insight into the way in which Mandela's political philosophy was evolving in a left-wing direction in the 1950s and early 1960s. It also helps us understand why communist ideas were attactive to many others in the freedom struggle.

- The source provides us with Mandela's definitive answer to a question that has long intrigued historians: that of whether he had ever been a member of the SACP. The accusation that he was a communist also formed the basis of the state's case against him during the Treason and Rivonia Trials.

Limitations

- Mandela may be deliberately downplaying the extent of his involvement with the SACP during the period. His autobiography was published in 1995, one year after the first non-racial elections after which Mandela became South Africa's first Black president. This was a time when Mandela was trying to promote reconciliation between the races by presenting himself as a unifying figure. He was trusted by many in the White community, and admitting that he had been a member of the SACP may have undermined this trust.

- Mandela had denied being a member of the SACP at the Rivonia Trial. He may have been lying in his autobiography in order to avoid accusations of inconsistency.

- Mandela's discussion of the relationship between the SACP and the ANC is very general in nature. He does not directly refer to the role of the SACP in any particular event or events. However, it may be surmised, since he refers to accusations that the communists "used" the ANC, that he is alluding to the period of the early 1960s and the debate over the armed struggle.

Source A

First question, part a – 3 marks

(See page 100.)

According to Source A, why did the ANC resort to armed struggle in 1961?

- The ANC has been given little option but to adopt armed struggle; according to the MK manifesto, "there remain only two choices: submit or fight".

- MK has been formed not to cause civil war but to avoid it, by awakening all South Africans to the errors of the NP government and the injustices of apartheid.

- Armed struggle has been adopted in order to overthrow the government and bring an end to racial oppression

Source B

First question, part b – 2 marks

A cartoon by Norman Mansbridge, *Punch* magazine, 1960.

DRAGON'S TEETH

What is the message of the cartoon in Source B?

- The cartoon shows a field which has been ploughed and sown by a tractor. The tractor is labelled "Apartheid". Rows of spears are beginning to emerge in the soil behind the tractor. This indicates that the apartheid system will reap a bitter harvest: armed struggle, represented by rows of spears.

- One of the spears is held aloft, meaning that Africans will finally take the fight to the apartheid system by adopting armed struggle. The message is that the South African government, which is shown seated with a gun in the tractor, is responsible for African resistance because of its apartheid policies and repression of the ANC.

- The caption "Dragon's teeth" implies that Africans will prove to be a formidable foe for the government. This is confirmed by the many spears emerging from the soil. The detail of the low dark clouds implies that there will be difficult times ahead for the country.

Source A

First question, part a – 3 marks

(See page 105.)

According to Source A, what were the results of Luthuli's "many years of moderation"?

The results of Luthuli's "many years of moderation" were:

- a reluctance on the part of the government to reciprocate his moderation

- the tightening of discriminatory legislation resulting in an "intensification of our subjugation"

- an awareness that the strategy of moderate opposition has not worked

- a realization that a "spirit of revolt" is now required.

Source B

The Black Christ, a painting by the White South African artist Ronnie Harrison, 1961. It depicts Chief Luthuli being crucified by Prime Minister HF Verwoerd and Minister of Justice John Vorster.

First question, part b – 2 marks

What is the message of Source B?

- Chief Luthuli, with his Christian compassion and non-violence, is a Christ-like figure.

- Black people, symbolized by the figure of Luthuli, have been "crucified" by the apartheid system.

- The government (represented by Verwoerd and Vorster) has destroyed the peaceful resistance of Africans.

Sources C and D

Second question – 4 marks

(See pages 104 and 105.)

With reference to its origin, purpose and content, assess the values and limitations of Source D for historians studying Chief Luthuli's involvement in the freedom struggle.

Values

- The article is written by an academic and is likely to have been well researched.

- As a minister and theologian himself, Couper is likely to have an intimate knowledge of Luthuli's religious beliefs and how these may have influenced his politics.

- Couper worked in Luthuli's Groutville parish, and may well have interviewed people who knew Luthuli personally in the place where he spent most of his time, even after he became ANC leader.

- Couper provides an alternative viewpoint to the mainstream position of the ANC. This position is that Luthuli came around to the idea of armed struggle after being perusaded by Mandela and others that the movement had run out of options.

Limitations

- As a lecturer in religion, Couper is likely to emphasize the spiritual dimensions of Luthuli's leadership, perhaps at the expense of a more rounded political analysis.

- The article was published in the *International Congregational Journal*, which is obviously a Christian publication. It is therefore hardly a surprise that Couper concludes that Luthuli was "first and foremost a Christian".

- Couper has set out to provide a revisionist account of Luthuli's role in the armed struggle controversy. This may have caused him to neglect certain evidence that contradicts his thesis, such as the testimony of other ANC leaders who argued that he finally agreed to the proposal and who were present at key meetings with Luthuli when the issue was being debated.

Third question – 6 marks

Compare and contrast the views of Chief Luthuli expressed in Sources C and D.

Comparisons

- Sources C and D agree that Chief Luthuli's acceptance of the Nobel Peace Prize was a crucial moment in the history of the liberation struggle because it focused the attention of the entire world on the injustice of racial oppression in South Africa.

- The sources agree that Luthuli was a conciliatory figure. Source C argues that he prevented African feelings of resentment from turning into a desire for revenge, while Source D claims he was responsible for holding together a broad coalition of competing interests.

- The sources agree that Luthuli was a pacifist who hated violence.

Contrasts

- Source D argues that while Luthuli was a secular politician, he was primarily a Christian. Source C makes no mention of his Christianity and suggests that he was entirely dedicated to the secular struggle against apartheid.

- Source C emphasizes Luthuli's role in pointing the ANC away from "petition politics" towards a more radical approach. Source D, on the other hand, emphasizes that his approach remained constant throughout.

- Source C suggests that Luthuli was "ready to embrace the new approach" of armed struggle. Source D disagrees, referring to his "consistent advocacy of non-violence" in the final years of his leadership.

- Source D argues that the mainstream of the ANC turned away from Luthuli after it embraced armed struggle. Source C, on the other hand, argues that Luthuli always remained at the heart of the ANC.

Fourth question – 9 marks

Using the sources and your own knowledge, to what extent do you agree with the claim that Chief Luthuli took the ANC "to greater heights"?

- Source A: Luthuli exhibits the qualities of a fearless and inspirational leader in his statement. The statement indicates that he is willing to adopt new, more radical strategies.

- Source B: The subject matter of the painting (crucifixion) might suggest that the ANC has been destroyed by the government under Luthuli's leadership. However, the fact that it has been painted by a White artist suggests that Luthuli's dignity has won the ANC the admiration and sympathy of some White South Africans. It also implies that Luthuli has become an icon of the struggle.

- Source C: Luthuli's achievement in winning the Nobel Peace Prize was a source of great pride for Africans at a time when the government was clamping down on the ANC. He was prepared to take the movement forward and embrace new strategies, for example armed struggle, as the situation demanded.

- Source D: Luthuli succeeded in unifying a diverse range of groups within the ANC. However, his commitment to non-violence became obsolete in the harsher context of the early 1960s and the ANC left him behind.

- Luthuli played an important role in the Defiance Campaign, and in planning the Resist Apartheid Campaign and the Congress of the People (COP).

- There were consecutive government banning orders against Luthuli, which limited his effectiveness as ANC leader.

- Luthuli failed to prevent the Africanists from breaking away from the ANC and forming the PAC.

- Luthuli carried out a symbolic burning of his passbook after the Sharpeville massacre and he organized other acts of resistance at the time.

- Luthuli's enduring legacy is as a moral leader and a man of peace.

Source A

First question, part a – 3 marks

(See page 110.)

According to Source A, in what ways did a young Nelson Mandela stand out as an ANC politician in the early 1950s?

- As a young man Mandela was highly conscious of his own authority and could appear haughty and arrogant.

- He had a tendency to dominate others.

- He was not afraid to upset his seniors by expressing his political ambitions.

- He was a radical who was determined to force the movement away from its policies of moderation and non-violence.

Source B

First question, part b – 2 marks

(See page 109.)

What does Source B reveal about Nelson Mandela's role in the ANC in 1952?

Volunteer-in-chief Nelson Mandela prepares to burn his passbook in the back garden of his home in Orlando West during the Defiance Campaign, 1952

- Mandela was volunteer-in-chief in the Defiance Campaign, the most senior organizer in the first major campaign against apartheid laws launched by the movement.

- As well as an organizer, Mandela was also involved in acts of defiance: in this photograph he is seen burning his passbook.

- Even though many of the acts of defiance were on a small scale (in this image he is acting alone in a deserted backyard), Mandela made sure that photographers were present to record the event and achieve maximum publicity for the Defiance Campaign.

Sources C and D

Third question – 6 marks

(See page 110.)

Compare and contrast the views expressed in Sources C and D about anti-government protests and Nelson Mandela's role in these demonstrations.

Comparisons

- Both sources describe Mandela's involvement in two important events: the protests against the Bantu Education Act and opposition to the forced removals in Sophiatown.

- Both sources stress Mandela importance to the ANC at an early stage in his political career: Source C shows him making speeches and organizing resistance, while Source D describes him as rescuing a dangerous situation at a protest meeting and playing a leading role in a party debate.

- Both sources indicate that Mandela was involved in the protests only because his banning orders had recently expired.

- Both sources describe the toughness of the government's response, and suggest that this was one the reasons for the failure of the campaigns in which Mandela was involved.

Contrasts

- Source C focuses solely on Mandela and his role in the protests. Source D mentions other figures as well, such as Huddleston and Cachalia.

- Source C indicates that the campaign to save Sophiatown was a failure but makes no mention of the outcome of the opposition

to the Bantu Education Act. Source D does the opposite.

- Source C refers to Mandela as a militant. Source D indicates that he a favoured "a more pragamatic approach".

Second question – 4 marks

With reference to its origin, purpose and content, assess the value and limitations of Source C for historians studying Mandela's involvement in ANC protests and campaigns in the 1950s.

Values

- The book is edited by Maharaj and Kathrada, two ANC veterans who knew Mandela well. They were politically active in the 1950s and would have been involved in the organization of some of the events they are describing, giving them intimate first-hand knowledge of the subject matter.

- The book was written in 2006, some 50 years after the events that are being described. The authors have the benefit of hindsight and are able to put the events of the 1950s into the context of subsequent political developments in South Africa, of which they were also a part.

- Apartheid had been dead for more than a decade by the time that the book was written. In the meantime, a process of reconciliation had taken place between the perpetrators and victims of the system. The authors are therefore less likely to be swayed by bitterness or other emotional factors.

Limitations

- Maharaj and Kathrada are very senior members of the ANC. Their assessment of the 1950s – a dramatic time in the history of the movement and indeed in the career of Mandela – is unlikely to be entirely impartial.

- The two spent many years with Mandela on Robben Island. Mandela was of course still alive in 2006, and it is highly unlikely that the authors would produce a critical biography of man who they revered and still regarded as a mentor and leader. The words "authorized portrait" in the title suggests that this may be a text in which details of his political career have been airbrushed.

- The passages describing the protests against the Bantu Education Act and the forced removals of Sophiatown are very brief. There is no in-depth analysis of Mandela's role in either. This suggests that the real focus of the book is Mandela's personality and celebrity rather than the protest and campaigns of the 1950s.

- There is no indication in the source that the opposition to the Bantu Education Act was a failure. This suggests that some of the less successful aspects of the ANC's campaigns have been glossed over.

Fourth question – 9 marks

Using the sources and your own knowledge, evaluate Nelson Mandela's contribution to the struggle against apartheid in the years 1948–55.

- Source A: Mandela was a confident and ambitious leader who refused to defer to his seniors. He had a natural authority and was not afraid to challenge accepted ways by advocating new, more radical strategies of resistance.

- Source B: Mandela was the main organizer of the Defiance Campaign, one of the most important campaigns in the struggle against apartheid. He led by example and was brave enough to court his own arrest by defying apartheid laws.

- Source C: Mandela played an important role in organizing the campaigns against Bantu education and forced removals. However, the success of these campaigns was limited – not for any shortcomings on his part, but because of the might of the apartheid state.

- Source D: Mandela was very quick-witted and was capable of defusing potentially dangerous situations. He was also prepared to be pragmatic, despite his radical reputation. However, some of the campaigns in which he was involved, such as that against Bantu education, were a failure.

- Mandela's leadership of the ANC Youth League and his success in radicalising the ANC in 1949 by persuading it to adopt the Programme of Action.

- He wrote the "M Plan", which later became the basis for founding Umkhonto we Sizwe (MK).

- Mandela's role in reaching out to other non-white anti-apartheid groups by forming the Congress Alliance, as well as his role in organising the COP and drafting the Freedom Charter.

- As a radical, Mandela took the ANC closer to the SACP and advocated turning the ANC into a genuine mass movement.

References

Bunting, B. 1998. *Moses Kotane: South African Revolutionary*. Cape Town, South Africa. Mayibuye Books, University of the Western Cape.

Couper, S. 2005. "My People Let Go". *International Congregational Journal*. Vol 5, issue 1.

Lodge, T. 2006. *Mandela: A Critical Life*. Oxford, UK. Oxford University Press.

Maharaj, M and Kathrada, A, eds. 2006. *Mandela: The Authorized Portrait*. Rowville, VIC, Australia. The Five Mile Press.

Mandela, N. 1995. *The Long Walk to Freedom*. London, UK. Little, Brown & Company.

Mbeki, G. 1992. *The Struggle for Liberation in South Africa: A Short History*.

Meredith. M. 1999. *Nelson Mandela: A Biography*. New York, USA. Public Affairs.

Sisulu, E. 2002. *Walter and Albertina Sisulu: In Our Lifetime*. Cape Town, South Africa. David Philip Publishers.

South African history prior to 1948

The first major clash of Black and White peoples in South Africa took place on the far frontiers of the Eastern Cape in the late 18th century. A definitive moment in the history of the region, it marked the point at which the vanguards of two great colonizing migrations came face to face for the first time. The first of these, the Bantu Migration, had already been underway for well over a millennium. It consisted of several waves of population movements, originally stemming from central parts of the continent (probably modern-day Cameroon), which had, over hundreds of years, swept slowly eastwards and then southwards along the African continent. As they pressed into Southern Africa, they displaced the indigenous San and Khoikhoi populations in the process. The Xhosa were at the farthest south-westerly prong of this great migration.

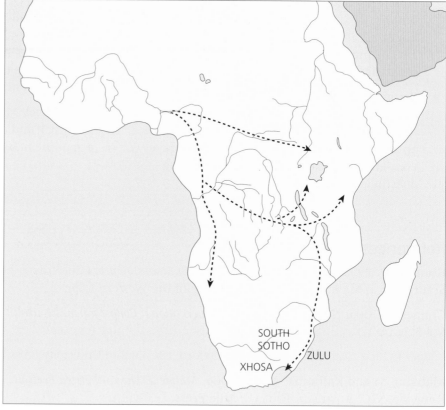

▲ The routes of the Bantu migration

The second of these migrations was on a smaller scale. The chartered Dutch East India Company (VOC) had established a tiny settlement at the Cape of Good Hope in 1652, on the site of modern-day Cape Town. Its purpose was to act as a refreshment post, supplying fresh fruit and vegetables to VOC ships plying the long and arduous journey to the spice islands of the Dutch East Indies. As time went on, the tiny group of VOC employees grew slowly in number. The settlement crept eastwards as some settlers tried to escape restrictive company rules and set up their own independent farms. These were the original *Trekboers*. There was little to stand in their way apart from the occasional Khoikhoi

▲ Van Riebeeck of the Dutch East India Company (VOC) landing at the Cape, in a 19th-century painting by Charles Bell. The Africans depicted in the image are indigenous Khoikhoi

resistance. By the late 18th century, these early Boer settlers had reached as far eastwards as the Great Fish River. Now they were confronted with a far more formidable foe: the Xhosa, who had reached the westward limit of their own migration. The resulting skirmishes were the first in a series of frontier wars that lasted a century. They went some way to shaping future relations between the races.

The arrival of the British and the Great Trek

By this time the British, who had established their own empire based on chartered company rule in India, had begun to take a keen interest in the region. The Dutch colony, on the southerly tip of the continent, occupied a strategically vital point on the sea route to the east. With Dutch power on the wane, the British used the Napoleonic Wars and the French occupation of Holland as an ideal opportunity to seize the Cape. Formal sovereignty was ceded by the Netherlands in 1806. In the 1820s, the British established the new settler towns of Port Elizabeth, East London and Grahamstown in the eastern part of the colony. Many Boer farmers were predictably disenchanted with the arrival of the British. They strained against the authority of the crown and resented what they felt to be undue bureaucratic interference in their traditional way of life. The British abolition of slavery across its empire in 1833 was the final straw. Beginning in 1835, thousands of Boers packed their ox-wagons and, unable to go any further east because of the Xhosa presence there, travelled deep into the more arid subcontinental interior. They spilled northwards and eastwards into what would later become the Orange Free State and the Transvaal, and then finally southwards into Natal. This series of journeys became known as the Great Trek.

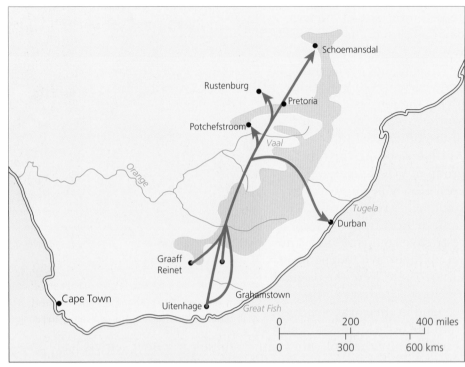

▲ The main routes of the Great Trek, 1835–1846

▲ Romantic depiction of the Great Trek by Tinus de Jongh

Meanwhile, a formidable new military force had emerged in the Natal region. Towards the end of the 1810s, the expanding Zulu nation under Shaka fought a series of aggressive wars against its neighbours. These conflicts initiated the terrible events that became known as the Mfecane. Groups that managed to flee Shaka's armies attacked other people where they settled, and this set off a chain reaction of warfare and destruction that resulted in the depopulation of much of the South African interior by the 1820s. Ironically, the Mfecane proved a major boon to the *Voortrekkers* (the name given to the Boers who took part in the Great Trek), who subsequently encountered little resistance when they established their homesteads. Nonetheless, armed engagements between Boers and Africans were not uncommon. The Boers had

an overwhelming edge in weaponry, and won a famous victory over Dingaan's Zulu army at the Battle of Blood River (Battle of "Ncome River" in Zulu) in 1838.

The independence of the Republic of Natalia that the Boers established in the wake of their victory was short-lived, however. Mindful of the strategic importance of controlling the entire coastline of the subcontinent, the British annexed Natal in 1843. However, they agreed to recognize Afrikaner sovereignty in the Transvaal

▲ Artist's illustration of the Battle of Blood River. The Boers formed a laager of ox-wagons and killed as many as 3,000 of the Zulu warriors who were storming the encampment. According to the legend, the nearby Ncome River turned red with blood

and the Orange Free State in conventions signed at Sand River in 1852 and in Bloemfontein in 1854. Growing European interest in the rest of the continent soon put an end to this status quo. The British attempted to federate South Africa by force in 1877 when an expeditionary party was sent to the Transvaal from Natal. It met with no initial resistance from the Boers. However, the Transvaalers organized their forces and won a famous victory over the British at the Battle of Majuba in 1881. This brought to an end the brief conflict that is sometimes known as the First Anglo–Boer War.

The mineral revolution and the South African War

Following this setback, it seemed as if British attempts to quash Boer independence might be put on hold indefinitely. However, some dramatic new developments completely altered this state of affairs. Diamonds had already been discovered in Kimberley in 1867. Now, in 1886, gold was found on the Witwatersrand in the heart of the South African Republic (the official name for the Transvaal). It soon became evident that the deposits were enormous. Labour and capital, from the rest of the subcontinent as well as from overseas, flooded into the reef. This movement of workers into the burgeoning city of Johannesburg would be of tremendous importance for two main reasons. First, it marked the real beginning of the mass migration of Africans into the cities, a phenomenon which subsequent segregationist laws tried to control and which the apartheid authorities would attempt, in vain, to reverse. Second, the flow of Whites into Johannesburg sparked a political contest between the government of the Transvaal led by Paul Kruger, which wanted to preserve the conservative Afrikaner character of the republic, and the so-called *uitlander* community of mainly English-speaking Whites, whose demand for the vote was

Jan Smuts

Jan Smuts was born in the Cape in 1870 and studied law at Cambridge University. When he returned to South Africa he moved to the Transvaal and served as political advisor to President Kruger, before leading a Boer commando unit during the South African War. He took part in negotiations leading to the Treaty of Vereeniging and became active in the politics of the Transvaal thereafter. A key figure in the national convention which resulted in the Union of South Africa, Smuts was instrumental in the creation of the South African Party (which later became the United Party) and was given three ministries in the first union government led by Louis Botha. He commanded South African troops against the Germans in the First World War and headed his country's delegation at the Paris Peace Conference, where he made a significant contribution to the creation of the League of Nations. He was appointed prime minister following the death of Louis Botha, and continued to serve, on an off, as national leader until the NP victory of 1948. The principal architect of the system of segregation, Smuts was nonetheless planning to reverse some of its more discriminatory laws before his defeat in the 1948 election. He died in 1950.

backed by the colonial authorities in Cape Town. In 1895, Cape Colony Prime Minister Cecil Rhodes was implicated in an abortive coup attempt which became known as the Jameson Raid. A small armed party was sent to invade the Transvaal and spark an *uitlander* uprising. Following its failure, the British appointed Alfred Milner to the post of high commissioner for South Africa. A self-described "British race imperialist", Milner was determined to bring the independence of the Transvaal to an end and used the *uitlander* franchise issue as a pretext for upping the political ante. The result was the South African War (sometimes known as the Anglo–Boer War or simply the Boer War), fought between the British and the two Boer Republics between 1899 and 1902. Early British hopes of a quick victory were confounded, but the imperial power gradually wrested back the initiative from the Boer armies. In the final two years of the war, the Boers waged a prolonged guerrilla campaign. They were finally brought to the negotiating table not by defeat in the field, but by the scorched earth tactics of the British and the internment of hundreds of thousands of Boer women and children in concentration camps.

The Act of Union and the segregation era

Despite the bitterness of the conflict, the Boer defeat was followed by an unlikely political reconciliation between the two White peoples of South Africa. The terms of the Treaty of Vereeniging offered to the Boers were relatively lenient. The Boer Republics, which had been brought under the direct control of the British, were soon granted a measure of self-government. In 1908, a South African National Convention (a body containing representatives from each region), met to consider the possibility of a full political union of the four colonies. The result was the agreement of the South African Act (also known as the Act of Union) of 1909. The new Union of South Africa, which came into being a year later, was given full dominion status in the British Empire. This meant that the country was now in effect a fully independent state.

Ironically, those Afrikaners who had fought the British with such tenacity just eight years previously now assumed political office. With the South African Party (SAP) winning the first general election, the former Boer War general Louis Botha was appointed prime minister, with Jan Smuts as his deputy. Africans were to be completely excluded from the new dispensation. With some very minor exceptions, only Whites could exercise the vote. Laws segregating White and Black people, which had been enforced to a greater or lesser degree in the British colonies and Boer Republics, were now applied with more vigour than before. In 1912, educated Africans responded to these worrying developments by forming the South African Native National Congress (SANNC), the forerunner of the ANC, in a vain attempt to defend their political interests. At the same time, die-hard Afrikaner nationalists objected to the "one stream" policy of the Botha–Smuts government, a strategy designed to promote further reconciliation

between the two White populations. The radical National Party (NP), under the leadership of JBM Hertzog, was formed in 1914. South African entry into the First World War and the failed Afrikaner rebellion which followed only served to harden these political divisions. Labour disputes in the early 1920s led to the Rand Revolt of White mine workers in 1922, which the Smuts government was able to end only by resorting to armed force. Meanwhile, agitation among the Black population was also growing, with tens of thousands of African workers joining the Industrial and Commercial Workers' Union (ICU) led by Clements Kadalie. In 1924, the SAP was swept from power as Hertzog replaced Smuts as prime minister. The NP leader extended the systematic discrimination of Africans still further through his so-called "civilized labour" policy.

The Great Depression of the early 1930s had a big impact on South African politics. With the economy reeling as countries across the world abandoned the gold standard, Hertzog and Smuts came together and unified their parties, forming the new United Party or UP. A new fusion government was formed. This was the cue for a second Afrikaner schism, with DF Malan breaking away from the Hertzogite nationalists to form the Gesuiwerde Nasionale Party (also known as the Purified National Party or GNP). The outbreak of the Second World War, and Smuts' decision to side with the British once again, meant that divisions among the Whites were again compounded. More radical Afrikaners, led by Malan, now stood clearly opposed to the moderates led by Smuts, who was supported by the majority of English-speakers. Hertzog left the UP and rejoined the GNP, which was now renamed the Herenigde Nasionale Party (Reunified National Party) or simply the National Party (NP). The political climate became even more tense with the creation of pro-Nazi organizations such as the Ossewabrandwag (Ox-wagon Sentinels), a group which counted future NP Prime Minister John Vorster as a member. Meanwhile, African politics was sharply radicalized by the war. South African industry expanded in order to meet the increased allied demand during wartime, and more and more Africans moved to the cities to fill the new jobs in manufacturing. Strike action became increasingly common. The ANC (which formed a radical Youth League in 1944) and the Communist Party of South Africa (CPSA) were both very prominent in the organization of strikes and other protests. With the war over, White South Africa seemed to be at a crossroads. Millions of Black Africans now lived alongside Whites in the cities. They were increasingly confident and vocal in demanding an end to the policy of racial discrimination. What should White policy makers do next? Was the dream of segregating the races still possible, or even desirable? In the 1948 general election, the White people of South Africa delivered their verdict. Their answer was Malan's National Party (NP) and its policy of apartheid.

Country profile

Political geography

During the apartheid era, South Africa was made up of four separate provinces. These were the Cape Province, Natal, the Transvaal and the Orange Free State. These areas had been independent of one another prior to 1910 but came together to form the Union of South Africa in that year. Two of the four, the Cape Province and Natal, had been British colonies of settlement and still, to a greater or lesser degree, retained a British identity; this very much depended on the area, and was truer in Natal than in the Cape. The other two areas, Transvaal and the Orange Free State, had formerly been Boer Republics, and for that reason were more typically Afrikaner in character (although the city of Johannesburg was a partial exception here, with its split Anglo-Afrikaner identity). In the Cape Province, the main urban settlement was Cape Town in the far south-west, the so-called mother city and the second most populous city in the nation. As the seat of the nation's parliament, Cape Town was also the legislative capital. There were also two large port towns in the eastern part of the Cape Province, Port Elizabeth and East London, as well as the diamond mining centre of Kimberley in the Cape interior. In Natal, the inland

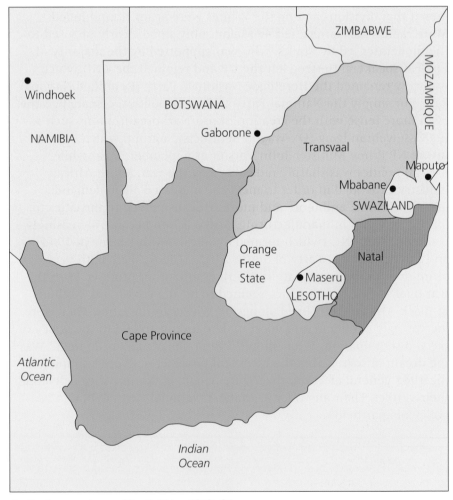

▲ The four provinces of South Africa, 1910–94

town of Pietermaritzburg was the provincial capital. However, by far the largest town in this province was the port city of Durban, which was also the third largest city in the country. Transvaal was the home of the country's seat of government, Pretoria. This meant that the city was also the national capital. However, the province's economy was dominated by the gold-mining city of Johannesburg, the largest city in the country as well as its financial powerhouse. The huge conurbation clustered around Johannesburg was known as the Witwatersrand. Located in the geographical heart of South Africa, the Orange Free State was very much a rural province. Its largest city, Bloemfontein, was also the judicial capital of the nation. The existence of three capitals – one administrative, one legislative, and one judicial – was a legacy of the Act of Union of 1910. The two British colonies, as well as the Transvaal and the Orange Free State, were each reluctant to concede the political initiative to their rival provinces in the new union. The result was a compromise whereby three national capitals were created.

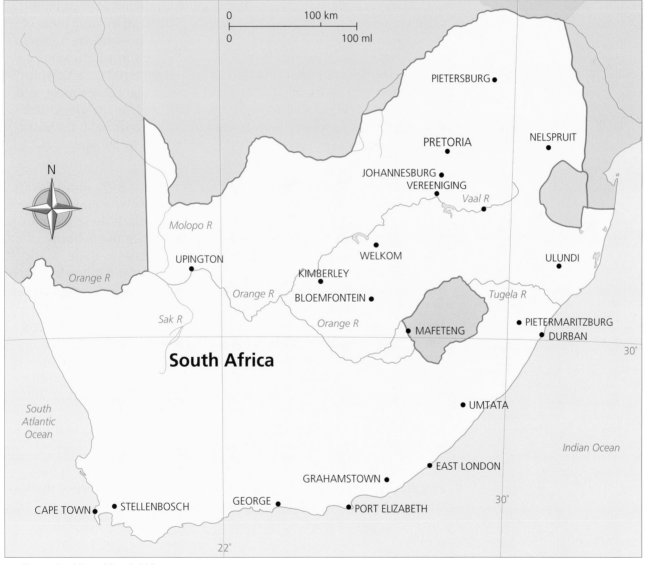

▲ The main cities of South Africa

People

Known today as the Rainbow Nation, South Africa, with its population of 52 million, has an amazingly diverse range of ethnicities. During the early apartheid period, the overall population of the country was significantly lower than it is today, ranging from 12 million in 1948 to 18 million in 1964. During this time, Whites, of whom there were roughly 3 million, constituted nearly one-fifth of the total population.

The White population of South Africa is made up of two main groups. The first group are the Afrikaners, sometimes referred to as **Boers**. The Afrikaners make up nearly 60% of the total White population. They are the descendants of the Dutch East Indies Company employees who first settled at the Cape of Good Hope in the 17th century, as well as of other European peoples, such as the French Huguenots who fled to the Cape to escape religious persecution at home. Their language still bears strong similarities to Dutch. Among the White population, the Afrikaners tend to be more numerous than the English in rural areas generally, in all of the Orange Free State, in the Transvaal (with the partial exception of Johannesburg), in the northern parts of Natal, and in some areas of the Cape, especially the western parts of the province and the northern Cape interior. The large majority of Afrikaners are Christians. Many are members of the protestant Dutch Reformed Church (DRC), a Calvinist denomination. This brand of Christianity is strict and conservative, and some historians argue that it had a strong influence on the ideological development of apartheid. During the early era of apartheid, the vast majority of Afrikaners supported the ruling NP led by DF Malan, JG Strijdom and HF Verwoerd.

The English, who make up much of the remaining 40% of the White population, are descendants of the British settlers who emigrated to the Cape and Natal in the 19th century, after both of these colonies were annexed by their government. They make up the majority of the White population in most of Natal and the Eastern Cape. Many English-speaking Whites moved to the Witwatersrand following the discovery of gold in 1886, a fact which explains the high proportion of English-speakers in the Johannesburg area. Most anglophone South Africans are members of various protestant churches. During the early apartheid era, they tended to support the United Party (UP). The UP was opposed to what was perceived as the Afrikaner favouritism of the NP. It was also against some of the more extreme elements of apartheid. However, with the notable exception of the famous anti-apartheid campaigner Helen Suzman, who was a member of the UP until 1959, this party supported the basic tenets of a system of racial segregation.

White South Africans as a whole were the main beneficiaries of the apartheid system. They were the only group who could exercise the vote and they held the vast majority of the country's wealth.

Boer

This term, which means "farmer" and refers to the Afrikaner people, is perfectly acceptable to use in a historical context. However, it is considered pejorative when used to describe Afrikaners today.

During the early apartheid period, of South Africa's majority non-White population, some 1.5 million were Coloured and nearly half a million Indian. The Coloureds were a group with an extraordinarily rich ethnic heritage. Broadly speaking, they were the descendants of the interracial offspring of Dutch farmers and their slaves. These slaves were mainly San, Khoikhoi or Malay. The latter group had been imported from the Dutch East Indies in the 17th and 18th centuries. The Coloured people also have a strong element of African ancestry. Most Coloureds are Afrikaans speakers, and many feel a strong cultural affinity with their White co-linguists, despite the legacy of the apartheid system. They constituted a majority of the population in the western and northern parts of Cape Province, but there were also large numbers of Coloureds in other major cities. Most Coloureds were Christian, and many were members of the DRC. Others, especially those who were considered "Cape Malay Coloured" during the apartheid years, were Muslim. The Indian community was mainly based in the cities of Durban and Johannesburg, although there were sizeable populations in other urban centres. Many of South Africa's Indians were descendants of indentured labourers who had been brought from India to work on Natal's sugar plantation in the 1860s. Others had arrived from India voluntarily to work as traders. Indian South Africans were mostly either Hindu or Muslim. In the complex hierarchy of apartheid, the Coloured and Indian populations occupied a sort of intermediate position. They were considered subordinate to Whites but superior to Black people. Most Coloureds and Indians were opposed to the apartheid system.

The various Black peoples who make up the large majority of South Africa's population can be divided into two main ethno-linguistic groupings: the Nguni and the Sotho-Tswana. Of the two, there are marginally more speakers of Nguni languages than Sotho-Tswana. By far the largest Nguni groups are the Zulu and the Xhosa, although there are sizeable populations of other groups such as the Tsonga (also called the Shangaan), Venda, Ndebele and Swazi. The main Sotho-Tswana populations are the Northern Sotho (sometimes known as the Pedi), the Southern Sotho and the Tswana. Under the old system of provinces, the Zulu were the dominant group in Natal and the south-eastern Transvaal, the Xhosa in the Eastern Cape, the Southern Sotho and Tswana in the Orange Free State, and the Northern Sotho, Tswana, Tsonga, Venda and Ndebele in the Transvaal. The large cities tend to be more mixed, with Johannesburg and Pretoria in particular containing large numbers of all of the country's African ethnicities. This was the result of huge numbers of Africans flooding into the cities from all parts of the country during the mineral revolution in the late 19th century, and again during the manufacturing boom of the Second World War. Many Africans still live in the enormous townships that skirt all of South Africa's major cities. The most famous of these is Soweto, whose population exceeds that of Johannesburg, the city it was built to serve.

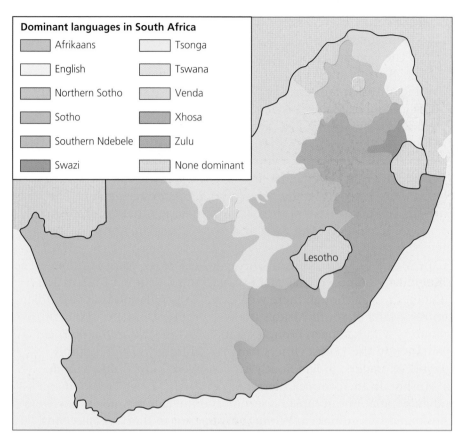

▲ The dominant language and ethnic groups by area in South Africa

Most Black South Africans are Christians, a legacy of nineteenth century European missionary activity. However, especially in rural areas, Christianity is often syncretized with traditional beliefs and cultural practices. A large number of Blacks belong to the so-called Africanist churches. These are independent Christian churches with a strongly African flavour, and they emerged in the early 20th century as a response to the perception among Africans that the missions churches were dominated by Europeans. The largest single denomination in South Africa today is the Zion Christian Church.

There are a number of other minority Black groups in South Africa. These are the descendants of the indigenous groups that had first settled the subcontinent and include the San, the Khoikhoi and the Griqua. The Griqua are, strictly speaking, a Coloured people, descended from Whites as well as the San and Khoikhoi. These groups were heavily marginalized by the apartheid system, and were mostly confined to the arid interior of the Cape Province.

During the period covered in this case study, the huge majority of the Black people of South Africa was opposed to the apartheid system and supported the liberation struggle of the ANC.

2 CIVIL RIGHTS MOVEMENT IN THE UNITED STATES (1954–1965)

2.1 Introduction to the Civil Rights Movement

Conceptual understanding

Key concept

→ Consequence

→ Continuity

→ Change

→ Perspective

Key questions

→ How were African Americans discriminated against socially, economically, and politically?

→ What methods, and with what effects, did opponents of desegregation employ to maintain the status quo?

▲ Civil Rights leaders in 1963 at the March on Washington for Jobs and Freedom

The US Supreme Court agrees to hear public school segregation cases brought by the National Association for the Advancement of Colored People (NAACP) in what will become known as *Brown v. Board of Education*

Malcolm X joins Nation of Islam.

1952

1954

The US Supreme Court overturns *Plessy v. Ferguson's* "separate but equal" doctrine in *Brown v. Board of Education of Topeka*; Mississippi responds by abolishing all public schools, starting the reaction to Brown that culminates in Massive Resistance

The White Citizens' Council is formed in Mississippi

The issue of remedy in Brown II is announced by the US Supreme Court, which declares that schools should desegregate with "all deliberate speed"

Rosa Parks refuses to give up her bus seat, beginning the Montgomery Bus Boycott

1955

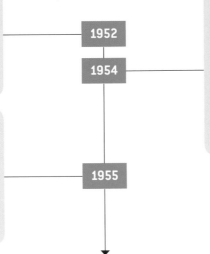

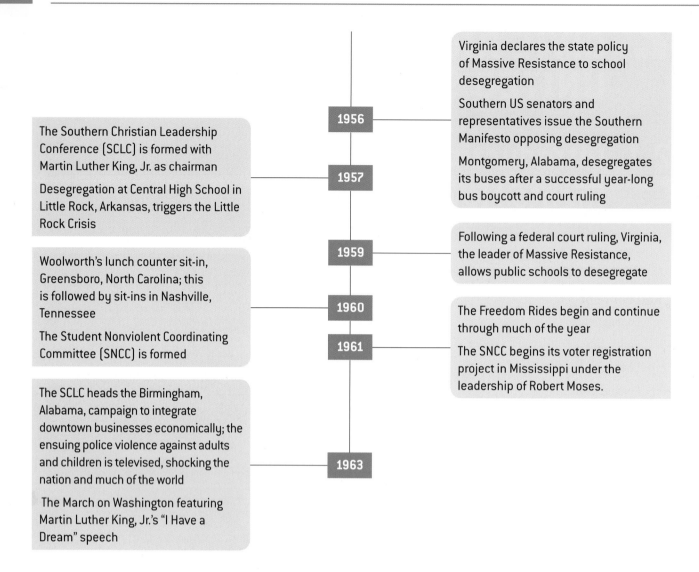

The Southern Christian Leadership Conference (SCLC) is formed with Martin Luther King, Jr. as chairman

Desegregation at Central High School in Little Rock, Arkansas, triggers the Little Rock Crisis

Woolworth's lunch counter sit-in, Greensboro, North Carolina; this is followed by sit-ins in Nashville, Tennessee

The Student Nonviolent Coordinating Committee (SNCC) is formed

The SCLC heads the Birmingham, Alabama, campaign to integrate downtown businesses economically; the ensuing police violence against adults and children is televised, shocking the nation and much of the world

The March on Washington featuring Martin Luther King, Jr.'s "I Have a Dream" speech

1956

1957

1959

1960

1961

1963

Virginia declares the state policy of Massive Resistance to school desegregation

Southern US senators and representatives issue the Southern Manifesto opposing desegregation

Montgomery, Alabama, desegregates its buses after a successful year-long bus boycott and court ruling

Following a federal court ruling, Virginia, the leader of Massive Resistance, allows public schools to desegregate

The Freedom Rides begin and continue through much of the year

The SNCC begins its voter registration project in Mississippi under the leadership of Robert Moses.

The African American Civil Rights Movement began long before the years covered by this case study. Its origins can be traced back to abolitionism during the antebellum period in the United States. However, the years beginning with the US Supreme Court's unanimous ruling in *Brown v. Board of Education* in 1954, which largely overturned the "separate but equal" doctrine firmly established in the *Plessy v. Ferguson* decision of 1896, set forth a period of mass action by African Americans. This marked a significant change in the quest for civil rights. In the first half of the 20th century, organizations such as the National Association for the Advancement of Colored People (NAACP) and the Congress of Racial Equality (CORE) formed in order to fight for the rights, and often the lives, of African Americans. The NAACP led the decades-long legal fight to overturn *Plessy v. Ferguson* and CORE organized small-scale "freedom rides" just after the Second World War, but the era of the Civil Rights Movement was one of protests of all sizes. These protests interacted with institutions in the United States that largely resisted both change and the legal, political, economic and social equality of African Americans.

To understand the importance of this chapter, which begins with *Brown v. Board of Education* and ends with the Voting Rights Act of 1965, it is helpful to know some of the history and the geography of the United States. The background to this can be found in Chapters 8 and 9 of the *History of the Americas* Course Companion and will briefly be reviewed here.

Source skills

As you read through this chapter, identify motives, actions and events that provide evidence in support of each of these five factors of racial discrimination. Copy the spider diagram and add any evidence you find.

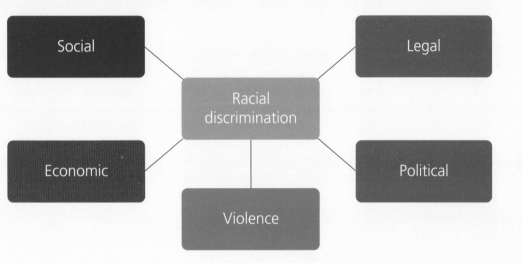

Background

Following the end of the American Civil War, the 13th, 14th and 15th Amendments were added to the US Constitution. The 13th Amendment abolished slavery, the 14th Amendment established citizenship and stated

> *nor shall any State deprive any person of life, liberty, or property, without due process of law; nor deny to any person within its jurisdiction the equal protection of the laws*

and the 15th Amendment provided for the right to vote regardless of *"race, color, or condition of previous servitude* [slavery]*"*. The intent of these Amendments was, along with the abolition of slavery, to provide for the legal and political equality of African Americans. Additionally, several civil rights laws were passed to guarantee rights further, regardless of race. The Civil Rights Act of 1866 added equal rights in contracts and employment, attempting to provide for equality of economic opportunity. White opposition to racial equality found many forms, including the intimidation and violence implemented by groups such as the Ku Klux Klan (KKK). Whatever gains African Americans had made in the states comprising the Confederacy during the Reconstruction period, these eroded quickly following the withdrawal of federal troops in 1877 in the deal that resulted in Rutherford B Hayes becoming president. Combined with US Supreme Court decisions that weakened and narrowed the 14th Amendment so that states had a great deal of latitude in application and enforcement, the

The **Great Migration** was the movement of many rural southern African Americans to northern cities, beginning a transition to the urban centers that would continue through much of the 20th century. By 1970, approximately 7 million African Americans had moved out of the South.

Peonage

Debt slavery, in which business owners required workers to labor until they paid off a debt. The wages paid were often so low that it took years or decades to pay the debt.

end of Reconstruction meant legal, economic and political inferiority for African Americans in the South. The legal and social structure that upheld the system of apartheid was known as Jim Crow. Laws defined a system that designated almost every area as "white" or "colored". Police, courts and groups such as the KKK punished any violation as a challenge to the system. (It should be noted that African Americans living in the northern states did not enjoy political or economic equality either, although there were significantly fewer legal obstacles and less racial violence in the North. However, the great majority of African Americans lived in the southern states, even after the first **Great Migration** of 1910–1930.)

African Americans in many places in the United States, but more so in the South, lived under a legal system that supported white supremacy, the constant threat of economic coercion and violence, state backed, individual, and mob. The legal system was used for the maintenance of political power and the economic gain of white Americans. According to Douglas A Blackmon (2009), shortly after the beginning of the 20th century approximately half of all African Americans lived in virtual servitude. Many were sharecroppers and worked in a system in which the owner of the land retained complete control over what African Americans produced, setting prices, rents and loan rates, and keeping African Americans in **peonage**, even though this was against federal law. The federal government did not enforce this law in the South. Southern states also used the penal system to set up and run a system of slavery. Black men were arrested for crimes such as vagrancy, drunkenness, or other minor violations, and were quickly convicted. The penalty was usually a choice between six months to a year in prison or a fine that was too high to pay. Imprisonment resulted in forced labour, where convicts were rented out by the prison system to private enterprises in agriculture or industry; the prison officials were monetarily compensated and the businesses gained labour at a rate well below going wages, while working conditions were often deplorable. In the case of a fine, either the fine-payer or the judge could opt for the fine to be worked off; either way the convict worked for months with no pay and usually in miserable working conditions. This system kept farms, factories and mines supplied with cheap labour.

One example Blackmon (2009) points to is the Tennessee Coal, Iron and Railroad Company (TCI), which was purchased by US Steel in 1907. The founder and chairman of US Steel, Elbert H Gary, was an abolitionist and was opposed to convict labour, ordering it to be stopped. However, TCI maintained the system for two reasons: it had contracts for the next four years to use thousands of such workers, and the prison contracts forestalled labour union difficulties. US Steel did implement modest improvements in the mines' working conditions, but TCI nonetheless signed new contracts for more convict labour. In fact, when the prison system cut the number of labourers available for the mines, US Steel complained. Thus, there was a substantial integration of northern economic interests with institutionalized involuntary servitude of African Americans in the South. However, since the federal government did not view these practices as involuntary servitude, it was able largely to ignore them.

TOK connections

Historian Robert Weisbrot (1990) explains:

> Daily humiliation of Negroes was woven into the fabric of Southern life in patterns as variegated as a community's imagination permitted. In 1905 Georgia prohibited Negroes and whites from using the same park facilities; donors of land for playgrounds had to specify which race could use them. Until 1940 Negroes and whites in Atlanta, Georgia, were not able to visit the municipal zoo at the same time. In 1915 Oklahoma authorized separate telephone booths for white and Negro callers ... Many public libraries permitted black and white to mingle only in the pages of books, while otherwise reserving the buildings exclusively for white use. Separate Bibles for oath-taking in courts, separate doors for whites and Negroes, separate elevators and stairways, separate drinking fountains, and separate toilets existed even where not required by law.

TOK guiding questions

- From what perspective does Weisbrot write? How does this perspective guide his construction of the paragraph?

- How does Weisbrot use vocabulary and the listing of evidence to help readers understand life in the Jim Crow South?

The killing of African Americans was commonplace from 1888 to 1923. In this period, more than 2,500 African Americans were **lynched** by white mobs. Individual African Americans were often hanged or burned for alleged crimes. A common accusation was sexual assault, or even the flirtation of an African American man with a white woman. Indeed, in 1955, African American teenager Emmitt Till was lynched simply for saying a few words to a white woman. While lynchings were not reserved for African Americans (white Americans had been lynched in the West for alleged horse theft or cattle rustling), the overwhelming majority of victims of lynchings during this period were African Americans.

The group most infamous for its racial violence was the Ku Klux Klan, or KKK. The Klan was formed in Tennessee in the winter following the end of the American Civil War. It was initially formed as a secret social organization but in a short time evolved into a vigilante group whose principal goal was to negate Reconstruction; beginning in 1869, the organization intimidated, assaulted and murdered African Americans and white Americans who were sympathetic to them. The Klan became active in all southern states and targeted African American political leaders and office holders. Acts of brutality were common, including the whipping of senior citizens and adults who refused to work for white Americans, lynchings, even in front of children, and the burning of churches. Many white government officials and police employees were Klan members. African Americans in the South lived in constant fear of extreme racial violence.

The Enforcement Acts of 1870 and 1871 were used by federal officials to crack down on Klan activity, and the states of Arkansas, Tennessee and Texas did organize police to target violent Klan actions. Government enforcement had some effect and, as Jim Crow laws achieved success in disenfranchising African Americans as well as forcing them into peonage, the Klan lost its reason for being and largely faded away.

In 1915, however, in light of the great wave of immigration that began in 1890, the Klan appeared again, this time as a patriotic and anti-Catholic, anti-Semitic and anti-African American organization. It grew

Lynching

Extra-judicial homicide. Sometimes referred to as "Frontier Justice" when a group of people take law into their own hands and hand down, then carry out, a death sentence.

to its largest membership within a decade. Interestingly, the film *Birth of a Nation*, which glorified the Reconstruction-era KKK and was screened in the White House for an enthusiastic President Woodrow Wilson, became effective pro-Klan propaganda, motivating more sympathizers to join. By 1925, the Klan counted an estimated four million adherents, including numerous elected officials. However, due to a combination of infighting, unfavourable newspaper coverage and public disapproval, the Klan faded once more as the United States became a combatant in the Second World War. The Klan was revived a decade later by the Brown decision.

◀ By the first decades of the 20th century the Ku Klux Klan had expanded beyond the South, rallying in Long Branch, New Jersey 7th April 1924.

Source skills

Source A

Sam Kilgore, a former slave, was interviewed and recorded as part of the Federal Writers' Project (FWP), 1936–1938. He was 92 when he gave his narrative.

Befo' we moved to Texas de Klu [sic] Kluxers done burn my mammy's house and she lost everything. Dey was 'bout $100 in greenbacks in dat house and a three hundred pound hawg in de pen, what die from de heat. We done run to Massa Rodger's house. De riders gits to bad dey come most any time and run de cullud folks off for no cause, jus' to be orn'ry and plunder de home. But one day I seed Massa Rodgers take a dozen guns out his wagon and he and some white men digs a ditch round de cotton field close to de road. Couple nights after dat de riders come and when dey gits near dat ditch a volley am fired and lots of dem drops off dey hosses. Dat ended de Klux trouble in dat section.

Born in Slavery: Slave Narratives from the Federal Writers' Project, 1936–1938. Texas Narratives, Volume XVI, Part 2, p. 258.

Source B

A description from the Public Broadcasting Service (PBS): *The Rise and Fall of Jim Crow: Jim Crow Stories: The Ku Klux Klan (1866).*

The Klan spread beyond Tennessee to every state in the South and included mayors, judges, and sheriffs as well as common criminals. The Klan systematically murdered black politicians and political leaders. It beat, whipped, and murdered thousands, and intimidated tens of thousands of others from voting. Blacks often tried to fight back, but they were outnumbered and out gunned. While the main targets of Klan wrath were the political and social leaders of the black community, blacks could be murdered for almost any reason. Men, women, children, aged and crippled, were victims. A 103-year-old woman was whipped, as was a completely paralyzed man. In Georgia, Abraham Colby, an organizer and leader in the black community, was whipped for hours in front of his wife and children… In Mississippi, Jack Dupree's throat was cut and he was disemboweled in front of his wife, who had just given birth to twins. Klansmen burned churches and schools, lynching teachers and educated blacks. Black landowners were driven off their property and murdered if they refused to leave. Blacks were whipped for refusing to work for whites, for having intimate relations with whites, for arguing with whites, for having jobs whites wanted, for reading a newspaper or having a book in their homes.

First question, part a – 3 marks

According to Source B, what were the implied and stated reasons for Klan violence against African Americans?

First question, part b – 2 marks

What is the message of Source A?

Second question – 4 marks

With reference to its content, origin and purpose, what are the values and limitations of Source B for a student studying the effects of KKK violence during and just following Reconstruction?

Race riots took hundreds of lives. There were numerous race riots, or acts of race-based mob violence, from the last decade of the 19th century into the first decades of the 20th century. These riots were sparked by a variety of circumstances, from alleged black on white crime to African American or African American-supported candidates being elected to office. Among the notable events of mass violence were: Wilmington, North Carolina (1898); Atlanta, Georgia (1906); Elaine, Arkansas (1919); and Tulsa, Oklahoma (1921).

In Wilmington, a city with a majority African American population, the catalyst for the riot was the electoral defeat of the segregationist Democratic Party in 1896 by a coalition of the white Populist Party "Fusionists" and African American Republicans. Democrats vowed revenge in the next election by appealing to white racial identity and fear of black males, in particular by playing on the idea that white women were constantly under the threat of rape by African American men. A Wilmington newspaper published a speech from a Georgia feminist, Rebecca Felton, in which she proposed,

If it requires lynching to protect a woman's dearest possession from ravening, drunken human beasts, then I say lynch a thousand negroes a week.

The 1898 election included the stuffing of ballot boxes by Democrats to ensure victory. Following the election, white Americans physically removed African American government officials, set the African American-owned newspaper office on fire and shot at African Americans on city streets; members of the mob asserting that they were protecting their rights. In the 24 hours after the election, at least 25 African Americans were killed and the actual number could have been well over 100 dead. Some African Americans and white Fusionists were loaded onto trains and banished from the city. Eventually, over 2,000 African Americans emigrated because of the effects of the race riot.

In September 1906, there was white mob violence in Atlanta, Georgia. The city had undergone rapid population expansion and had, as a result, become a leading economic city in the South. Racial tensions rose over several factors, including a mayoral election campaign in which the white candidates portrayed each other as pandering to African Americans, and stories carried by major newspapers telling of alleged assaults by African American males against white women. Other news stories discussed "uppity" black elites wanting to achieve social, economic and political equality.

On 22 September, four alleged assaults by African American men on white women were reported in the newspapers. Within hours, thousands of white men had assembled downtown. After midnight, the mob attacked hundreds of African Americans, destroyed businesses and even boarded street cars to beat black men and women. The next day, many African Americans armed themselves and law enforcement and militias patrolled; nonetheless, white vigilante groups attacked some African American areas of Atlanta and African Americans defended themselves. A third day brought more vigorous police enforcement and a confrontation between armed African Americans and law enforcement officers that resulted in the death of one policeman and the arrest of 250 African American men. Estimates of the total number of deaths range from 25–40 for African Americans, with two white Americans losing their lives. The riot received national press coverage and threatened Atlanta's reputation as a prospering city. As a result, Atlanta became much more segregated, Georgia restricted black suffrage two years later, and there emerged a motivation for more forceful African American advocacy of rights.

The race-based mob violence in Elaine, Arkansas, and Tulsa, Oklahoma, is considered to be the most violent of the period. According to the Encyclopedia of Oklahoma History and Culture, the Tulsa Race Riot is the *"single worst incident of racial violence in American history"*. Occurring over 18 hours, the white mob violence was responsible for the deaths of 50–300 African Americans (official records are inaccurate) and the destruction of more than 1,000 homes and businesses in Greenwood, (the African American neighbourhood in Tulsa).

The violence was apparently started when an African American man, a shoe shiner called Dick Rowland, accidentally stepped on the foot of a white woman, Sarah Page, in an elevator. The incident was reported in the newspapers as attempted rape and a mob gathered the next evening, amid calls to lynch Rowland. African Americans fought against thousands of armed white Americans and were overwhelmed: the entire African American neighbourhood in Tulsa was burned to the ground.

Two years prior to the Tulsa Race Riot, the 1919 Elaine Massacre had occurred in the Red Scare period following the First World War. After white security officers and deputy sheriffs confronted armed African Americans guarding a union meeting at Hoop Spur Church, shots were exchanged, resulting in the wounding of the Phillips County deputy sheriff and the death of a white security guard. The next day, the sheriff led a posse into the black quarter of Elaine to arrest the alleged perpetrators. The posse grew to between 500 and 1000 white men. US troops were also sent to Elaine to put down the "insurrection". Reports differ on the number of deaths. Close to 300 African Americans were arrested and 122 were charged with crimes; of these, 12 were tried and convicted of murder, motivating scores of others to plead guilty to second degree murder. The murder convictions of the Elaine Twelve were appealed all the way to the US Supreme Court. and, in the decision of *Moore v. Dempsey* the court ordered a rehearing. Political scientist Megan Ming Francis ([year])argues that *Moore v. Dempsey* was the critical basis for changing the US Supreme Court's approach from deference to state authority towards more of a federal role in guaranteeing rights of Americans, thus creating a path for the NAACP's civil rights litigation strategy that culminated in *Brown v. Board of Education*.

These four episodes of race-based mob violence – Wilmington, Atlanta, Elaine and Tulsa – have been largely ignored in mainstream US history texts. It is only within the past several decades that historians and the communities themselves have written these events into state and local histories.

Self-management and research skills

Create a table like the one below to gather and sort important historical evidence about the race riots that took place from 1898–1921. Research may be divided within a student group in which each student investigates one city.

Location/dates	Causes	Participants	Results [e.g. human and property damage/ long term effects]	Source
Wilmington/				
Atlanta/				
Elaine/				
Tulsa/				

Source skills

The following sources are both part of an online exhibit of the Tulsa Race Riot on the Oklahoma Historical Society's website, the Encyclopedia of Oklahoma History and Culture.

Source A

A photograph of African Americans sifting through the rubble after the Tulsa Race Riot

Source B

Two excerpts from the *Encyclopedia of Oklahoma History and Culture.*

Over the next six hours Tulsa was plunged into chaos as angry whites, frustrated over the failed lynching, began to vent their rage at African Americans in general. Furious fighting erupted along the Frisco railroad tracks, where black defenders were able to hold off members of the white mob. An unarmed African American man was murdered inside a downtown movie theater, while carloads of armed whites began making "drive-by" shootings in black residential neighborhoods. By midnight fires had been set along the edge of the African American commercial district. In some of the city's all-night cafes, whites began to organize for a dawn invasion of Greenwood …

Shortly before dawn on June 1, thousands of armed whites had gathered along the fringes of Greenwood. When daybreak came, they poured into the African American district, looting homes and businesses and setting them on fire. Numerous atrocities occurred, including the murder of A. C. Jackson, a renowned black surgeon, who was shot after he surrendered to a group of whites. At least one machine gun was utilized by the invading whites, and some participants have claimed that airplanes were also used in the attack.

digital.library.okstate.edu/encyclopedia/entries/T/TU013.html

First question, part a – 3 marks

What evidence is there in Source A to suggest that a race riot occurred and that property was damaged?

Second question – 4 marks

With reference to its content, origin and purpose, what are the values and limitations of Source A for students researching violence against African Americans in the early 1900s?

Third question – 6 marks

Compare and contrast Sources A and B in terms of what they show about anti-African American violence in Tulsa, Oklahoma.

Violent acts carried out against African American women was another way in which some white Americans sought to oppress African Americans. A slave was a chattel (personal possession) and, as such, a slave's body did not belong to the slave but to the slave's owner. Danielle L McGuire writes that, after the abolition of slavery, *"former slaveholders and their sympathizers used rape as a 'weapon of terror' to dominate the bodies and minds of African-American men and women"*. McGuire also reports that *"sexual and racial violence functioned as a tool of coercion, control, and harassment"* (2010). The rape of African American women continued into the 20th century, usually without legal punishment despite the claims of victims. Indeed, sexual abuse continued into the 1950s and 1960s as female civil rights workers were jailed and subjected to the whims of prison guards. The role of sexual violence combined with race relations remains an active area of research.

A critical means for the maintenance of white control in the Jim Crow South was the disenfranchisement of African Americans. During Reconstruction, African Americans in the former states of the Confederacy were able to vote, run for and hold office. After 1876, white Americans in those states quickly worked to reclaim political power by disenfranchising African Americans through various methods, including violence and intimidation, election fraud, and both substantive and procedural legal barriers. Soon after the ratification of the 15th Amendment and the Enforcement Act of 1870, African

Americans were threatened and sometimes assaulted when going to the polls. In 1873, more than 100 African Americans were killed in mob violence while defending local Republican government officials in Colfax, Louisiana. Federal enforcement of the right to vote was basically nullified in *United States v. Cruikshank*, a case that grew out of the Colfax incident. Still, African Americans continued to go to the polls. The second phase of disenfranchisement was known as "Redemption." The **stuffing of ballot boxes** and the disposal of, or failure to count, African American votes was common; furthermore, the US Supreme Court significantly weakened the ability of the federal government to enforce legal voting practices in *U.S. v. Reese* in 1875. An additional practice was to count out ballots cast by African Americans for the chosen white candidates instead.

These practices were both inefficient and brought unwanted legal challenges, and often unwanted attention. White supremacists sought more efficient and longer lasting means to deny African Americans the vote. The path was through the passage of laws that effectively disenfranchised African Americans without ever mentioning race. The most common methods employed included a **poll tax,** which was used to prevent the poor (and most African Americans in the South were sharecroppers or in extremely low paid employment) from voting, and a **literacy test**, which facilitated the disqualification of almost every potential African American voter at the hands of biased registrars. Approximately one half of all African Americans were illiterate, having been denied an adequate education. However, even those who could read were disqualified by election officials.

One potential problem with the poll tax and literacy test was the disqualification of white voters as well. This obstacle was circumvented with what came to be called the "**Grandfather Clause**", which allowed most white Americans, no matter how impoverished or illiterate, to cast legal votes. The Grandfather Clause allowed those whose grandfathers and sometimes great grandfathers were eligible to vote to cast ballots legally, regardless of the new election laws. As almost all the grandfathers of African Americans had been slaves, the Grandfather Clause effectively applied only to white Americans.

Another tactic was the "Whites-only primary". The Democratic Party, being a non-government entity, was allowed to set its own rules for participation and membership. As this was the dominant political party in all southern states, excluding African Americans from the selection of candidates negated African American votes as well. The Whites-only primary was finally declared unconstitutional in *Terry v. Adams* in 1953, but federal enforcement was at best ineffective. Consequently, as a result of the variety of tactics employed by white supremacists in the last quarter of the 19th century and the first 50 years of the 20th century, the 15th Amendment providing African Americans with the right to vote was nullified.

The United States is a federal system: there is a central government with a Constitution and laws, and there are 50 state governments, each with its own Constitution and laws. The US Constitution

---

Ballot stuffing

The practice of election officials who cast significant numbers of fraudulent ballots to be counted with the intent, and usually the result, of the preferred candidate (or slate of candidates) winning the election.

A **poll tax** is one usually due at the time of voting and must be paid in order for a vote to be cast.

Literacy test

When registering to vote, citizens had to read and demonstrate understanding of a passage, often from the state constitution. The interpretation had to receive the approval of the registrar, who was almost always white and understood the unwritten purpose of the test.

A **grandfather clause** allows an exception for acts which were previously legal but made illegal. Today the term grandfathering refers to any rule, regulation, or law that allows those people under a previous set of circumstances to continue, while new persons are subject to the new regulations.

reserves for the state governments those legal areas over which the federal government does not have authority, but the interpretation of those reserved powers has evolved and varied over the life of the United States. The incorporation of the Bill of Rights as applicable to the states did not begin in earnest until the 1920s, but even then it was a gradual process. Consequently, the Jim Crow laws could vary from state to state, and the state and local governments almost completely excluded African Americans from the official government functions of legislating, policing and contract enforcement, as well as other civil rights. There was little the federal government could or would do; even when it could do something, the realities of party politics largely prevented white officeholders from taking action. The Democratic Party became a coalition of white Southerners and northern labour, while the Republican Party grew to include northern business interests, rejecting a progressive wing in the early 1900s. The Democratic Party that emerged as a majority with Franklin D Roosevelt in 1932 was a coalition of progressives from the North, many of whom were former Republicans, and white segregationist Southerners who regarded the Republican Party as the party of Lincoln and "Radical Reconstruction". For the most part, Democrat leaders ignored the rights of African Americans in order to keep the diverse coalition together. The result was little progress on civil rights from the federal government during the New Deal years, a period of dramatic governmental growth.

The Second World War largely focused the nation on fighting the war in Europe and the Pacific, but despite the participation of millions of African Americans as soldiers and defence workers, segregation remained. Just months before the United States entered the war, A Philip Randolph, leader of the Brotherhood of Sleeping Car Porters, threatened a march on Washington to protest against discrimination in defence factories and the armed forces. Roosevelt averted the confrontation by ordering an end to employment discrimination in the defence industry, but the problem festered as the armed forces of a country fighting Nazi Germany stayed segregated. As African American soldiers returned at the end of the war, they returned to a Jim Crow South. Many of the veterans felt they had earned the right to be treated as equals and began to act on their demands. Such activists included Medgar Evers, Amzie Moore and Charles Sims.

The decade following the war saw some progress as President Harry Truman ordered the army desegregated, as well as supporting civil rights legislation in 1948. However, Jim Crow remained the way of life in the southern states and increased pressure on the system resulted in a hardening of positions, especially as challenges came from African American activists and the federal government. The first large challenge to Jim Crow came in 1954 when the US Supreme Court declared segregated schools to be inherently unequal, violating the equal protection clause of the 14th Amendment.

Historical Framework

As the struggle for civil rights evolved in the 20th century, developments can be classified into three strands: legal challenges, using the courts to secure rights that were being violated, essentially to force commercial and government institutions to adhere to the US Constitution; demonstrations and boycotts on various scales to force public and private institutions to stop a range of Jim Crow practices, from the refusal to serve African Americans to the prevention of African Americans from voting; the writing and passage of laws to allow the power of government to enforce civil rights. These strands were not mutually exclusive and often progress resulted from a combination of two or three strands working together, sometimes unintentionally, sometimes grudgingly, to achieve results. Examples of combined strands include: *Brown v. Board of Education* (1954); Montgomery Bus Boycott (1955–1956); the Little Rock Crisis (1957); the Civil Rights Act (1964); the Voting Rights Act (1965).

Segregation and education; *Brown v. Board of Education* decision (1954); Little Rock (1957)

Possibly the most well-known US Supreme Court decision of the 20th century, *Brown v. Board of Education of Topeka* changed the landscape of legal support for segregation, specifically racial segregation in public education. It was a paradigm shift. If the 14th Amendment can be considered the "African American Bill of Rights", as partially incorporated by *Gitlow v. New York* (1925), Brown made it official, even though the overturning of *Plessy v. Ferguson* (1896) was specifically only in the area of public education. However, Brown was not simply a sudden shift that came from the new Chief Justice of the Supreme Court, Earl Warren; rather, the steps to overturning Plessy had been paved by the decades-long effort of the

NAACP's legal arm, with the continued support of Walter White and the strong leadership of Charles Hamilton Houston. The NAACP devised and implemented a legal strategy to reverse Plessy, the legal foundation for Jim Crow. Hamilton's contributions were so critical to the effort, he became known as "the man who killed Jim Crow".

The foundation for the NAACP's strategy came from the Margold Report. After assessing the climate and the prospects of dismantling Jim Crow, Nathan Ross Margold wrote a report that suggested attacking segregation through the courts: "*if we boldly challenge the constitutional validity of segregation if and when accompanied irremediably by discrimination, we can strike directly at the most prolific sources of discrimination*" (1930). Specifically, the NAACP would use the courts to challenge whether the "equal" part of "separate but equal" really meant "equal" in the case of public schools. Rather than ask the courts to order the mixing of races, the NAACP would try to get the courts to allocate as much per pupil for African American students as was spent on white Americans. Study after study showed that per pupil spending on white children was two to five times as much as on African American children, pay for African American teachers was much less than that of white educators, facilities within schools were completely unequal, and the school year for African Americans was significantly shorter; forcing school districts to comply with "equal" would be quite expensive. As the strategy of the NAACP's legal division evolved to focus on education (lynching was also a major focus), the thinking was that, in the end, making separate facilities equal would be cost-prohibitive and the practical result would be the end of segregated schools.

The legal strategy also had to consider the importance of judicial restraint and legal precedent. Consistency in law is critical to its acceptance and applicability. Judges' rulings usually follow previous rulings and lower courts follow the rulings of higher courts. In the United States, the Supreme Court sets forth legal decisions (called Opinions) that guide lower courts. When subsequent rulings are based on an opinion, that opinion acts as a precedent. The overturning of a precedent upon which a series of legal decisions is based is quite difficult, as judges value consistency and predictability as critical. The reluctance to overturn long-standing precedents, along with respect for the intent of legislators, is what is known as "judicial restraint". Thus, the legal basis for segregation, Plessy, which was the culmination of numerous rulings in the 1880s and 1890s and had been in force for several decades, would be extremely difficult to reverse.

Of equal importance, the integration of white and African American children in schools would strike at the heart of Jim Crow, but it would also strike at the core fears of segregationists: equal status and miscegenation (the interbreeding of people of different races). Despite the great injustices, it would be difficult to find plaintiffs in public school cases due to the fear of economic and violent reprisals. African Americans who had tried to assert rights in Jim Crow states had lost their jobs and been lynched. Charles Hamilton Houston, who had become the chief of the NAACP's legal team, had modified Margold's strategy to start with graduate schools, the highest level of education. This approach would not upset entire local populations, which could pressure judges, and would also have the advantage of pointing out obvious inequalities, for example where no African American medical or law schools existed. However, it was necessary to find a client with the standing to bring a lawsuit.

Opportunity came in the person of Donald Murray in early 1935. Murray had applied for admission to the University of Maryland School of Law; his application had not even been considered, his letter of application had been rejected and the fee returned, and he had been told to apply to the Princess Anne Academy, the only post-secondary school available to African Americans in Maryland. The Princess Anne Academy was at best of junior college level; it offered no graduate courses whatsoever and had no law school. He was also told that he could apply to an out-of-state law school and that he would be eligible for tuition assistance, but the offer was a hollow one as the legislature had appropriated no funds for that purpose. Here was a willing plaintiff with standing, and certainly no "equal" facility. The "equal" part of Plessy could be tested.

The case was first designated *Murray v. Pearson* (Raymond Pearson was the President of the University of Maryland).

In June 1935, the case went to court, with Charles Houston, assisted by Thurgood Marshall, arguing for Donald Murray in *Murray v. Maryland*. The NAACP lawyers argued successfully, calling both the president of the University of Maryland, Raymond Pearson, and the dean of the School of Law as witnesses. The Princess Anne Academy was exposed as offering an education far below the level of the first two years of undergraduate education at the University of Maryland, not to mention that of a law school. Judge Eugene O'Dunne decided in favour of Murray, ordering the law school to admit him. The decision was appealed and in 1936 the state Supreme Court affirmed the decision.

The Supreme Court cannot be forced to hear a case, rather it chooses the cases it will hear. A minimum of four justices must vote to hear a case. An affirmative vote results in a *writ of certiorari*.

While *Murray v. Maryland* (1936) was a victory, it was only a first step. The decision only applied to Maryland and then only effectively to graduate schools. At this time in the United States, for a decision to apply to the entire country it had to reach the US Supreme Court.

This would mean selecting cases that would likely be appealed all the way to the Supreme Court. A way to guarantee this process was to choose cases that the NAACP would be likely to lose, and that they could then choose to appeal. Soon after Murray, the NAACP took up the equalization of teacher salaries in South Carolina. An African American school principal who asked the district superintendent for the salary increase saw his contract terminated, but the NAACP saw a ruling that equalized teacher salaries.

The next step was the case of *Gaines v. Missouri* (1938), also a law school case, in which the state refused to let African Americans attend the state university's law school. Missouri provided remedy in that it agreed to pay any additional tuition incurred by African Americans attending schools out of state but, unlike Maryland, fully funded that option. The Missouri Supreme Court decided against Lloyd L Gaines, allowing an appeal to the US Supreme Court. The Supreme Court reversed the decision of the Missouri Supreme Court: the law school was ordered to admit Gaines. Essentially, separate facilities had to be equal within a state, but the Supreme Court did not comment on segregated facilities themselves. Although this was Houston's last case for the NAACP, he continued to attack, by legal means, segregation in transportation, labour and public facilities. These cases, too, helped pave a legal road to overturning Plessy. In 1940, Houston was followed by his chosen successor, Thurgood Marshall. It was the task of Marshall and the NAACP legal team to establish that separate facilities could never be equal, even if equally funded.

The cases of *Sweatt v. Painter* (1950) and *McLaurin v. Oklahoma State Regents* (1950) were the final two steps before Brown that chipped away at the "separate but equal" doctrine. In 1946, Herman Sweatt had applied for admission to the University of Texas School of Law. Texas had built a second law school just for African Americans, but in 1950 the US Supreme Court issued an opinion that, even if the facilities were equal, a law school was more than a legal education, involving interaction with fellow students, professors, access to a law library, and reputation. Consequently, no separate law school could ever be equal. Here the Supreme Court had ruled that, at least in the area of graduate schools, separate facilities could never be equal. *McLaurin v. Oklahoma*, a case involving the Oklahoma State School of Education, further established that being segregated within the same school also violated the equal protection clause of the 14th Amendment.

The public school cases were getting underway in various states: in Clarendon County, South Carolina, elementary and high school students brought suit in *Briggs v. Elliot*; in Prince Edward County, Virginia, the plaintiffs in *Davis v. County School Board* were high school students; in New Castle County, Delaware, elementary and high school students sued in *Gebhart v. Belton*; and in *Brown v. Board of Education of Topeka* the plaintiffs were elementary school students. The US Supreme Court agreed to hear these four cases – along with the District of Columbia case, *Bolling v. Sharpe* – as one consolidated case, calling it *Brown v. Board of Education*. The case ended up being argued twice before the justices. It was first heard in the spring of 1953, but the Court was unable to reach a decision and both sides were ordered to present their arguments again in the autumn of the same year.

The following extract tells how Barbara Johns organized students at the African American Moton High School to walk out in 1951 in support of achieving integrated schools in Prince Edward County. Johns also contacted the NAACP for legal support. In total, 117 of the students who walked out became the plaintiffs in Davis v. County School Board, one of the cases that became the basis for Brown.

Kluger, R. 2011. *Simple Justice: The History of Brown v. Board of Education and Black America's Struggle for Equality*, Kindle edition, locations 11804–11811. Knopf Doubleday Publishing Group.

At the appointed moment in the auditorium, 450 students and a faculty of two dozen teachers less one principal hushed as the stage curtains opened. The student strike committee was seated behind the rostrum. Standing at it and in command of the suddenly murmuring room was Barbara Rose Johns. She asked the teachers to leave, and as the excitement grew, most of them obliged. And then the beautiful sixteen-year-old girl at the rostrum told her schoolmates what was in her heart. It was time that Negroes were treated equally with whites. It was time that they had a decent high school. It was time for the students themselves to do something about it. They were going to march out of school then and there and they were going to stay out until the white community responded properly. The Farmville jail was too small to hold all of them, and none of them would be punished if they acted together and held fast to their resolve. In the long run, said Barbara Johns, things would never be really equal until they attended school with white students on a non-segregated basis.

Questions

1 What were Barbara Johns's motivations in organizing the strike?

2 Why do you think Johns asked all the teachers to leave?

3 In light of what you know about Jim Crow and potential consequences for Johns and her family, what qualities of the Learner Profile would you ascribe to Barbara Johns?

Front page of New York Times 18 May 1954, banner headline announces the Brown decision. The other headlines illustrate the Cold War context of the period.

During the summer of 1953, an important change occurred at the US Supreme Court. Chief Justice Fred Vinson had died and President Dwight D Eisenhower had appointed the former three-term governor of California, Earl Warren, as the new Chief Justice. Although he had never been a judge, Warren had been both a prosecutor and a magistrate and, as historian Richard Kluger writes, had favoured *"a sweeping civil rights program, beginning with a fair employment practices act. ... I insist upon one law for all men"* (2011). Eisenhower did not voice the same support for civil rights, but Warren was a fellow Republican and a rival for party leadership. Over his career as Chief Justice, Warren became known as the leader of the most liberal or progressive Supreme Court in US history. Eisenhower later called his appointment of Earl Warren *"the biggest damned-fool mistake I ever made"*. Nonetheless, it was the change from Vinson to Warren that made the difference.

After reargument, the Supreme Court, which had been deadlocked months before, several justices' positions gradually changed as the case was discussed within the chambers, with Warren guiding discussions. In May 1954, the Supreme Court ruled unanimously that segregation by race in public schools was inherently unequal and that *"Any language in Plessy versus Ferguson contrary to this finding is rejected"*. The strategy originally proposed by Nathan Margold had finally been realized in law.

The ruling in Brown was a monumental decision that, while not specifically overturning all laws supported by Plessy, was understood to have greatly undermined any legal support for Jim Crow. Reactions to the ruling were mixed across geographical regions and races. The ruling shook up segregationist white Americans who saw their Jim Crow society being destroyed, while other white Americans reacted with caution or in support. Some African Americans celebrated the decision, but few with overt enthusiasm; many acknowledged Brown as an important step, with the highest court in the United States finally supporting their position.

However, fulfilling Brown was not an easy task. Soon after the opinion was read, many southern states began to organize resistance. Furthermore, the Supreme Court had avoided the issue of remedy in the ruling. Remedy, or what each school district was actually supposed to do in order to correct the "de jure" segregation, was of critical importance. The question was discussed in the following term and, in what became known as "Brown II", the Court stated that schools must be desegregated "with all deliberate speed".

Even before the words "with all deliberate speed" were uttered, it was possible to see the resistance that was to come in the desegregation plans submitted to the Supreme Court for the Brown II deliberations. One good example is Florida, which placed the burden of desegregation on each individual student, requiring them to make a formal request to the local school board. If they were turned down, then an appeal to various administrative offices and the state school board was required before a court would even consider a hearing. Additionally, the student was required to give the local school board unspecified but sufficient advance notice while submitting the original request. This excessively complicated system was designed so that no African American student would ever enter a white school. Several other states were equally creative.

Beyond the obvious state intransigence, the difficulty the Supreme Court had with crafting the order is well documented, and the question of determining a reasonable time frame for action involved factors such as community culture, facilities, enforcement mechanisms, local responsibility, and the reputation of the Supreme Court itself. Could one date be plausible for all districts, in all places, and for all populations, large and small, urban and rural? As Brown had established a constitutional right to attend a non-segregated school, was any time frame longer than "immediately" acceptable, when delay effectively continued the denial of a student's rights? The Eisenhower administration weighed in, requesting that no exact commencement or completion date be required. Furthermore, a date far in the future would encourage inaction by resistant communities and states. In effect, the decree required African American plaintiffs to bring compliance lawsuits to federal district courts, but the Supreme Court also provided guidance for those courts. The phrase "with all deliberate speed" was an attempt to provide both flexibility and firmness, but it became justification for resistance by school districts and states throughout the South.

Reactions to Brown

Brown was celebrated as a significant, if a partial, victory by most African Americans and some white Americans. Some school districts in southern states started to desegregate during the 1954–1955 school year, including Fayetteville, Arkansas, Baltimore, Maryland, Louisville, Kentucky and St Louis, Missouri. Nonetheless, the overwhelming majority of school districts throughout the South opposed the ruling and remained segregated. Political leaders soon organized resistance through various means. Of the 11 former Confederate states, all but one passed laws requiring, or at least allowing, segregated schools. The majority of these states also prohibited tax dollars from being spent on desegregated schools. In 1956, 96 southern legislators (19 US senators and 77 congressmen) signed the Southern Manifesto, pledging not to allow desegregated public schools. Virginia's programme of Massive Resistance exemplifies the dedication of most states to keeping white and African American children separate in public schools. With opposition ongoing, federal courts held more than 200 desegregation hearings over the next six years, often issuing court orders to desegregate. The integration of Central High School in Little Rock, Arkansas, in 1957, illustrates the process well, showing: the actions of local, state and federal government officials; public opposition; local support; and the actions of students, both those of the initial integrators and those of the white students at Central High School.

Virginia: From planned inaction to Massive Resistance

As the US Supreme Court deliberated Brown II, the governor of Virginia, Thomas B Stanley, appointed a commission of 32 state lawmakers, all white Americans, to craft a plan responding to Brown. The Gray Commission proposed a plan with a local option that technically allowed desegregation, but its goal was to inhibit any actual desegregation. The plan met with opposition for being too compliant with Brown. When Arlington County, a suburb just south of Washington, DC, announced a plan to desegregate its schools, the state legislature sprang to action, prohibiting elected school boards. In numerous newspaper editorials, James K Kilpatrick, editor of the Richmond News Leader, called for the state to **interpose** itself to nullify the Supreme Court's ruling.

Segregationist Democratic Senator Harry F Byrd's state-wide political machine acted with force. In February 1956, Byrd made a speech calling for Massive Resistance to federally mandated school desegregation. The Gray Plan was discarded in favour of proposed legislation created under the guidance of Governor Stanley, the Stanley Plan. In July, two separate federal judges ordered the desegregation of public schools in Charlottesville and Arlington County. African Americans sued more school districts throughout the state. In the midst of the federal court rulings, Governor Stanley declared that Virginia would not permit integrated public schools within the state.

On 29 September, after a contentious debate regarding methodology, tactics and constitutionality both within the Gray Commission and in a month-long special legislative session, a compromise plan was passed. The main features of the plan included the automatic closure of any school that integrated, not just those that chose to follow Brown but even schools forced to do so by federal court orders. Schools could be reopened if they remained exclusively for white students. The law mandated that state funding be cut off to any school district that allowed any school in its system to desegregate. To ensure no African Americans were placed in white schools, applications for pupil placement were removed from local authority and the power to approve or deny became the responsibility of the state. Appeals had to follow a lengthy path through the state court system before US district courts. Additionally, the legislature provided for a publicity campaign to support continued segregation by creating the Virginia Commission on Constitutional Government, with James J Kilpatrick hired as its

Interposition

The concept, widely discussed in the South in the pre-Civil War period, that states could place themselves between the federal government and the citizens of the state when state officials felt the federal government had exceeded its constitutional powers.

publications director. By early autumn, just two years following the original Brown decision, the Commonwealth of Virginia had decided to fight the federal government to maintain its segregated school system. The legislation and accompanying government actions are what became known as Massive Resistance.

A new governor, the Democratic supporter of Massive Resistance J Lindsay Almond, took office in January 1958. His support of continued resistance to Brown was tested in September 1958. Schools in three geographically divergent districts – Norfolk, Charlottesville and Warren County – were ordered by federal courts to integrate, but Governor Almond closed the schools, locking out 13,000 students. The Stanley Plan allowed for private school tuition grants, but these proved completely inadequate in the attempt to open white-only private schools for upwards of 10,000 students. A debate quickly developed between white Americans who favoured reopening the public schools and following the court orders and segregationist private school advocates. In early December, those white parents favouring public schools formed the Virginia Committee for Public Schools; this was the largest citizen-led organization involved with the integration crisis, illustrating that the white community was not of one mind on the subject. Further pressure came from 29 of Virginia's most important businessmen, who informed Governor Almond that they feared defying the court decree was damaging the state's economy. Almond held out, keeping the schools closed.

On 19 January 1959, a federal court and the Virginia Supreme Court agreed in separate cases that the state's action of closing public schools violated the US Constitution. After an initial impassioned speech, Almond proposed repealing elements of the Stanley Plan and, beginning with the new semester in February, and without incident, several African American students entered previously white-only schools in Norfolk and Arlington. The Almond administration directed that a new plan be created. The Perrow Plan relied on the idea of "freedom of choice", where parents could select a school in which to enrol their child, to pass – narrowly – legal muster; in this way, the plan kept most schools segregated by placing the burden of pupil placement on parents, who had to appeal to a Pupil Placement Board. It also repealed state compulsory attendance requirements, making it optional for any locality to fund public schools.

Despite strong support for continued Massive Resistance, the Perrow Plan passed both houses of the Virginia Legislature and became law. Most school districts, including those that the governor had closed, slowly began integrating schools. One district, Prince Edward County, held out, keeping its school doors shut until 1964. Yet even with the last resisting school finally allowing integration, by 1964 only 5% of African American students in Virginia attended school with white children. It was only after the US Supreme Court ruling of *Green v. New Kent County* that the farce of "freedom of choice" was abolished and significant inroads made towards public school desegregation in Virginia. Brown was a landmark decision, but Virginia was not unique in its attempts at interposition and the erection of legal and procedural obstacles designed to inhibit desegregation throughout much of the South. Long-term patterns of segregated schools also existed in urban areas in the North.

Little Rock, Arkansas, 1957

On 22 May 1954, soon after the *Brown* ruling, the Little Rock School Board stated that they would comply with the Supreme Court ruling. Within months, the Arkansas branch of the NAACP, led by its president, Daisy Bates, petitioned for immediate integration of the city schools; by May 1955, the school board had approved Superintendent Virgil Blossom's proposal, a gradualist plan that allowed the superintendent to choose the African American students who would be integrated into previously white-only schools. The purpose of this Blossom Plan, as it become known, was to comply with Brown on a minimal basis, with tokenism that would effectively limit enrolment of African Americans in white schools to a handful. The plan was to begin with the integration of elementary schools and move on to the integration of high schools several years later. However, as many white parents objected most vociferously to beginning with younger children, the plan was revised to begin a token integration of high schools in 1957 and to start elementary school desegregation in 1963.

The NAACP sued for immediate integration, but the federal court ruled that the Blossom Plan met Constitutional requirements and this decision was upheld by the US Eighth Circuit Court of Appeals. The district's gradualism was assisted by the segregated housing patterns of Little Rock. Of the three high schools, Horace Mann was located in the African American quarter of the city, the newest high school, Hall High School, was in the wealthier western white area, and the attendance area of Central High School was mostly white, although it did include 200 African Americans of high school age. Opposition to any integration grew as the Capital Citizens' Council (CCC) was formed to build support against integration. The CCC organized rallies and brought in guest speakers to promote white supremacy and demand segregation. The CCC also sponsored a second anti-integration organization, the Mother's League of Central High School (MLCHS), to provide a "feminine" slant to the effort. Only 20% of its membership were mothers of Central High School students.

Talk of racial mixing, the emotional and physical health of vulnerable white children, and miscegenation was employed to stir up resistance. Of the 75–80 applications, the school board had identified nine black students to attend for the 1957–58 school year. Segregationists, including the CCC and MLCHS, requested that Governor Orval Faubus prevent implementation of the first steps of integration at Central High, citing potential violence. The school district, also fearing violence, requested the state's help in making sure the plan was not impeded by disruptions. The governor requested assistance from the federal government to maintain order in advance of the school opening, but was refused on the grounds that public safety was primarily a local and state responsibility. Faubus's response was to declare that the federal government was mandating a policy but placing all responsibility for implementation on the states. Pulaski County, in which Little Rock is situated, issued an injunction to halt integration, but this was reversed one day later by Federal District Judge Ronald Davies.

The crisis had reached a peak of *federal v. state authority*. Governor Faubus took action and ordered the Arkansas National Guard to Central High School to prevent violence, not by ensuring the entry of African American students to the school, but instead by surrounding the school to prevent their entry. Governor Faubus chose interposition in the context of public order. Despite the Governor's actions and supported by Judge Davies's order, the nine African American students attempted to attend Central High School on 4 September 1957. They were met by an angry crowd of white Americans, including both students and adults, who saw the Arkansas National Guard prohibit their entry. A vivid scene was captured by news photographers as Elizabeth Eckford arrived separately by mistake and, after being turned away, was hounded off the campus by the yelling crowd.

With state and local officials refusing to obey the decision of the US Supreme Court and a federal judge mandating compliance, the confrontation which gradualists had hoped to avoid was national and international news. Furthermore, news of the crisis reached President Eisenhower, who had at best given tepid support to the original Brown decision, commented in 1954, *"I think it makes no difference whether or not I endorse it. The Constitution is as the Supreme Court interprets it, and I must conform to that and do my very best to see that is carried out in this country"*. Kluger writes that Eisenhower's declaration that he had to support Brown because it was his duty rather than because it was right gave *"aid and comfort to the forces of resistance"* (1975). Eisenhower, while not voicing personal support for racial equality, strongly believed in the supremacy of federal powers as expressed in the Constitution.

As tension mounted in Little Rock, there were discussions with the Eisenhower administration as attempts were made to reach an agreement. Negotiations included a visit by Governor Faubus to Eisenhower's vacation home in Newport, Rhode Island, on 14 September. On 20 September, Judge Davies ordered an immediate halt to Arkansas National Guard activities blocking the enrolment of African American students. Faubus removed the troops and, on the morning of 23 September, the nine African American students entered Central High School through a side door. An angry crowd of more than 1,000 white Americans gathered and soon the police removed the students from the school. Federal assistance was requested by Mayor Woodrow Mann via a telegram which read, *"The immediate need for federal troops is urgent. The mob is much larger… mob is armed and engaging in fisticuffs and other acts of violence. Situation is out of control"*.

Eisenhower acted. A governor had challenged the authority of the federal government, a move the President would not countenance. Despite appeals from the governor and other state and local officials, Eisenhower ordered 1,200 troops from the 101st Airborne Division to go immediately to Little Rock. Speaking from the White House on 24 September, over radio and television, Eisenhower told the American public, *"Whenever normal agencies prove inadequate to the task …to uphold the Federal Courts, the President's responsibility is inescapable"* (1957). Later in the same speech he added, *"Mob rule cannot be allowed to override the decisions of the courts"*. On 25 September, the Little Rock Nine were escorted into Central High School by US Army soldiers. The soldiers entered the school and the students were escorted from class to class. Eisenhower also federalized the Arkansas National Guard, removing the troops from the governor's control. On 1 October, the US Army troops were replace by the National Guard, who remained at Central High School for the remainder of the year.

▲ Arkansas Governor Orval E Faubus holds a photo of federal troops with drawn bayonets hustling white students from Central High School area during his radio-TV address to the nation. Faubus accused the Eisenhower administration of using "police state" methods in what he branded an "unwarranted" use of federal troops to force school integration in Little Rock.

▲ This 1957 photo shows the nine African American students leaving Central High School at the end of the school day escorted by federal troops

Eisenhower's actions were met with opposition and anger. Governor Faubus went on television, stating,

My fellow citizens, we are now an occupied territory. In the name of God, whom we all revere, in the name of liberty we hold so dear, in the name of decency, which we all cherish, what is happening in America?

(26 September 1957). The next day Senator Richard Russell sent a telegram to the White House:

I must vigorously protest the highhanded illegal methods employed by the armed forces of the United States under your command who are carrying out your orders to mix the races in the public schools.

On 3 October, in an action organized by the MLCHS, white students walked out of Central High School. The organization accused the federal troops of improper behaviour and opposition continued throughout the whole year.

The president's orders were all received warmly by numerous supporters of immigration, including by the parents of the Little Rock Nine, who sent the president a telegram on 30 September, telling him, "*We the parents of nine negro children enrolled at Little Rock Central High School want you to know that your action in safe guarding their rights have strengthened our faith in democracy*". Martin Luther King, Jr, who had sent a telegram to the White House on 9 September telling the President, "*If the federal government fail to take a strong positive stand at this time it will set the progress of integration back fifty years*", now sent another telegram stating, "*I wish to express my sincere support for the stand you have taken to restore law and order in Little Rock, Arkansas*".

The Little Rock Nine had to endure constant harassment inside the school walls. The youngest was 14-year-old Carlotta Walls, who enrolled as a sophomore, and the only senior was Ernest Green, who had just turned 16 when he first attended classes at Central High School. While the reception that the African American students received from the other students was generally cold, and accompanied by daily verbal and sometimes physical abuse by a group of about 50 of them, there were several white students who befriended the Nine. However, the few openly friendly white students were themselves threatened and some even physically attacked. The few kind faces disappeared. Unless an incident was witnessed by a teacher or administrator, no disciplinary action was taken. Teachers often ignored the Nine, and they were not permitted to participate in extra-curricular activities. Additionally, several former classmates of the Nine urged them to leave Central High School. Nonetheless, of the Nine, only one, Minnijean Brown, did not complete the school year. In December, she was suspended for spilling chilli on two white boys; and in February, after she was taunted and hit with a purse, she was expelled for calling the girl who had attacked her "white trash". Ernest Green graduated on 27 May 1958, with an inconspicuous Martin Luther King, Jr, in the audience.

The Lost Year

Arkansas authorities were not satisfied with token integration. After the school year ended, they acted quickly to stop it altogether. The Little

Rock School Board asked Federal District Judge Harry Lemley for an implementation delay until 1961, which he granted. Immediately, the NAACP directly petitioned the US Supreme Court for an emergency reversal. While the case was in court, the state legislature went into special session, passing numerous laws, including one that allowed the governor to close any school ordered to desegregate and another that granted tuition funding for displaced students. In *Cooper v. Aaron*, the US Supreme Court ruled that integration at Central High School had to proceed immediately and the Blossom Plan continue as scheduled. Governor Faubus closed all four high schools in Little Rock that same day, a move later approved by Little Rock voters, and the schools remained closed for the entire year.

Of approximately 3,000 white students who found themselves shut out of school, the great majority found placements at other schools, public and private, but only half of the 700 African American students were as lucky. This was partially because the NAACP felt that private schools for African American students would support the segregation that Brown was intended to eliminate. White proponents of public schools clashed with segregationists. Arkansas tried to intimidate the NAACP from challenging segregation by enacting laws such as Act 115, which banned NAACP members from employment by the state, and Act 10, which required all state employees to list political membership, thus exposing the NAACP members. Act 115 was voided by a federal district court in June 1959 and Act 10 was overturned by a 5–4 decision of the United States Supreme Court in *Shelton v Tucker*, 1960. The voters of Little Rock elected a less confrontational School Board which opened the schools early for the 1959–60 school year, beginning a period of federal court supervised integration.

Protests and action

Schools were not the only focus of the Civil Rights Movement in the 1950s and early 1960s. The desegregation of public facilities, especially public transport, was the target of spontaneous and planned actions, small and large. Similarly, voting rights, the key to political power, were also a focus of organized campaigns. Spurred on by the protests and campaigns, the US Congress and US presidents, in particular President Lyndon B Johnson, crafted legislation that put the federal government firmly on the side of equal access and voting rights, regardless of race or ethnicity. This section will detail the evolution of the protests, the results of the Montgomery Bus Boycott and the Freedom Rides that led to the Civil Rights Act of 1964, and Freedom Summer, which provided the impetus for the Voting Rights Act of 1965. These two laws will also be examined, along with the major protagonists and major groups involved in civil rights during this period.

The Montgomery Bus Boycott

The Montgomery Bus Boycott, which began in December 1955 and ended a year later, is often considered to be the starting point of the African American Civil Rights Movement. The boycott was the first community action that brought nationwide attention to the civil rights struggle, and was the first sustained, large-scale, community-wide protest by African Americans in a southern city. Perhaps as importantly, it triggered the emergence of the charismatic, 27-year-old civil rights leader, the Reverend Dr Martin Luther King, Jr, and catalyzed the creation of the Southern

Christian Leadership Conference (SCLC), the organization that would often lead significant protests and demonstrations over the next decades.

The boycott, while an inflection point, was not the beginning of the challenges to the Jim Crow transportation laws. Not only had Charles Hamilton Houston worked for action against lynching and segregated public schools, he had also challenged segregated transportation. In 1946, NAACP attorneys William Hastie and Thurgood Marshall argued that the Commerce Clause of Article I of the US Constitution made segregation of interstate bus travel unconstitutional and the US Supreme Court agreed, striking down a Virginia law in *Irene Morgan v. the Commonwealth of Virginia* (1946). In 1947, the Congress of Racial Equality (CORE) conducted "freedom rides" on interstate buses, which led to arrests, but garnered little notice. In June 1953, a bus boycott in Baton Rouge, Louisiana, resulted in partial integration of city buses. Later that year, in Montgomery, Alabama, a group of African American women formed the Women's Political Council (WPC), led by an English teacher from Alabama State College, Jo Ann Robinson. The group met with city officials to discuss the bus company's racial policies, but to no effect. There was no legal precedent to turn to, as *Irene Morgan v. the Commonwealth of Virginia* was only concerned with interstate travel, not intrastate or city transportation systems.

▲ Rosa Parks being fingerprinted by Deputy Sheriff DH Lackey, 1 December 1955

On 2 March 1955, Claudette Colvin, a 15-year-old African American girl was arrested for refusing to give up her seat to a white woman. Later that month, ED Nixon, former president of the Alabama NAACP, Jo Ann Robinson, NAACP Secretary Rosa Parks, voter registration activist Rufus A Lewis, and the recently appointed pastor of Dexter Avenue Church, Martin Luther King, Jr, met with city officials to discuss city bus seating policies. In April, Aurelia S Browder refused to give up her seat and she, too, was arrested. Another African American woman, Mary Louise Smith, was arrested in October, also for refusing to give up her seat. By the time Rosa Parks was arrested for the same crime on 1 December 1 1955, a series of civil disobedient acts by several African American women had occurred.

What was different about the Montgomery Bus Boycott were the actions of local activists. This boycott was a grassroots movement, not one organized or led from above. The main protagonist, Rosa Parks, had worked actively for civil rights for two decades. Beginning in 1932, Parks and her husband Raymond, a founder of the Montgomery NAACP chapter, secretly raised money and hosted meetings for the defence of the Scottsboro Boys. The Parks also promoted voter registration. In 1943, after her second failed attempt to register to vote, Parks encountered the bus driver who, 12 years later, would have her arrested. To ride a bus, African Americans had to pay the driver at the front of the bus, exit the bus and re-enter through the rear door. Parks refused to leave the bus after paying.

She was forced out of the bus, then the driver, James F Blake, drove off, leaving Parks behind. It was after this incident that she officially joined the NAACP and was elected the Montgomery chapter secretary, a dangerous job that required her to document violent acts and investigate murders, voter intimidation and rape.

It was the same driver who was driving the bus on 1 December 1955. Blake ordered Parks and three other African Americans to give up their seats and move to the back. The other three obeyed but Parks refused, was arrested and taken to jail. On 2 December, the WPC, led by Jo Ann Robinson, decided to organize a one-day bus boycott; over 50,000 leaflets were printed to publicize the event, and were distributed in less than 24 hours. ED Nixon set up a meeting with Montgomery's African American leaders, including the Reverends Ralph David Abernathy and Martin Luther King, Jr, to coordinate support. At this meeting, the leaders decided to make three demands: a pledge from city and bus company officials that African Americans would be treated with courtesy; a revision of the city code that would seat white Americans from front to back and African Americans from back to front, with no reserved areas; and the hiring of African American drivers for routes that carried all or mostly African American passengers. It was hoped by the leadership that the third demand would make the first two seem as mild as they were. The next day King told reporters, *"We are not asking for an end to segregation. That's a matter for the legislature and the courts… All we are seeking is justice and fair treatment in riding the buses"* (1955). The boycott was scheduled for Monday, 5 December, and the leaders hoped for a turnout of a little over half of all African American passengers.

The boycott was successful; almost no African Americans boarded city buses that Monday. There was no action from the city or bus company. Rosa Parks appeared in court, was found guilty of violating the law and was fined US$14. The following day, the Montgomery civil rights leaders, including Abernathy, Nixon, Lewis and King formed the Montgomery Improvement Association (MIA); King, a surprise choice at just 27 years old, was elected president. The MIA was created for the sole purpose of overseeing a longer boycott. That evening, a mass meeting of the MIA at Holt Street Baptist Church attracted thousands from Montgomery's African American community. Covered by press and television, the meeting opened with hymns and prayer, followed by a speech by King. This speech carried what became his trademark: building enthusiasm through parallelism, cadence and imagery. He connected the ideal of American democracy to the peaceful weapon of protest, and non-violence to Christianity. The speech was the beginning of King's national prominence as a civil rights leader.

▲ Reverend Martin Luther King, Jr, speaking at a meeting of the Montgomery Improvement Association (MIA), 1956

The boycott continued. Almost all African Americans and some white Americans chose to walk or got rides through an organized transportation operation, including car pools, that began on 13 December. Enough support money was raised to fund the purchase by the MIA of two new cars. On 16 December, an allegedly biracial committee formed by Montgomery Mayor WA Gayle met with the vice-president of the Chicago, Illinois, based bus company and representatives of the MIA, but no agreements were reached. Many of Montgomery's white citizens believed that no boycott involving Montgomery's 40,000 African Americans could be the result of voluntary cooperation: African Americans were surely being coerced by "goon squads". Motorcycle police were ordered to follow buses to ensure that those waiting to ride were free to do so, but there were no such "goon squads" to be found.

▲ The White Citizens Council maintained activities in Montgomery during the civil rights era. Here, KKK and White Citizens Council members join teenagers in protesting school desegregation in 1963.

The boycott continued into January 1956. On the night of 30 January, King's home was bombed while his wife, Coretta, and his young daughter were home. The explosive shattered windows and blasted a hole in the porch. ED Nixon's home was bombed two days later on 1 February. On the same day, a lawsuit, whose principal plaintiff was Aurelia S Browder – the woman arrested the previous April (*Aurelia S Browder, et al v. W A Gayle, et al*) for challenging the constitutionality of segregated buses (see page 152) – was filed in federal court. The boycott continued and, with the support of the White Citizens' Council, city officials tried to break it, even bringing conspiracy charges against 90 boycott leaders on 21 February. The trial and conviction of King brought national attention to the cause in March, including funds and strong support.

Montgomery's civic leaders were determined to maintain segregated buses. In late April Mayor Gayle stated that he would enforce segregation and arrest any drivers who defied Montgomery's segregation laws. A state judge ruled in favour of the mayor. With such resistance and defiance by city leaders months into the campaign, the daily focus of the MIA's leadership was on maintaining the boycott as the weeks and months wore on without results. On 5 June, the federal court in Montgomery ruled that Alabama's bus segregation laws violated the 14th Amendment. The defendants appealed while the boycott continued. On 13 November, city leaders obtained a court injunction that disabled the car pool system for the remainder of the boycott. The same day, the US Supreme Court affirmed the lower court ruling in *Aurelia S Browder, et al v. WA Gayle, et al*. On 14 November, MIA members voted to continue the boycott until city leaders agreed to implement the US Supreme Court order. Finally, on 20 December and a year after the boycott had begun, city leaders ended the policy of segregated buses.

Montgomery bus passengers, white American and African American, rode the newly desegregated buses in an atmosphere of some tension, but peacefully; most passengers filled the buses as they had before,

but now with some racial mixing in rows where buses were full. However, segregationists used deadly violence on numerous occasions to intimidate passengers and boycott leaders. On 24 December, five white men attacked a 15-year-old girl at a bus stop. Two gunshots hit the buses, the first one shattering a window and wounding a passenger in both legs. Four churches and two homes, including that of the Reverend Abernathy, were bombed on 10 January 1957. At the time of the bombing, Abernathy was at an organizing meeting in Atlanta, Georgia, but his wife and infant daughter were at home; they escaped uninjured.

While the buses did desegregate and passengers became used to the new norm, most historians, including Robert Weisbrot, assert that the Jim Crow system of apartheid persisted in the city, with buses being the sole exception. Nonetheless, it can be argued that the success of the Montgomery Bus Boycott transformed the attitude of southern African Americans from one of fear of white Americans, especially the Ku Klux Klan, to a growing defiance in the face of threats and brutality. However, the effect was greater than this. Montgomery showed that a united African American community could successfully challenge Jim Crow and it spawned movements in numerous other southern cities. It elevated Martin Luther King, Jr, to a national figure as well as promoting non-violent resistance as a means of achieving racial equality. Lastly, Montgomery served as a spark for the creation of the Southern Christian Leadership Conference (SCLC) – by King, Abernathy, Bayard Rustin, Ella Baker, Joseph Lowery, Fred Shuttlesworth and numerous black ministers – in Atlanta, Georgia, in January and New Orleans, Louisiana, in February 1957.

Source skills

The following documents concern events that occurred between 1955 and 1957 relating to the Montgomery Bus Boycott.

Source A
A WPC boycott leaflet printed on 2 December 1955.

This is for Monday, December 5, 1955

Another Negro woman has been arrested and thrown into jail because she refused to get up out of her seat on the bus for a white person to sit down.

It is the second time since the Claudette Colbert case that a Negro woman has been arrested for the same thing This has to be stopped.

Negroes have rights, too, for if Negroes did not ride the buses, they could not operate. Three-fourths of the riders are Negroes, yet we are arrested, or have to stand over empty seats. If we do not do something to stop these arrests, they will continue. The next time it may be you, or your daughter, or mother.

This woman's case will come up on Monday. We are, therefore, asking every Negro to stay off the buses Monday in protest of the arrest and trial. Don't ride the buses to work, to town, to school, or anywhere on Monday.

You can afford to stay out of school for one day if you have no other way to go except by bus.
You can also afford to stay out of town for one day. If you work, take a cab, or walk. But please, children and grown-ups, don't ride the bus at all on Monday. Please stay off of all buses ██████

Source B

Excerpts from Martin Luther King's speech on 5 December 1955 at the Holt Street Baptist Church in Montgomery, Alabama.

The rally to promote the start of a continued bus boycott drew an audience of several thousand.

You know my friends there comes a time when people get tired of being trampled over by the iron feet of oppression. There comes a time my friends when people get tired of being flung across the abyss of humiliation where they experience the bleakness of nagging despair ...

We are here this evening because we're tired now. Now, let us say that we are not here advocating violence. We have overcome that. I want it to be known throughout Montgomery and throughout this nation that we are a Christian people... We believe in the teachings of Jesus Christ. The only weapon that we have in our hands this evening is the weapon of protest. And secondly, this is the glory of America with all its faults. This is the glory of our democracy.

And we are not wrong, we are not wrong in what we are doing. If we are wrong, then the Supreme Court of this Nation is wrong. If we are wrong, the Constitution of the United States is wrong. If we are wrong, God Almighty is wrong. If we are wrong, Jesus of Nazareth was merely a Utopian dreamer and never came down to earth. If we are wrong, justice is a lie.

Source C

Excerpts from Montgomery City Code (1952), Chapter 6, Sections 10 and 11

Sec. 10. Separation of races—Required.

Every person operating a bus line in the city shall provide equal but separate accommodations for white people and negroes on his buses, by requiring the employees in charge thereof to assign passengers seats ... in such manner as to separate the white people from the negroes where there are both white and negroes on the same car.

Sec. 11. Same—Powers of persons in charge of vehicle; passengers to obey directions.

Any employee in charge of a bus operated in the city shall have the powers of a police officer of the city while in actual charge of any bus, for the purpose of carrying out the provisions of the preceding section, and it shall be unlawful for any passenger to refuse or fail to take a seat among those assigned to the race to which he belongs, at the request of any such employee in charge, if there is such a seat vacant.

IIT Chicago-Kent Library Blog, blogs.kentlaw.iit.edu/
library/exhibits/montgomery-1955/
images-documents/montgomery-city-code/

Source D:

Excerpts from *And the Walls Came Tumbling Down*, the autobiography of Ralph David Abernathy.

Abernathy discusses the bombing of his house and the First Baptist Church and recalling several telephone conversations with his wife, Juanita, in January 1957, in the aftermath of the Montgomery Bus Boycott

She had been asleep in our bedroom with Juandalynn close by, still in a baby bed. Suddenly she had been awakened by a loud explosion that almost deafened her. It had obviously been a bomb. The house was in splinters. ...

After several phone calls during the rest of the night, I eventually pieced together the whole story. Someone had planted a bomb on our front porch, right next to the bedroom. Obviously whoever it was had known precisely where we slept and had tried to place the explosive at precisely the point where it would do the most damage. ...

I found one detail of the story particularly chilling: her account of what had happened while we were talking on the telephone the second time. As she had been huddled in our bedroom, talking to me, the sky had suddenly flashed, and then she had heard a distant blast.

"What's that?" Juanita had asked, trembling with renewed terror.

A nearby policeman had looked down at his watch. Then looked back at her with a frozen face.

"That would be your First Baptist Church," he had said.

She had stared for a moment into the coldest eyes she had ever seen, and suddenly the full horror of the situation had dawned on her. The police had known all along. They were in on the plans.

First question, part a – 3 marks

What is the message of Source B?

First question, part b – 2 marks

What evidence does Source A provide for the causes of the Montgomery Bus Boycott?

Second question – 4 marks

With reference to its content, origin and purpose, what are the values and limitations of Source D for students researching the risks to leaders of the Montgomery Bus Boycott.

Third question – 6 marks

Compare and contrast Sources B and C regarding the causes of the Montgomery Bus Boycott.

Fourth question – 9 marks

Using the sources and your own knowledge, assess the impacts of the Montgomery Bus Boycott.

The Freedom Rides, 1961

The Freedom Rides of 1961 were a way of exerting pressure on governments at all levels – local, state and federal, but predominantly the federal government – to enforce the right of African Americans to use interstate transportation unencumbered by segregation and segregationists. Just a year before, the US Supreme Court had reinforced *Irene Morgan v. the Commonwealth of Virginia* (1946) with *Boyton v. Virginia* (1960). Consequently, both segregated interstate transportation and its associated facilities, such as terminals, waiting rooms, restaurants and restrooms, were prohibited by the US Constitution's Commerce Clause and the Interstate Commerce Act.

Civil rights leaders, such as CORE's director, James Farmer, had high expectations of newly-inaugurated President John F Kennedy and his administration. After tepid endorsement and enforcement of civil rights laws and rulings by the previous administration, it was hoped that Kennedy would focus on civil rights. Testing the commitment of the new president, two mixed groups of African American and white passengers would travel from Washington, DC, to New Orleans, Louisiana, via the Deep South, passing through Virginia, North Carolina, South Carolina, Georgia, Alabama and Mississippi. One group of men and women would ride a Greyhound bus, the other would travel on Trailways. Lack of compliance and overt defiance by cities and states would compel Kennedy to act. As Farmer explained, "*We put on pressure and create a crisis (for federal leaders) and then they react*". The Freedom Riders expected threats, multiple arrests. and possibly severe violence.
It was a journey that would test Farmer's Gandhian beliefs.

Prior to departure, the Freedom Riders received promises of support from the SCLC and the NAACP for housing and food. The concept of the rides was not universally appreciated by the civil rights community. NAACP Mississippi Field Secretary Medgar Evers, a man of great courage who had been a combat soldier in a segregated US army in Europe during the Second World War and who was a veteran of civil rights activism in the rural Deep South, thought that the rides would reverse the progress the NAACP had made in Mississippi. Conversely, Roy Wilkins of the NAACP urged that the organization support the rides. Direct confrontation was a risk to those involved and possibly to the communities along the way,

▲ Freedom Riders John Lewis and James Peck after being beaten during the 1961 Freedom Rides. Lewis, who endured several attacks, later became a United States Congressman.

but it was Wilkins's view, and that of the Freedom Riders themselves, that the cautious ways of the 1950s had not garnered nationwide support, especially from the political leaders of the country.

One reason for this lack of support was the Cold War. The post-war period had brought thermonuclear weapons, confrontations and crisis between US allies on the one hand and the Soviet Union and its sphere in Berlin, Korea, Egypt and Hungary on the other, and the withdrawal of the French in Vietnam. Sputnik had catalyzed the space race and school children were taught to "duck and cover" on the order of their teachers or upon seeing a flash. It was a time of great fear and overreaction in the United States, exemplified by McCarthyism. Additionally, the emerging middle class, mostly white Americans, wanted to live the suburban dream, and most did not want to see the racial and economic disparities that existed throughout the country. Singer-songwriter Bob Dylan asked, *"How many times can a man turn his head pretending he just doesn't see"* (1962), using a melody adapted from a Negro spiritual. The Freedom Riders wanted to force America to answer that question.

A biracial contingent of thirteen Freedom Riders, six white and seven African American, began their trip on 4 May 1961, just two weeks after the failed Bay of Pigs effort to overthrow Fidel Castro, and as President Kennedy was preparing for his first meeting with Soviet leader Nikita Khrushchev. The Riders encountered few problems in Virginia and North Carolina, but three of them, two white and one African American, were beaten in Rock Hill, South Carolina. The Riders continued into Atlanta, Georgia, where they met with Martin Luther King on the evening of 13 May; King declined an invitation to join the Riders, warning them that he had been told that the Ku Klux Klan was planning violent action. When the buses entered Alabama, the situation changed. The leader, James Farmer, reluctantly left to attend his father's funeral. Then, on 14 May, the 11th day of the Freedom Rides, came incidents that turned the Rides into a national news story. As the first bus, the Greyhound, pulled up to the bus terminal in Anniston, Alabama, 30–50 men armed with sticks and metal bars surrounded the bus. Police stayed away from the terminal by order of Anniston officials. Rocks were thrown through bus windows and two tyres were slit. A driver steered the damaged bus away from the terminal, taking the road to Birmingham. Forty cars followed.

When the bus tyres went flat, the driver stopped on the side of the highway, in front of a roadside general store. The driver inspected the tyres and walked away from the bus, leaving the passengers to fend for themselves. A mob emerged from the 40 cars that had followed, then surrounded and tried to storm the bus. A white male passenger with a gun kept them at bay for several minutes. The man was not an

▲ The Freedom Rider's bus, destroyed by a mob in Alabama, 1961

ordinary passenger, but rather an undercover member of the Alabama Highway Patrol, there by order of Governor John Patterson, an outspoken segregationist. Patterson did not want the negative publicity of lynchings or beatings of Freedom Riders, but he also wanted white Alabamans to think he was supporting them. An incendiary bomb was thrown into the bus through a smashed rear window, causing a fire and filling the bus with smoke. The passengers streamed out, coughing and shielding their eyes. As they left the bus, they were attacked and beaten until a gunshot rang out.

The patrolman, Eli Cowling, warned that he would kill the next person who attacked anyone. As the violence ended, the store owner's 12-year-old daughter, Janie Forsyth, who had witnessed the attack, came out with water and towels, wiping the faces of victims. Other white witnesses invited the Riders inside.

TOK connections

Janie Forsyth Kinney describes the scene of the Greyhound bus attack on 14 May 1961.

The people on the bus were gagging, she recalled. While some of the passengers lay down on the bus floor in search of air to breathe, others, including an elderly black woman, panicked. Meanwhile, the crowd yelled out epithets, McKinney recalled. "They were saying things like, 'Roast those n*****s alive.'" There were reports of people outside the bus holding the bus doors shut to prevent anyone from escaping. Then, something in the bus exploded, forcing the mob back and giving the passengers a chance to break out of the burning vehicle.

The door burst open, and there were people just spilling out of there. They were so sick by then they were crawling and puking and rasping for water. They could hardly talk.

Lee, C. UCLA Today, 10 May, 2011. UCLA Newsroom. newsroom.ucla.edu/stories/civil-rights-activists-still-remember-203453

TOK guiding question

Create three TOK questions based on McKinney's description of the attack. In these questions, address the roles of memory, reason and emotion in the attack itself, and of McKinney's recollection.

The Trailways bus was attacked in Anniston as well, but was relatively undamaged and, unaware of the fate of the burned Greyhound and its passengers, drove on to Birmingham, Alabama. At the Trailways bus terminal in Birmingham, a KKK mob of 30 men armed with baseball bats, chains and pipes first attacked reporters and news photographers, smashing cameras, before beating the Freedom Riders and several bystanders. After the 15 minutes, the mob melted away as the police arrived. Casualties included James Peck, who needed 53 stiches for his wounds. The Riders took refuge in the parsonage of Reverend Fred Shuttlesworth who, through force of will, fended off attempts by Sheriff Bull Connor and the police to arrest the group for violating segregation laws. After surgery, Peck gave interviews from his hospital bed, insisting that he would be back on the bus the next day heading to Montgomery. Photographs of the beaten Riders and stories of the Klan's mob attack were featured in major newspapers. Newsman Howard K Smith witnessed the event, interviewed several victims and attempted to get the story on that evening's news, but was thwarted by the local station director.

Before the Rides began, the FBI and the Attorney General Robert Kennedy were aware of potential violence. The FBI also knew that

Sheriff Connor had given the KKK 15 minutes, but did nothing other than alert the Attorney General to a vague possiblity of potential violence. Kennedy notified the local police, ignorant of the complicity of local law enforcement. Following the attacks, the White House administration was unhappy with the Freedom Riders, the KKK, Governor Patterson and the local police. Publicly, the president called for calm, but did not place blame on anyone. Privately, he voiced his opinion that the Freedom Riders should stop. James Farmer had hoped the administration would be forced to defend the civil rights activists and allow them to continue with their federally protected interstate trip, but the administration would not act.

The Freedom Riders wanted to continue, but drivers from Greyhound and Trailways refused to pilot buses with the Freedom Riders on board, so the group was stranded at the Birmingham bus terminal. With the assistance of John Seigenthaler, aide to the Attorney General and sent to negotiate with local officials for the safety of the Freedom Riders, the group was taken to the airport. From here, after a bomb scare and having racial abuse yelled at them by Alabama state police, the Riders were flown to New Orleans, ending the first of the Freedom Rides.

The Freedom Rides did not end, although CORE no longer directed them. Student Non-violent Coordinating Committee (SNCC) leaders John Lewis and Diane Nash immediately organized a second trip of 10 riders, many of them fellow students from Fisk College in Nashville, Tennessee. Members of SNCC thought that the North-based CORE had not understood the fervour with which southern segregationists would fight for their way of life. The new Freedom Riders were aware of the danger and, before leaving, wrote their last wills and testaments. President Kennedy was furious and Seigenthaler was ordered to contact Diane Nash and persuade her to stop the new Freedom Ride. In response to Seigenthaler's demand that the Ride be stopped, Nash informed him that it would continue despite the president's wishes. Moreover, the administration did order Greyhound to supply a bus and driver or be in violation of federal law, so the Freedom Ride from Nashville south to Montgomery, Alabama, went on.

Upon disembarking at the Greyhound station in Montgomery, the Freedom Riders and Seigenthaler were beaten. That night, there was a rally led by Martin Luther King, Jr, Fred Shuttlesworth, John Lewis and Ralph Abernathy, held at theAbernathy's church. A crowd of 1,500 African Americans and several Freedom Riders attended. A mob surrounded the church, yelling and tossing rocks, followed by tear gas, through a window. Attorney General Robert Kennedy hastily called in 500 unarmed deputized federal marshals, who barely kept the mob at bay. Inside the church, Abernathy and King spoke to the frightened crowd. King telephoned the Attorney General, informing him of the situation and of the increasing risk of violence and death. President Kennedy then called Governor Patterson, who refused to come to the phone. Finally, an assistant of Patterson's told him that unless the governor declared martial law the mob would soon explode in violence. Patterson relented and approved calling in the Alabama National Guard to establish order.

President Kennedy called for a "cooling off period", but the Riders refused. They finally had the attention of the White House and the press, both national and international. The administration forced Governor Patterson to agree to protect the Freedom Riders until the bus entered Mississippi. The following day, the Freedom Riders were set to continue into Mississippi and invited King to join them. The most nationally recognized face of the movement declined for a second time, citing a need not to violate probation, but several Riders pointed out that they, too, were on probation. As a result, King lost a significant amount of respect in the eyes of SNCC members, some Riders believing he was afraid. Many began to refer to him disrespectfully as "De Lawd".

The Kennedy administration, fearing more violence when the bus entered Mississippi, made a deal with Mississippi Senator James Eastland: in exchange for a guarantee of protection from physical violence, the state could arrest the Riders for disturbing the peace and similar violations. Consequently, the Riders were arrested, spending time in the notorious Parchman Prison. As people around the country became aware of their fate, several hundred untrained and unsolicited Freedom Riders from across the United States travelled to Jackson, Mississippi, by plane, train and bus, eventually crowding the prison with over 300 Riders. The Kennedy administration pressed the Interstate Commerce Commission (ICC) for a ruling. On September 22, the ICC issued a ban on segregation on interstate travel. Just as in 1956, when the bus boycott had continued until Montgomery city buses allowed integrated seating, the Freedom Rides continued until 1 November, when the ICC ruling took effect. Many facilities were desegregated with little publicity in the succeeding months, the Kennedy administration threatening legal action to localities that disobeyed the order. CORE reported that, by the end of 1962, segregation of interstate travel had ended.

The Freedom Rides achieved the specific goal of integrating interstate travel. They did not, however, achieve James Farmer's overall objective of obtaining overt, active and continued support for civil rights from the federal government. Support from the Kennedy administration was grudging, limited and slow. Furthermore, the Freedom Rides accelerated a split within the civil rights movement itself: active confrontation and decentralized grassroots activism as exemplified by SNCC on the one hand, and the centralized, established leadership of the NAACP and the SCLC on the other. The SCLC, formed just five years earlier in the wake of the Montgomery Bus Boycott, its leaders and their families targets of bombings and other violence, was seen by many members of SNCC as too cautious to achieve significant change.

ATL Social, communication and self-management skills

While the Freedom Riders were under assault on buses and jailed in the notorious Parchman Prison, they found ways to remain calm, organized and to communicate a feeling of togetherness with fellow activists. Managing one's emotions and behaviour under tremendous pressure is key to success. One way civil rights activists did this is through singing. Bernice Johnson Reagon writes,

> *What is interesting about the songs that end up as freedom songs is the fact that they function in the Movement as "congregational" songs. Congregational songs are started by a songleader – a songleader is different from a soloist. A soloist is someone who can execute the entire song. A songleader is someone who starts the song, and if that performance is successful, it is successful not only because of the prowess of the leader but because people who are located within the sound of that voice join in to raise the song into life.*

www.pbs.org/wgbh/amex/eyesontheprize/
reflect/r03_music.html

On the buses, Freedom Riders sang "Hallelujah! I'm A-Travelin'", making up additional lyrics, such as the following, as they rode from Nashville into Jackson:

> *I'm taking a ride on the Greyhound bus line,*
> *I'm riding the front seat to Jackson this time,*
> *Hallelujah, I'm a-travelin',*
> *Hallelujah, ain't it fine,*
> *Hallelujah, I'm a-travelin'*
> *Down Freedom's main line.*

www.pbs.org/wgbh/amex/eyesontheprize/story/
05_riders.html

While in Parchman Prison, they sang in response to mistreatment, upsetting the guards who threatened further mistreatment, including the confiscation of their mattresses. The Riders responded by singing:

> *You can take our mattress, oh yes!*
> *You can take our mattress, oh yes!*
> *You can take our mattress,*
> *You can take our mattress*
> *You can take our mattress, oh yes!*

Questions

Reflect on how the Freedom Riders functioned under stress and kept each other motivated. What methods do you have to:

1 manage your emotions and make positive decisions that help you reach your goals?

2 motivate others to achieve their own or group goals?

Class discussion

In what ways and to what extent were freedom songs important to the Freedom Riders achievements?

Full document skills: School desegregation and Little Rock, Arkansas

Source A

Richard Kluger, a journalist and social historian, writing in his comprehensive work, *Simple Justice: The History of Brown v. Board of Education and Black America's Struggle for Equality* **(1975)**

Not everyone agreed, of course. The white-supremacists of the South were swift and shrill in their outcry. Governor Herman Talmadge of Georgia asserted that the Court's decision had reduced the Constitution to "a mere scrap of paper." The Justices "had blatantly ignored all law and precedent and usurped from the Congress and the people the power to amend the Constitution, and from the Congress the authority to make the laws of the land." Senator Byrd of Virginia called the decision "the most serious blow that has yet been struck against the rights of the states in a matter vitally affecting their authority and welfare." Governor Umstead of North Carolina was "terribly disappointed." Governor Byrnes of South Carolina was "shocked." Senator Eastland of Mississippi was defiant: the South, he said, "will not abide by or obey this legislative decision by a political court." Any effort to integrate Southern schools would lead to "great strife and turmoil."

Source B

United States President Dwight D. Eisenhower addressed the American people on the radio and television during the Little Rock Central High School desegregation crisis on 24 September, 1957.

As you know, the Supreme Court of the United States has decided that separate public educational facilities for the races are inherently unequal and therefore compulsory school segregation laws are unconstitutional. Our personal opinions about the decision have no bearing on the matter of enforcement; the responsibility and authority of the Supreme Court to interpret the Constitution are very clear. Local Federal Courts were instructed by the Supreme Court to issue such orders and decrees as might be necessary to achieve admission to public schools without regard to race-and with all deliberate speed. During the past several years, many communities in our Southern States have instituted public school plans for gradual progress in the enrollment and attendance of school children of all races in order to bring themselves into compliance with the law of the land. They thus demonstrated to the world that we are a nation in which laws, not men, are supreme. I regret to say that this truth-the cornerstone of our liberties-was not observed in this instance. It was my hope that this localized situation would be brought under control by city and State authorities. If the use of local police powers had been sufficient, our traditional method of leaving the problems in those hands would have been pursued. But when large gatherings of obstructionists made it impossible for the decrees of the Court to be carried out, both the law and the national interest demanded that the President take action.

Source C

Elizabeth Eckford, one of the Little Rock Nine, describes the day she attempted to enter Central High School as told by Daisy Bates in her work, *The Long Shadow of Little Rock* **(1962).**

… I turned around and the crowd came toward me.

They moved closer and closer. Somebody started yelling "Lynch her! Lynch her!"

I tried to see a friendly face somewhere in the mob – someone who maybe would help. I looked into the face of an old woman and it seemed a kind face, but when I looked at her again, she spat on me.

The came closer, shouting, "No nigger bitch is going to get in our school. Get out of here!"

I turned back to the guards but their facers told me I wouldn't bet any help from them. Then I looked down the block and saw a bench at the bus stop. I thought, "If I can only get there I will be safe." I don't know why the bench seemed a safe place to me, but I started walking toward it…

When I finally to there, I don't think I could have gone another step. I sat down and the mob crowded up and began shouting all over again. Someone hollered, "Drag her over to this tree! Let's take care of that nigger." Just then a white man sat down beside me, put his arm around me and patted my shoulder. He raised my chin and said, "Don't let them see you cry."

Source D

Elizabeth Eckford ignores the hostile screams and stares of fellow students on her first day of school. She was one of the nine negro students whose integration into Little Rock's Central High School was ordered by a Federal Court following legal action by NAACP. 6 September, 1957.

First question, part a – 3 marks

According to Source B, what were the reasons why Eisenhower decided to intervene in Little Rock?

First question, part b – 2 marks

What message is conveyed by Source D?

Second question – 4 marks

With reference to its origin, purpose and content, analyze the value and limitations of Source C for a historian studying school desegregation in the South.

Third question – 6 marks

Compare and contrast the views Sources A and B convey on efforts to desegregate schools following the *Brown Decision*.

Fourth question – 9 marks

Using the sources and your own knowledge, assess the opposition to federally mandated school desegregation and the federal response in the first years after *Brown*.

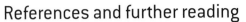

References and further reading

Jerrold M. Packard, *American Nightmare: The History of Jim Crow*, New York, St. Martin's Press, 2002.

For a study on Black Women in the Jim Crow South and during the Civil Rights Movement see:

Danielle L. McGuire, *At the Dark End of the Street: Black Women, Rape, and Resistance – A New History of the Civil Rights Movement from Rosa Parks to the Rise of Black Power*, New York: Alfred A. Knopf, 2010.

For a first-hand account of the Montgomery Bus Boycott see:

Jo Ann Gibson Robinson, *Montgomery Buss Boycott and the Women Who Started it: The Memoir of Jo Ann Gibson Robinson*, Knoxville: University of Tennessee Press, 1987.

For a history of the campaign to reverse school segregation see:

Richard Kluger, *Simple Justice: The History of Brown v. Board of Education and Black America's Struggle for Equality*, New York: Vintage Books, 1975, 2004.

For a history of the Civil Rights Movement focused on the years of these chapters see:

Robert Weisbrot, *Freedom Bound: A History of America's Civil Rights Movement*, New York: Penguin Books (PLUME), 1990, 1991.

Taylor Branch, *Parting the Waters, America in the King Years 1954–1963*, New York: Simon & Schuster, 1988

For a biography of Martin Luther King, Jr. and the SCLC see:

David Garrow, *Bearing the Cross: Martin Luther King, Jr., and the Southern Christian Leadership Conference*, New York: William Morrow, 2004.

For information on the Freedom Rides see:

Richard Arsenault, *Freedom Riders: 1961 and the Struggle for Racial Justice*, Oxford: Oxford University Press, 2011. (Abridged Edition)

For a collection of documents from the civil rights movement see:

Clayborne Carson et al. editors, *The Eyes on the Prize Civil Rights Reader: Documents, Speeches, and Firsthand Accounts from the Black Freedom Struggle, 1954–1990*, New York: Penguin Books, 1991.

▲ CORE Member Dave Dennis

Conceptual understanding

Key Concept

→ Consequence

→ Continuity

→ Change

→ Perspective

Key questions

→ How did African Americans and their allies challenge and overcome discriminatory practices?

Freedom Summer in Mississippi, promoting voter registration; volunteers Chaney, Goodman and Schwerner are murdered

Malcolm X forms the Organization of Afro-American Unity; "The Ballot or the Bullet" speech garners national attention

The Mississippi Freedom Democratic Party (MFDP) attempts to be seated at the Democratic National Convention in place of the state's all-white Democratic Party

The Civil Rights Act of 1964 is passed and signed into law by President Lyndon B Johnson

The 24th Amendment to the US Constitution, prohibiting poll taxes, is ratified

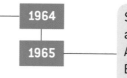

1964

1965

State troopers attack civil rights marchers at the Edmund Pettus Bridge in Selma, Alabama, in what becomes known as Bloody Sunday

The Voting Rights Act of 1965 is signed

After the eventful year of 1963 – with Project C's protests and marches in Birmingham, Alabama, in April and May, President Kennedy's Civil Rights Address on 11 June, the March on Washington on 28 August, Kennedy's proposed civil rights bill, and the assassination of the president on 22 November – civil rights organizations and leaders wanted to expand activities into the Deep South to create even greater pressure on the federal government and the new Johnson administration. This time, their target would be political power, specifically voting rights and political representation. This campaign in Mississippi in 1964 became known as Freedom Summer.

Source skills

An excerpt from President John F. Kennedy's Address on Civil Rights, 11 June 1963.

The heart of the question is whether all Americans are to be afforded equal rights and equal opportunities, whether we are going to treat our fellow Americans as we want to be treated. If an American, because his skin is dark, cannot eat lunch in a restaurant open to the public, if he cannot send his children to the best public school available, if he cannot vote for the public officials who represent him, if, in short, he cannot enjoy the full and free life which all of us want, then who among us would be content to have the color of his skin changed and stand in his place? Who among us would then be content with the counsels of patience and delay?

First question, part a – 3 marks

According to Source B, why should action be taken immediately to resolve unequal treatment by race?

Examiner's hint: Kennedy sites specific inequities as the reason to act on inequities.

- Segregated lunch counters
- Poor public school options for African Americans
- Inability to vote in elections.
- Kennedy also cites a general concept of an inability to live a "full and free live" due specifically to skin colour.

Mississippi was a state known for its racial violence, including an active KKK, whose members included government officials, businessmen, and police, as well as employees at Parchman Prison. Mississippi was also the state where the "respectable" white supremacist Citizens' Councils had originated, with the city of Jackson home to the organization's monthly newspaper. Despite the violence and the multiple means by which white Mississippians maintained Jim Crow, SNCC member Robert (Bob) Moses, a former high school mathematics teacher with a master's degree in philosophy from Harvard, came to the state in 1961 to encourage voter registration. The constant violence and economic intimidation, which included job losses and home evictions, greatly curtailed the success of the SNCC's work. When Moses was beaten in 1961, his assailants were acquitted by an all-white jury. The same year, voting rights activist Herbert Lee was murdered in front of several witnesses by state legislator EH Hurst, who was never brought to trial. To overcome the intimidation and violence, and to promote voter registration, a more coordinated effort was needed.

The Council of Federated Organizations (COFO) was formed to coordinate the NAACP, the SCLC, CORE, the SNCC and the National Urban League (NUL), to administer and carry out the newly funded Voter Education Project (VEP). The funds came with help from Attorney General Robert Kennedy, but the federal government offered no protection. Despite constant harassment, the effort was modestly successful in several southern cities, where approximately 500,000 African Americans were registered to vote by 1964. Mississippi was not part of this success, however, due to obstacles that included literacy tests, and violence and intimidation by segregationist groups such as the KKK and the police. In 1963, Moses and a fellow activist were in a car when they were fired at numerous times. Moses's colleague, who was driving, was wounded. Other civil rights workers were arrested and sometimes beaten, sometimes by police. Due to the character of Mississippi's opposition, only 1% of 400,000 potential African American voters were registered. In 1964, rejecting the finality of Mississippi's opposition to racial equality, COFO leaders decided to flood Mississippi with volunteers in order to change the status quo. The campaign was called Freedom Summer.

Freedom Summer was to combine voter education, registration and political activism, as well as running Freedom Schools to teach literacy and civics to both adults and children. It was to be a fully integrated project, bringing in middle and upper class white student volunteers from across the nation, adding to voter education work done in the same area by a small group of college student volunteers in 1963. A number of African American activists preferred an all African American campaign, reasoning that well-educated and mostly wealthy white Americans working with African Americans might further enrage segregationists, and also that the students would usurp leadership positions.

In 1986, Moses explained:

> [a] *concern which existed within the Mississippi staff which was predominantly people who grew up and lived in Mississippi, were from Mississippi, had spent their lives in, under the Mississippi condition which was strict segregation and really living in this closed society. So they had very little working contact with white people, and they weren't anxious to introduce them into the project which they viewed as, and rightly so, as their project, their effort, something which they had created out of nothing really and at great risk to themselves.*

Moses acknowledged their concerns, but firmly rejected their objections in favour of the "**Beloved community**" ideal.

Beyond the notion of the Beloved Community, however, was a reason that could only be shared privately among the COFO leadership: only if middle and upper class white Americans were threatened or became victims of violence would the federal government provide the protection that the White House claimed it was powerless to give. The pressure coming from well-connected parents on their local congressmen and senators was a means of penetrating the white power structure. The press would give more coverage to the deaths of white Americans than to those of African Americans. The nationwide reaction to photos of beaten and bloodied white Freedom Riders James Peck and James Zwerg in 1961 supported this supposition. Another leader of Freedom Summer, Dave Dennis, explained that the "*death of a white college student would bring on more attention*", while also acknowledging the "cold" calculation of inviting those students to Mississippi. Thousands of applications arrived and, ultimately, 900 mostly white applicants were accepted. The volunteers were usually idealistic, but often realistic as to the dangers. They were told to provide US$500 for bail money in case of arrest. The training emphasized the likelihood of violence and gave volunteers the opportunity to drop out, leaving a force ready to go into African American communities for their summer vacation.

Beloved community

A term popularized by Martin Luther King, Jr. that comes from love and a commitment to nonviolence. The Beloved Community would not tolerate any form of discrimination, poverty, hunger or homelessness. Disputes, whether local or international would be resolved through the process of conflict resolution with the dual goals of peace and justice.

TOK connections

The recruitment and use of volunteers in the hope that some would get hurt or killed in order to further the goals of the Civil Rights Movement can prompt a number of questions about ethics.

Review these three approaches to ethics: Utilitarianism, Consequentialism and Universalism. Keep each approach in mind while reading the following excerpt from an interview with Dave Dennis, a leader of Freedom Summer, in 1985.

Interview with Dave Dennis. Blackside, Inc. November 1985.

> Number one is that with whites coming in, it would, uh, bring on a stiffer type of retaliation on the part of the state, which would mean is, is that that would bring in much more publicity, and at the same time that would, would bring about the main attempt, and that was to emphasize the inequities of the problems that existed in terms of blacks becoming part of the political structure. Uh, we also knew that if a black was killed that there would not be the type of attention uh, on the state as would be if a white was killed,

or if a white was injured badly, uh, it would bring on more attention than if it's a black was injured. You see there had been blacks killed and blacks beaten in Mississippi for years and although there would be some small uh, little publicity on it the government never did really act in any type of affirmative manner in order to try to stop that type of violence against black people, and we felt that they would if in terms if that existed towards whites.

TOK guiding questions

1 Apply each the three approaches to ethics – Utilitarianism, Consequentialism and Universalism – to the reasoning of Dave Dennis. What do you think his ethical approach was?

2 By yourself, in a group or in a class discussion, apply Universalism, Utilitarianism, and Consequentialism to the decision to use volunteers in this way. What is the result of each application? Why?

3 What is the value of asking ethical questions about the methods used to achieve ethical goals?

The first major setback to Freedom Summer occurred during the training period, when three civil rights workers were reported missing in Neshoba County, Mississippi. James Chaney, a black Mississippian from Meridian, and white-Jewish New Yorkers Mickey Schwerner, a veteran CORE activist, and Andrew Goodman had come to Oxford, Mississippi, to find housing for the summer volunteers and to recruit churches in which to hold Freedom Schools. Schwerner had worked in Mississippi for a year and had recruited Chaney. Despite the news, the volunteers headed south under the uncertainty of the missing activists. As we will see, Chaney, Schwerner and Goodman would be found murdered.

The project went forward. A total of 41 Freedom Schools were established, many in churches and under the threat of arson, and more than 3,000 African American youths attended. The curriculum included reading, mathematics, African American history and also leadership skills, so that the civil rights activism could continue once the volunteers had returned home. Voter registration efforts continued, too. Potential voters were tutored in how to interpret the Mississippi Constitution, as an applicant could be asked to interpret any section of the document to the satisfaction of the registrar. Thousands came to classes and 17,000 applied for the right to vote, but obstacles to registration were such that only 1,600 were accepted. Freedom Summer leaders had anticipated the resistance of white Mississippians and had worked with local African American Mississippians to promote an alternative political party. The Mississippi Freedom Democratic Party (MFDP) had been formed in April to challenge the all-white Mississippi Democratic Party.

The state of Mississippi did not accept the "invasion" passively. Before the Freedom Summer project was underway, even the announcement of the plans had spurred anger. John R Rachal writes how state and local politicians, including Senator James Eastland and Governor Paul Johnson, along with many leading newspapers, used terms such as "carpetbaggers", "intruders", "communists", "integrationists" and "racial zealots" (1999) to describe the mostly white college students who were coming to Mississippi for the summer. Rachal describes how, when running for governor the year before, Johnson had said the NAACP stood for "niggers, alligators, apes, coons and possums". and how the murders of Chaney, Schwerner, and Goodman was called a "Communist hoax" by the KKK (1999). Rachal goes on to point out that the Mississippi KKK also warned in its publication *The Klan Ledger*,

> We have taken no action as yet against the enemies of our State, our Nation, and our Civilization, but we are not going to sit back and permit our rights, and the rights of our posterity to be negotiated away by a group composed of "Jewish" priests, bluegum black savages and mongrelized money-worshippers.

Many local newspapers echoed the same thoughts in editorials. The link of communism to civil rights was not a new one. In fact, some socialists had long been involved with the Civil Rights Movement, and some members of civil rights organizations had previously been members of socialist or communist organizations. The USSR had used films of the violence in Birmingham, Alabama, to criticize the United States. However, the SNCC, the SCLC, the NAACP and other participating groups were not communist-affiliated; in fact, the quest to vote and for full economic participation was a fight to enjoy the benefits of the democratic capitalist system.

Name calling was the least of the threats, as shown by the murders of Chaney, Schwerner and Goodman. Arrests of civil rights workers were common and were often on dubious charges, such as reckless driving or running a stop sign, when the driver concerned was driving below the speed limit and had come to complete stops. With drivers even arrested for car theft when driving their own vehicles, obeying the law was not an effective defence. Beyond the arrests and the time in prison, there was violence. The SNCC recorded "*35 shooting incidents, with three persons injured; 30 homes and other buildings bombed; 35 churches burned; 80 persons beaten; at least six persons murdered*".

During the summer, the bodies of the Chaney, Schwerner and Goodman were discovered underneath an earthen dam by a search team headed by the FBI. Later investigations would prove that the KKK, working with local law enforcement and using information provided by the State Sovereignty Commission, had committed the murders. Despite the evidence, the state of Mississippi did not bring any charges; even when two men, Horace Barnette and James Jordan, later admitted killing the three activists, no charges were brought. (Later, federal prosecutors did charge 18 suspects with civil rights violations. Seven of these, including KKK Grand Wizard Sam Bowers, were convicted and served sentences from three to ten years.) But as persistent as the threats, harassment and violence were, the overwhelming majority of Freedom Summer volunteers survived and worked but left to go back to college at the end of the summer. The African American residents of Mississippi remained, their churches burned, homes destroyed, and jobs and property lost.

As Freedom Summer progressed, the MFDP prepared to offer alternative delegates at the Democratic National Convention (DNC) in Atlantic City, New Jersey. President Johnson, who had signed the Civil Rights Act on 2 July, wanted a united Democratic Party, as well as the support of all the state delegations, including the all-white delegations of the Deep South. The white supremacist Mississippi delegation was included in this, but the MFDP hoped that they might be able to pressure the Democratic Party to renounce the segregationist state parties, or at least be able to expose its hypocrisy in including them.

The convention was to begin on 24 August. The MFDP had selected its own delegates to be seated. On 22 August, before the convention began, a credentials hearing took place, in which several MFDP delegates presented their case. Fannie Lou Hamer, who had grown up a Mississippi Delta sharecropper and who had been beaten by police and prison guards for attempting to register to vote, argued forcefully that MFDP delegates should be seated instead of the Mississippi Democratic Party regulars. As Hamer began, President Johnson, fearing that he would lose control of the convention as well as the support of southern white Democrats, held a press conference to divert media attention away from Hamer's speech. Hamer's testimony was filmed, however, and excerpts in which she described the shootings and prison beatings endured by herself and by other women attempting to register to vote were shown later, as was her powerful conclusion.

> ### ᴬᵀᴸ Research skills
>
> Read about Fannie Lou Hamer in an online encyclopedia, such as the Kind Institute Encyclopedia:
>
> mlk-kpp01.stanford.edu/index.php/encyclopedia/encyclopedia_contents
>
> so that you know a little of her background. Then read the excerpts below, from her 22 August speech.

Source skills

Source A

Fannie Lou Hamer: Testimony Before the Credentials Committee, DNConvention, delivered 22 August 1964.

[The] plantation owner came and said, "Fannie Lou, do you know – did Pap tell you what I said?"

And I said, "Yes, sir."

He said, "Well I mean that."

Said, "If you don't go down and withdraw your registration, you will have to leave." Said, "Then if you go down and withdraw," said, "you still might have to go because we're not ready for that in Mississippi."

And I addressed him and told him and said, "I didn't try to register for you. I tried to register for myself."

I had to leave that same night.

On the 10th of September 1962, sixteen bullets was fired into the home of Mr. and Mrs. Robert Tucker for me. That same night two girls were shot in Ruleville, Mississippi. Also, Mr. Joe McDonald's house was shot in. …

All of this is on account of we want to register, to become first-class citizens. And if the Freedom Democratic Party is not seated now, I question America. Is this America, the land of the free and the home of the brave, where we have to sleep with our telephones off the hooks because our lives be threatened daily, because we want to live as decent human beings, in America?

americanrhetoric.com/speeches/fannielouhamercredentialscommittee.htm

Second question – 4 marks

With reference to its content, origin and purpose, what are the values and limitations of Hamer's speech for a student researching voting rights and political representation in the Deep South and the national Democratic Party?

A compromise was worked out with the help of Hubert Humphrey, the vice-presidential candidate, and supported by Martin Luther King. However, the compromise deal only gave the MFDP two delegates while seating all regular Democratic Party delegates, and was therefore rejected by the MFDP. Hamer stated, "*We didn't come all this way for no two seats*" (1964). Interestingly, all but three of the regular (segregationist) Mississippi delegates left the convention because they would not support the Johnson–Humphrey **slate**. A number of MFDP members obtained credentials from sympathetic delegates from other states and sat in the vacant Mississippi delegation seats.

Freedom Summer was a series of setbacks with few successes, if progress is measured at the summer's end. However, the lack of registered voters most emphatically demonstrated the need for federal enforcement of voting rights, thus paving the way for the Voting Rights Act of 1965. The need was further demonstrated early in 1965 by three voting rights marches from Selma, Alabama, to the capital, Montgomery, infamous for its police beatings of civil rights leaders and marchers. Efforts to enfranchise African Americans continued in the South into the 1970s and were usually met with substantial resistance, sometimes violence. The controversy at the DNC in Atlantic City spurred the Democratic Party to change its rules. In 1968, the MFDP delegation was seated to represent Mississippi at the Democratic National Convention in Chicago, Illinois.

Legislative changes: The Civil Rights Act of 1964 and the Voting Rights Act of 1965

The Civil Rights Act, 1964

The Civil Rights Act of 1964 is the most famous of all civil rights legislation. Indeed, author Clay Risen calls it "The Bill of the Century" (2014). Relying on the 14th and 15th Amendments as well as the Commerce Clause in Article 1 Section 8 of the US Constitution, the act encompassed voting rights, public accommodations, desegregation of public facilities, limits on discrimination within federally funded programs, employment discrimination, and authorized higher court review of district court referrals to state courts. It also reauthorized and expanded the US Commission on Civil Rights. While the act did not resolve many problems of racial discrimination, it was a significant step in federal responsibility and power in the enforcement of equal rights.

The act came about as a result of the constant and rising pressure created by a decade of actions and events, including the bus boycotts, business boycotts, lunch counter sit-ins, the Freedom Rides, demonstrations and marches. These actions highlighted the unceasing organizational, political and individual – and often violent – resistance to integration, economic opportunity and voting rights. After the nationally televised police violence in Birmingham, Alabama, in April 1963, which featured the use of cattle prods, fire hoses, clubs and biting dogs on demonstrators, the pressure on President Kennedy to act increased significantly. Demonstrations continued across the country, increasing the pressure; in the next three months there were approximately 1,000 demonstrations in 209 different cities and towns.

During the first two years of Kennedy's presidency, his administration proposed no civil rights legislation and, as stated previously, considered civil rights activists an annoyance, at best. The White House wanted to focus

A slate

A list of candidates presented by an organization, faction or a party for nomination or election.

on foreign relations, defence and the economy. However, the rising tide of violence against civil rights workers, both African American and white, could not be ignored, and by many accounts it disgusted and shocked the president. On 11 June 1963, in the midst of the continual demonstrations, Kennedy went on national television to propose a comprehensive bill covering discrimination in public accommodations and employment, as well as strengthening voting rights enforcement mechanisms. Violence continued unabated. The murder of Medgar Evers outside his home on the evening after Kennedy's speech, the substantial impact of the March on Washington for Jobs and Freedom in August, and the KKK bombing, on 15 September, of a church in Birmingham that killed four girls all served to reinforce the president's message. Nonetheless, the passage of a bill through Congress was far from guaranteed.

ATL Communication skills

Presidents use nationally televised speeches to command attention on what they consider to be critical issues. This was particularly true in the 1960s, when many viewers only had access to two or three channels; when national networks interrupted regularly scheduled programmes for a Presidential Address, the impact was much greater than it is today, with hundreds of channels and other media available to most viewers.

The excerpts below are from President Kennedy's Address on Civil Rights, 11 June 1963.

Good evening, my fellow citizens:

This afternoon, following a series of threats and defiant statements, the presence of Alabama National Guardsmen was required on the University of Alabama to carry out the final and unequivocal order of the United States District Court of the Northern District of Alabama. That order called for the admission of two clearly qualified young Alabama residents who happened to have been born Negro. …

I hope that every American, regardless of where he lives, will stop and examine his conscience about this and other related incidents. This Nation was founded by men of many nations and backgrounds. It was founded on the principle that all men are created equal, and that the rights of every man are diminished when the rights of one man are threatened. …

It ought to be possible for American consumers of any color to receive equal service in places of public accommodation, such as hotels and restaurants and theaters and retail stores, without being forced to resort to demonstrations in the street, and it ought to be possible for American citizens of any color to register and to vote in a free election without interference or fear of reprisal.

It ought to be possible, in short, for every American to enjoy the privileges of being American without regard to his race or his color. In short, every American ought to have the right to be treated as he would wish to be treated, as one would wish his children to be treated. But this is not the case. …

This is not a sectional issue. Difficulties over segregation and discrimination exist in every city, in every State of the Union, producing in many cities a rising tide of discontent that threatens the public safety. …

The heart of the question is whether all Americans are to be afforded equal rights and equal opportunities, whether we are going to treat our fellow Americans as we want to be treated. If an American, because his skin is dark, cannot eat lunch in a restaurant open to the public, if he cannot send his children to the best public school available, if he cannot vote for the public officials who represent him, if, in short, he cannot enjoy the full and free life which all of us want, then who among us would be content to have the color of his skin changed and stand in his place? Who among us would then be content with the counsels of patience and delay?

millercenter.org/president/speeches/speech-3375

Questions

1 How did Kennedy use this speech to educate and to persuade the American public?

2 What evidence does the speech contain to indicate pressure caused by recent and ongoing events?

3 What rhetorical techniques does Kennedy employ in his speech? In what ways and to what extent are these devices effective?

4 Why, given the reach of a national broadcast, was the effect of the speech limited?

The bill made little progress in the next few months. The assassination of President Kennedy on 22 November placed Lyndon B Johnson in the White House. Until 1957 Johnson had opposed all civil rights legislation during his years in the House of Representatives and the Senate. During consideration of the 1957 Civil Rights Act, Johnson, a powerful senator, had worked to weaken the legislation, although he ultimately voted in favour. As slow as Kennedy had been to reach an understanding of the need for action on civil rights, most mainstream civil rights leaders had considered him a friend to the freedom fight and they had little confidence in the new president. However, Johnson proved to be an important and powerful ally, who used the full force of his office to push the Civil Rights Act through.

Over the next several months, the bill went through numerous rewritings. Title II, the banning of discrimination in public facilities, was so controversial that it was separated from the rest of the legislation and shepherded through committee work by Democrat Mike Mansfield and Republican Everett Dirksen. Some compromises to gain votes, or at least guarantee a floor vote, weakened parts of the bill. A surprise amendment by Virginia Senator Howard Smith added the word "sex" to Title VII (equal employment opportunities), making gender a protected class, along with race, ethnicity and religion. Historians cannot agree whether Smith, who had previously supported equal rights for women, was serious about women's rights, or whether he added the word as a wrecking amendment to make it politically unattractive to enough senators to cause the bill to fail. The amendment stayed.

More modifications and legislative manoeuvering took place, including an almost three-month delay in the Senate due to a **filibuster** by a bloc of 19 southern senators. However, on 2 July 1964, following pressure from civil rights leaders and organizations, lobbying groups and church congregations (some of whose members sat in legislators' offices day after day, demonstrating a refusal to accept another delay or dismissal), exhaustive work by Senator Dirksen, and President Johnson's full engagement and political hardball, the bill passed in the Senate by a vote of 73 to 27, and in the House by 289 to 126. Votes in both chambers were divided by region rather than by political party, with more than 90% of southern legislators voting against and 90% of northern legislators voting for. President Johnson signed the bill the same day, surrounded by an audience that included Martin Luther King, Jr.

The 1964 Civil Rights Act addressed critical areas of civil rights, including voting rights, public accommodations, school desegregation, federally funded projects, and enforcement. More specifically, it required privately owned and operated businesses that served the public to serve customers and clients regardless of race, colour or national origin. The caveat was that the businesses had to be engaged in interstate commerce. Essentially, unless a restaurant, hotel, stadium or concert hall served only customers from within the state and purchased all its supplies from within its state, it was conducting interstate commerce and was therefore subject to the law. Thus, all businesses, with the exception of undefined private clubs, fell

A **filibuster** occurs when one or more Senators continually speak on the floor of the Senate so that no votes can be taken. United States Senate rules (at that time) allowed for non-stop debate (speaking), unless two-thirds of the Senators voted to end the debate. That vote is called a "cloture" vote. Presently 60 of 100 votes are required for cloture."

under the jurisdiction of the law. Under Title III of the act, states and localities were compelled to stop discrimination in their own facilities as well.

Transition was not immediate and some areas resisted the law. Over time, however, with the constant assistance of civil rights activists and African Americans who exercised their legally protected rights, Titles II and III of the act increasingly replaced Jim Crow traditions. In addition, federal funds could be denied to any government agency that discriminated and the voting rights section of the act, Title I, outlawed the practice of unequal voting requirements. For example, if a literacy test was used, all voters would be subject to the same qualifying exam and the same qualifying standard.

The Civil Rights Act and the legislative actions surrounding it are often cited as causing a shift in the major political parties. In the "Solid South", the Democratic Party quickly began to lose members as legislators switched to independent parties or became Republican. In 1964, Johnson, a Texan, lost five states in the Deep South, all of which had been won or split by the Massachusetts-born Kennedy four years earlier. In 1968, Republican Richard Nixon ran for and won the White House, employing a "Southern Strategy" against sitting Vice-president Hubert Humphrey, a consistent supporter of civil rights. Nixon did not capture the entire South, though. George Wallace, the Alabama Governor famous for his "segregation now, segregation tomorrow, segregation forever", statement and who had attempted to block the integration of the University of Alabama, ran as the American Independent Party candidate and won the states of Arkansas, Louisiana, Mississippi, Alabama and Georgia. Texas, Johnson's home state, went to Humphrey, while Nixon won five states in the South. The defection of the white South from the Democratic Party, at least in presidential elections, was fully underway by the end of the 1960s. However, legislative electoral maps show a more gradual transition and indicate that the movement was not monolithic, and other factors, including the foreign and domestic policies, shifting demographics, and social unrest in the 1960s and 1970s also played a significant role in the shift of Southern states to the Republican Party.

The Voting Rights Act, 1965

While the Civil Rights Act of 1964 was the most important civil rights legislation of the 20th century, the voting rights section of the act was not up to the task of ensuring equal voting rights and access to political participation. As evidenced by Freedom Summer and the reception the Democratic Party leaders gave the MFDP at the Democratic National Convention in Atlantic City, New Jersey, there was a need for further legislation. However, the Johnson administration, the US House of Representatives and the US Senate had only just finished their hard fight over the 1964 Civil Rights Act, and to move another related bill as quickly through the legislative obstacle course of committees, floor amendments, votes, a conference committee and more votes, was not feasible.

Yet voting rights activists would not rest. In January 1965, the SCLC, led by Martin Luther King, Jr, built upon previous voting rights work by the SNCC and opened a voting rights campaign in Selma, Alabama. As with previous voter registration efforts, responses by the white community included threats and violence. Following the beating and fatal shooting by state troopers of Jimmie Lee Jackson as he walked in a voting rights march in Marion, Alabama, the SCLC's James Bevel called for a protest march from Selma to Montgomery. On 7 March, which would become known as "Bloody Sunday", a group of more than 500 assembled on the Edmund Pettus Bridge under the leadership of the SNCC's John Lewis and the SCLC's Hosea Williams. Dallas County Sheriff Jim Clark, who had deputized KKK members previously, ordered white male residents to report to headquarters to be deputized, escalating the tension and threat of violence. Clark had previously been caught by news cameras personally attacking several activists, including CT Vivian and Amelia Boyton, leaving the latter unconscious from the clubbing. Even though Selma's mayor had hoped to minimize the effect of the protest by limiting confrontations and minimizing police involvement, Selma police and Alabama patrolmen responded to the beginning of the protest march with tear gas, billy clubs and riders on horseback with bull whips. More than 50 people were injured and images of the beatings appeared on evening news programmes across the country. The campaign showed once again the extent to which white supremacists had gone and would go to prevent African Americans from voting.

The heightened pressure of the events in Selma motivated President Johnson and the US Congress to act. Johnson appeared on television just one week after Bloody Sunday, on 15 March. His outrage was evident:

> *I speak tonight for the dignity of man and the destiny of democracy.*
>
> *I urge every member of both parties—Americans of all religions and of all colors—from every section of this country—to join me in that cause.*
>
> *At times history and fate meet at a single time in a single place to shape a turning point in man's unending search for freedom. So it was at Lexington and Concord. So it was a century ago at Appomattox. So it was last week in Selma, Alabama.*
>
> *There is no Negro problem. There is no southern problem. There is no northern problem. There is only an American problem.*
>
> — Johnson, 1965

Johnson ended his speech with the powerful phrase "we shall overcome", from the protest song closely association with the Civil Rights Movement:

> *This great, rich, restless country can offer opportunity and education and hope to all—all black and white, all North and South, sharecropper and city dweller. These are the enemies—poverty, ignorance, disease—they are our enemies, not our fellow man, not our neighbor. And these enemies too— poverty, disease, and ignorance—we shall overcome.*
>
> — Johnson, 1965

The result of these events was the Voting Rights Act of 1965, which was written, passed and signed into law by 6 August 1965, a rare legislative time frame of four months. The act outlawed literacy tests and directed

the US Department of Justice to challenge poll taxes, which it did. The act also gave the Attorney General the power to assign federal examiners to observe and direct voter registration where less than half of the eligible residents were registered to vote. According to the act, jurisdictions with such a history

> could not implement any change affecting voting until the Attorney General or the United States District Court for the District of Columbia determined that the change did not have a discriminatory purpose and would not have a discriminatory effect.

This was a major change from the costly and slow lawsuit remedy provided for in previous voting acts: now the Department of Justice could work actively to guarantee voting rights. Two US Supreme Court decisions – *Harper v. Virginia State Board of Elections* and *South Carolina v. Katzenback* (both 1966) – upheld the many requirements of the Voting Rights Act, concluding that placing the burden of proof of compliance on the states and localities that had a history of voting rights violations was constitutional. The effect of the law was swift: within two years more than half of southern African Americans of legal age were registered to vote and in Mississippi the percentage of eligible African Americans registered to vote moved from the lowest to the highest in the South. As the Congress of Racial Equality states,

> The law's effects were wide and powerful. By 1968, nearly 60 percent of eligible African Americans were registered to vote in Mississippi, and other southern states showed similar improvement. Between 1965 and 1990, the number of black state legislators and members of Congress rose from two to 160.

Source skills

Source A

Excerpts from President Lyndon B Johnson's Voting Rights Act Address, 15 March 1965.

This was the first nation in the history of the world to be founded with a purpose. The great phrases of that purpose still sound in every American heart, north and south: "All men are created equal" — "Government by consent of the governed" — "Give me liberty or give me death."…

Many of the issues of civil rights are very complex and most difficult. But about this there can and should be no argument. Every American citizen must have an equal right to vote. There is no reason which can excuse the denial of that right. There is no duty which weighs more heavily on us than the duty we have to ensure that right.

Yet the harsh fact is that in many places in this country men and women are kept from voting simply because they are Negroes. …

The command of the Constitution is plain. There is no moral issue. It is wrong—deadly wrong—to deny any of your fellow Americans the right to vote in this country. There is no issue of States rights or National rights. There is only the struggle for human rights.

Source B

Excerpts from the text of the Voting Rights Act of 1965.

SEC. 2. No voting qualification or prerequisite to voting, or standard, practice, or procedure shall be imposed or applied by any State or political subdivision to deny or abridge the right of any citizen of the United States to vote on account of race or color. …

SEC. 3. (b) If in a proceeding instituted by the Attorney General under any statute to enforce the guarantees of the fifteenth amendment in any State or political subdivision the court finds that a test or device has been used for the purpose or with the effect of denying or abridging the right of any citizen of the United States to vote on account of race or color, it shall suspend the use of tests and devices in such State or political subdivisions as the court shall determine is appropriate and for such period as it deems necessary.

Source C

R. Weisbrot. *Freedom Bound* (1990).

As in the passage of the Civil Rights Act of 1964, legal change found its catalyst in social disorder. The historian David Garrow has argued persuasively that at Selma, Martin Luther King refined to new sophistication the tactic of precipitating racist violence in order to win media coverage and, in turn, public support that could translate into legislation. The spasm of one-sided violence at Selma helped solidify a stronger, more quickly formed consensus for civil rights action than had occurred in 1963, when violence in Birmingham involved black rioters as well as rampaging white police. The nation had also traveled far in those two years, becoming more sensitive to the indignities as well as the dangers blacks endured in seeking their rights.

Source D

A news photograph taken during the Selma to Montgomery March, March 1965.

First question, part a – 3 marks

What is the message of Source C?

First question, part b – 2 marks

What evidence is there in Source A to suggest that President Johnson supported voting rights legislation?

Second question – 4 marks

With reference to its content, origin and purpose, what are the values and limitations of Source D for students studying the activities of Civil Rights Movement activists in working for voting rights?

Third question – 6 marks

Compare and contrast Sources A and B with regard to the federal government's commitment to voting rights.

Fourth question – 9 marks

Using the sources and your own knowledge, assess why, how and to what effects civil rights activists fought to secure voting rights for African Americans.

The role and significance of key individuals and groups

This section considers the roles of some of the significant individuals and groups involved in the Civil Rights Movement from 1954 to 1965. The key leaders and organizations designated represent significant and varied actors. Lyndon B. Johnson was the President of the United States, while Malcolm X and Martin Luther King, Jr., were both ministers and great orators, but represented differing goals while advocating and applying different strategies and tactics. The NAACP is one of the oldest civil rights organizations, founded in the first decade of the 20th Century. The Nation of Islam was founded in 1930 as a religious order with a goal of improving the lives of African Americans, focusing in northern urban areas. A quarter of a century later, the Southern Christian Leadership Conference was formed in the wake of the Montgomery Bus Boycott, rooted in the beliefs of Christianity, and concentrating on southern cities. The Student Non-violent Coordinating Committee was a grass-roots organization whose membership combined the SCLS's practice of non-violent resistance with less centralized leadership and a focus on the rural areas of the South. An examination of the varied actors provides a deeper comprehension and appreciation of the breadth of the African American civil rights movement.

▲ President JF Kennedy invited a group of civil rights leaders to the White House. Pictured in the front row (left to right) are Martin Luther King, Jr., Attorney General Robert Kennedy, Roy Wilkins and Vice President Lyndon B. Johnson

Martin Luther King, Jr.

Dr Martin Luther King, Jr. was the young pastor of the Dexter Avenue Baptist Church when he first became known for his involvement in the Montgomery Bus Boycott. He had followed the family tradition of entering the ministry: his grandfather, then father, led Atlanta's Ebenezer Baptist Church. He earned his doctorate in systematic theology from Boston University in 1955. King had been active in civil rights before Montgomery, as evidenced by his membership of the NAACP and his position on its executive committee. Following his leadership of the 382-day bus boycott, King emerged as an important figure in the Civil Rights Movement. In the months following the boycott, King and other pastors from African American churches met to create a new civil rights organization, the Southern Christian Leadership Conference (SCLC), of which he was elected president. The SCLC took its ideals from Christianity and its non-violent tactical methods from Mahatma Gandhi. In the 13 years from 1955 to his assassination in 1968, Martin Luther King, Jr. became the single most recognized and influential civil rights leader in the United States.

King was active in many protests and actions during the period from 1954 to 1965. Examples of some of the important placed he worked, spoke and marched to advance the cause of equal rights include: Albany, Georgia; Birmingham, Alabama; Washington, DC; and Selma, Mississippi. The Nobel Prize reports that, from 1957 to 1968, King *spoke over twenty-five hundred*

Note: The key actors in the Civil Rights Movement were not limited to the several listed in this course. A study of the civil rights years is incomplete without understanding the roles played by a variety of the numerous leaders and organizations. Protagonists from the era could have included Thurgood Marshall, Ella Baker, Fannie Lou Hamer, John Lewis, James Farmer, Joanne Robinson, or Earl Warren. Antagonists that had an important impact include Orval Faubus, Harry Byrd, or Eugene "Bull" Connor. White Citizen Councils and the Ku Klux Klan fought desegregation and equal rights at every step, using legal, extra-legal, and violent means. Pro-civil rights organizations counted CORE, COFU, the Urban League among them, and the American Civil Liberties Union was active as well in the legal battle. The Federal Bureau of Investigation and Director J. Edgar Hoover repeatedly investigated and interfered with the major civil rights groups and leaders, but also tracked the KKK as well. Certainly the actions of the United States Congress and Senate, and the Federal District, Appeals, and Supreme Court were critical to both the successes and setbacks of the movement.

times, appearing wherever there was injustice, protest, and action...wrote five books, was arrested upwards of twenty times and assaulted at least four times". He is not only famous for his leadership, but for his words. Two of the most well-known and important examples of his powerful use of language are his "Letter From a Birmingham Jail" and the "I Have a Dream" speech from the March on Washington for Jobs and Freedom. Both were authored and made public in 1963.

In his "Letter From a Birmingham Jail", 16 April 1963, King responds to an editorial by eight Alabama clergymen, all white, in which they criticize the actions and methods of King and others for choosing to protest in Birmingham, first because they are outsiders and also in light of the "moderate" new city administration. King was arrested along with hundreds of other protesters in Birmingham, but King was placed in a solitary cell; without sufficient paper, he began to write his response in newspaper margins and on the scraps of paper available. King's reply explained the movement's philosophy and its choice of tactics. His powerful words may not have convinced Birmingham's white clergy, but they articulated the conditions in the Jim Crow South, the ethical reasons behind the choice made by himself, other members of the SCLC and African Americans from other locations to protest in Birmingham, and an integrationist, pro-American philosophy that advocated the full participation of African Americans in every aspect of life in the United States.

Martin Luther King, Jr is perhaps most famous for the words, "I have a dream". The "I Have a Dream" speech was delivered in August 1963. It was the last of many speeches given that day and was the first time that many white Americans had heard King speak. The cadences and techniques he used were in the long tradition of the African American Church. The speech pointed to injustice, religion and faith, but was also a call for justice. The end of the speech with the repetition of "I have a dream", also pointed to a goal of racial, religious and ethnic integration in a harmonious America.

As a major civil rights leader, King developed contacts and influence in both the Kennedy and the Johnson administrations. In the midst of his campaign for the presidency in 1960, just a week before the election, Kennedy called King's wife, Coretta, to express concern for her then imprisoned husband while Kennedy's brother, Robert, used his influence to secure King's release on bail. While President Kennedy and his brother were often annoyed with the Civil Rights Movement, King's participation was key in the growth of support for a civil rights act. When Lyndon B Johnson became President on 22 November 1963 following Kennedy's assassination, King worked to develop a relationship with him, in spite of some doubts as to the new president's commitment to civil rights. In fact, Johnson proved to be a more forceful ally than Kennedy, though King's influence with the Johnson lessened when the civil rights leader spoke against the war in Vietnam.

Martin Luther King, Jr. was criticized by others within the Civil Rights Movement, including some members of the SNCC, for his reliance on non-violence, perceived gradualism and for expanding his advocacy to issues beyond civil rights. Younger activists, many with the SNCC, questioned his courage due to an apparent reluctance to be arrested and his unwillingness to join the Freedom Rides. To organizers, in Albany for example, it seemed as though King would arrive in a city after all the organizing work was done, bring added attention to the protest, then return to Atlanta, leaving the organizers to cope with the ramifications of his participation. While recognizing King's ability to lead mass movements and attract attention from the national media, other leaders voiced concerns that the media and politicians paid more attention to King as a person than to the issues themselves. Malcolm X, who called the March on Washington a "farce", was critical of King's dream of an integrated society, and the lack of a threat of violent retaliation invited white-on-black violence. Nonetheless, Martin Luther King, Jr. remained committed to non-violence and integration.

Malcolm X

Malcolm X was an important civil rights leader who, unlike the rest of the movement's leaders discussed in this section, focused on the deplorable conditions of African Americans living in the urban North. His childhood experiences of racism, threats and violence against his family, as well as the break-up of his family and the placement of the children in different homes, contributed to his views of American society. However, just as many of the most influential leaders of CORE, the SCLC and the SNCC came to their civil rights work by way of their religious faith, so too did Malcolm X, following his conversion to the Nation of Islam (NOI) during his time in prison for armed robbery. The NOI was unlike mainstream civil rights organizations such as CORE and the NAACP; Elijah Muhammad preached racial solidarity and racial superiority. African Americans were God's chosen people who would triumph with the help of Allah. However, Muhammad taught that discipline and economic self-reliance was critical, too. African Americans should become more highly educated and practice small-scale community capitalism, owning local businesses and patronizing only black-owned stores. Abstinence from vice was critical. It was a message that appealed to many African Americans in the northern urban ghettos, including those of Detroit, Chicago and New York; here, the Civil Rights Movement, with most of its focus on desegregation in southern states, had not resulted in significant change. Unemployment was high, housing was dilapidated and schools were run down and often over-crowded. Jim Crow laws may not have been in place, but the domination of political and economic institutions by the white establishment had resulted in practices that had denied opportunity to African Americans for decades.

Malcolm X became a spokesperson and editor for *The Messenger*, NOI's print publication, soon after leaving prison in 1952. Articulate and witty, Malcolm X appealed to the desperation of urban blacks. He started in Chicago, then moved to Harlem, a section of New York in Upper Manhattan, in 1954. There, he attracted thousands to the NOI Mosque No 7, giving impassioned speeches promoting the ideals of self-reliance and faith, as well as defining white Americans as the enemy. As a result of Malcolm X's work and charisma, membership surged upwards of 50,000, making the NOI a household name in the United States, and one feared by many white Americans and some middle and upper class African Americans.

▲ Malcolm X speaks in support of the Harlem school boycott at a rally, 1964

Malcolm X

It was common practice among converts of the Nation of Islam to change their last name from their "slave surname" to an "X" which was representative of the unknown African name of their ancestors. Malcolm X's "slave surname" was Little.

Source skills

Malcolm X, spokesperson for the Nation of Islam, Black Revolution speech, June 1963.

> I must point out that The Honorable Elijah Muhammad says a desegregated theater, a desegregated lunch counter won't solve our problem. Better jobs won't even solve our problems. An integrated cup of coffee isn't sufficient pay for four hundred years of slave labor. He also says that a better job, a better job in the white man's factory, or a better job in the white man's business, or a better job in the white man's industry or economy is, at best, only a temporary solution. He says that the only lasting and permanent solution is complete separation on some land that we can call our own.

Second question – 4 marks

With reference to its origin, purpose, and content, analyse the values and limitations of this source for a student studying the views of the NOI regarding civil rights leaders' and groups' actions and goals?

Examiner's hint: Some of the points that you may consider are listed below.

Values:

- As a leading spokesperson Malcolm X can be relied upon to explain the views of NOI.

- The purpose the speech is to make the views of NOI clear and as such the speech is valuable by expressing the views of Elijah Muhammad, the leader of NOI, not Malcolm X's alone.

- The content has value in that the speech identifies major actions and accomplishments of civil rights actors while explaining that separation from the "white man" is the only solution to the problem of unequal treatment.

Limitations:

- Because it was a public speech it may not reveal the actual views of NOI, and it is also possible that Malcolm X may be misinterpreting the views of Elijah Muhammad.

- Malcolm X purposely used speeches and chose language to provoke a reaction and as such avoided nuance and explanations of the actions and goals mentioned.

- While the speech does point out specific actions, it fails to provide reasons for the insufficiency of civil rights groups actions. It also identifies only one solution, but fails to identify reasons.

Mainstream periodicals including *Time Magazine* and *The New York Times* wrote detailed stories about Malcom X, who belittled established civil rights leaders' goal of integration as fantasy, saying, *"These Negroes aren't asking for any nation—they're trying to crawl back on the plantation"* (1963). Black nationalism was identified as the correct path. White society was corrupt and corrupted everything it touched. African Americans needed to control their own education, politics and economy. In perhaps his most famous speech, "The Ballot or the Bullet" speech of 3 April, 1964, Malcolm X explained that black nationalism

> *only means that the black man should control the politics and the politicians in his own community…that we will have to carry on a program, a political program of re-education… make us more politically conscious, politically mature.*

The message garnered support from urban African Americans who were not members of NOI. Malcolm X's forceful advocacy of African Americans helped bring about the Black Pride movement, which celebrated African heritage as well as strongly advocating solidarity in a society that worked to keep them weak and fragmented. Indeed, the FBI worked hard to sow discord within and across the various civil rights organizations. Additionally, opposition to Malcolm X from within the civil rights movement was substantial. Leadership complained that his inflammatory speeches and interviews attracted disproportionate media coverage, diverting the nation's attention from critical issues. They also claimed he did not propose viable solutions to the issues he raised.

In 1964, Malcolm X went on a pilgrimage to Mecca. He returned to the United States a Sunni Muslim and changed his name to El-Hajj Malik El-Shabazz. He no longer espoused the inherent evilness of white Americans, but still strongly condemned pervasive racism within the

United States. He spoke in favour of Pan-Africanism while admitting its limits, and criticized capitalism, but advocated black nationalism and praised African American entrepreneurship. He still favoured self-defence, rather than turning the other cheek, in response to violence. He further argued that African Americans were justified in using any means necessary to defend themselves if the government was incapable of protecting them or chose not to do so. That year, millions of African Americans would act with their ballots. If they were not allowed to do so, or the process rendered their votes useless, the bullet was the alternative. Malcolm X proclaimed, *"this country can become involved in a revolution that won't take bloodshed. All she's got to do is give the black man in this country everything that's due him, everything"* (1964).

Malcolm X spent much of the rest of 1964 trying to establish deeper ties with civil rights leaders. He formed the Organization of Afro-American Unity (OAAU) and evoked both cooperation and militancy by voicing support for any action by any group that worked, while still advocating fighting over talking. In an act of support for the then imprisoned Martin Luther King, Jr., whom he had only met once, Malcolm X met privately with King's wife, Coretta Scott King, explaining, *"If white people realize what the alternative is, perhaps they will be more willing to hear Dr. King"* (1965).

Malcolm X's efforts at building the OAAU and working with other civil rights leaders were tragically cut short. On 21 February 1965, Malcolm X was assassinated while giving a speech in the Audubon Ballroom in Harlem, leaving a legacy that both united and divided the Civil Rights Movement. However, this legacy also brought significantly greater awareness to all of the United States of the grievances and frustrations of African Americans – in particular those outside the South, whose plight had been largely ignored by the national press and white civic leaders – as well as a sense of pride in African identity that has lasted for decades beyond his death.

Lyndon B Johnson

Lyndon Baines Johnson became a key figure in the fight for civil rights only after being elected as president. A white Texan who had been Senate Majority Leader and was an expert at using the many levers of power, Johnson was also known to use racial epithets. Having ignored, then opposed and weakened legislation during the 1950s, his conversion to the cause of equal rights came late in his political career.

Johnson grew up in small-town Texas and began his professional career teaching Mexican-American children in a segregated school. At the height of the Great Depression, he ran the National Youth Administration (NYA) in Texas before starting his long career in elected office in the late 1930s. He was an admirer of Franklin D Roosevelt's New Deal and remained so as he rose ambitiously in power, becoming the most powerful Democrat in the US Senate during the 1950s. As president, Johnson wanted to leave his own legacy, which included civil rights as part of his vision for a "Great Society".

▲ Johnson speaking on the telephone on 17 August 1965, 11 days after signing the Voting Rights Act

Johnson became president just as Kennedy's civil rights bill had largely stalled in the US House of Representitves and US Senate. The focus of the government was still on foreign policy; the Cold War, thermonuclear bombs and missiles, and the expanding Vietnam conflict were critical parts of the President's agenda. Unrest in the Caribbean also grabbed the new administration's attention. Still, the new president was concerned with domestic issues of poverty and civil rights. In the opening remarks of his first State of the Union Address, which focused on what came to be called the War on Poverty, Johnson made civil rights a key component of his administration: "*Let this session of Congress be known as the session which did more for civil rights than the last hundred sessions combined*" (1964). Later in the same speech, he re-emphasized the commitment to racial equality:

> *Let me make one principle of this administration abundantly clear: All of these increased opportunities — in employment, in education, in housing, and in every field — must be open to Americans of every color. As far as the writ of Federal law will run, we must abolish not some, but all racial discrimination. For this is not merely an economic issue, or a social, political, or international issue. It is a moral issue, and it must be met by the passage this session of the bill now pending in the House.*

— Johnson, 1964

Johnson used his knowledge of Senate strategy and the political debts owed to him by wavering senators to help the Civil Rights Act pass the US Senate in 1964. As much as Johnson celebrated the hard-won act, however, discrimination and unrest continued, both in the South and in the North. With increasing pressure from Civil Rights Movement demonstrations, from leaders, and as a result of the violent responses of segregationists, as well as racial violence in Harlem and Rochester, New York, as well as other northern cities in the summer, Johnson realized that further legislation and government action was needed.

Events in early 1965 further pushed the president. On 9 February, Martin Luther King, Jr. met with Johnson in the White House to push for voting rights legislation, eliciting a promise that the president would act. Two weeks later, Malcolm X was assassinated and, on 7 March, televised pictures and film footage of the violence in Selma prompted Johnson to make a speech to a joint session of the US Congress, a rare event. The speech was completely focused on voting rights and televised nationally. As noted previously, the Voting Rights Act of 1965 was passed quickly.

Johnson's advocacy of civil rights did not end there. The urban riots of 1965 angered the president. At first, Johnson was taken aback by a perceived lack of gratitude shown by the African American community. He thought he deserved great praise for pushing civil rights bills into law, which was more than his predecessors had done in almost a century. The urban unrest made it clear to Johnson and others in the US House of Representatives and the US Senate that more legislation was needed. He sent another civil rights bill to the US Congress in 1966, proposing the banning of discrimination in housing and in the selection of jurors on both federal and state levels. As urban unrest continued, Johnson condemned the violence and even sent troops into Detroit in 1967 to stop the rioting, but he also proposed more legislation. The result was the Civil Rights

Act of 1968, better known as the Fair Housing Act, which banned most discriminatory practices in the sale and rental of homes and apartments, and provided additional protection for civil rights workers. The act was signed into law one week after Martin Luther King, Jr. was assassinated.

Johnson's presidency was critical to the passage of important civil rights bills. Some of his biographers argue that his public support for civil rights was not matched by his private racial prejudices, and that he came to support civil rights only in the last years of his three-decade-long political career. However, it is also argued that his later speeches articulated a firm commitment to equal rights, regardless of his personal feelings. Additionally, as the level of Johnson's importance in civil rights legislation is still being examined in the context of grass roots activism and key legislators, both Republican and Democrat, in the US House of Representatives and the US Senate, it is also evident that he was critical to the passage of federal civil rights legislation.

Civil rights organizations

The National Association for the Advancement of Colored People (NAACP)

The National Association for the Advancement of Colored People (NAACP) was instrumental in the fight for the rights of African Americans, beginning with its founding on 12 February 1909. Established following a race riot in Springfield, Illinois, in 1908, the NAACP was a racial and religiously integrated organization from the start. Charter members and early members included WEB Du Bois, Mary White Ovington, Joel and Arthur Spingarn, Mary McLeod Bethune, and famous reformers of the era Lincoln Steffens and Jane Addams. The NAACP's purpose was to *"secure for all people the rights guaranteed in the 13th, 14th, and 15th Amendments to the United States Constitution, which promised an end to slavery, the equal protection of the law, and universal adult male suffrage"*. Included in its work was its publication, *The Crisis*, whose editor was WEB Du Bois.

▲ John Lewis, chairman of the Student Nonviolent Coordinating Committee (SNCC), and Hosea Williams, of the Southern Christian Leadership Conference (SCLC). The civil rights organizations sometimes worked together during campaigns.

The NAACP grew quickly, with the fight against lynching one of its prime areas of advocacy and with membership rising from 9,000 in 1909 to approximately 500,000 by the end of the Second World War. Chapters first opened in northern cities, but field offices opened in several southern states as well. The rapid growth came in the wake of the NAACP's long battle against lynching, its lobbying for civil rights legislation and its decades-long legal battle against segregation and discrimination in education. The campaign progressed under the leadership of NAACP Executive Secretary Walter White, who was chosen for the position in 1929, and the chief legal strategist, Charles Hamilton Houston. As part of the campaign, Thurgood Marshall and other NAACP attorneys recruited the plaintiffs in South Carolina, Virginia, and other southern states that became the foundation for *Brown v. Board of Education of Topeka* (1954).

During the post-war civil rights era, the NAACP continued its legal work through the NAACP Legal Defense and Education Fund (LDF), led by future Supreme Court Justice Thurgood Marshall. The NAACP's efforts resulted in the landmark decision of Brown in 1954. When opposition to Brown threatened progress, the NAACP went to court after court and led the battle for enforcement. The NAACP also lobbied congressmen and senators for civil rights legislation, with the modest successes of the Civil Rights Acts of 1957 and 1960.

As other civil rights organizations were born and became increasingly influential in the 1950s and 1960s, the NAACP continued its work. As the Civil Rights Movement focused on the South, so did the NAACP. The NAACP Youth Council was formed and its members participated in sit-ins. NAACP members worked with other organizations to provide bail for Freedom Riders and working for voter rights, and were subject to KKK and segregationist violence as well. Mississippi Field Secretary Medgar Evers's home was bombed in 1962 and Evers was assassinated in 12 June 1963, just hours after President Kennedy's first major civil rights address. Important NAACP members of the Civil Rights Movement included: Rosa Parks; Daisy Bates, the force behind the Little Rock Nine; Ella Baker, who helped create the Student Nonviolent Coordinating Committee (SNCC); and Martin Luther King, Jr.

The NAACP was also a primary organizer of the March on Washington for Jobs and Freedom in 1963, and the following year the NAACP joined the Council of Federated Organizations (COFO), a leading organizer of Freedom Summer. However, as other organizations gained traction, the NAACP became seen as part of the cautious establishment, no matter the risks that its members took. This casting of the NAACP is an indicator of the shift in the Civil Rights Movement, as only a decade earlier many African Americans had viewed the NAACP as risk-takers and had considered the organization much too radical.

Finally, the NAACP's advocacy also was important in shaping and securing the passages of the Civil Rights Act of 1964 and the Voting Rights Act of 1965.

The Southern Christian Leadership Conference (SCLC)

The Southern Christian Leadership Conference (SCLC) was critical to the Civil Rights Movement. It led, co-led or participated in scores of campaigns and events from its inception in 1957 and throughout the civil rights period under study. It was instrumental in advancing the cause of civil rights, tirelessly employing non-violence as a tactic and assisting other civil rights groups as well. While accused of becoming cautious in its approach as the 1960s wore on, the SCLC was often at the forefront of protests, even if the organizations participation was sometimes reluctant. Its churches provided sanctuaries and its leaders used their courage and charisma to build the Civil Rights Movement.

The origin of the SCLC is directly associated with the Montgomery Bus Boycott and the important role of African American ministers, principally the Reverends Ralph David Abernathy and Martin Luther King, Jr., in this year-long effort. On 10–11 January 1957, a group of 60 activists from 10 southern states met in Atlanta, Georgia. The purpose of the meeting was tied deeply to religious duty. As stated in a 7 January press release by the Montgomery Improvement Association (MIA), *"This conference is called because we have no moral choice, before God, but to delve deeper into the struggle and to do so with greater reliance on non-violence and with greater unity, coordination, sharing and Christian understanding"* (1957).

Bayard Rustin prompted this conference with seven working papers suggesting the expansion of the Montgomery movement to many cities in the South. In February, the new organization became the Southern Leadership Conference with King, Abernathy, the Reverend CK Steele of Tallahassee, Florida, and the Reverend TJ Jemison from Baton Rouge, Louisiana, as officers. The first convention took place in Montgomery, Alabama, where the leadership added "Christian" to the organization's name. The charter members committed to a role coordinating affiliated local organizations rather than directing of a single, large group. SCLC membership was open to all races, religions and backgrounds. It would become evident that, as a result of the success of the Montgomery Bus Boycott, non-violent mass action was its chosen strategy.

A southern-based and urban organization, the SCLC was active in various ways. As a coordinating organization, the SCLC considered training leaders as one of its primary responsibilities. Across the South, it trained thousands of activists in the philosophy of Christian non-violent resistance. For example, together with the American Missionary Association (AMA) it operated a leadership training and citizenship school at the Dorchester Center in Midway, Georgia. This centre was where the 1963 Birmingham, Alabama, campaign was planned. The SCLC filed class action lawsuits against state and local governments for maintaining segregated public facilities, conducted voter registration drives, and organized numerous boycotts against stores that did not hire African American workers. The organization also began Operation Breadbasket in Atlanta in 1962 to combat poverty by creating jobs in African American neighbourhoods; in this way, the SCLC echoed Malcolm X's call for economic self-reliance, the difference being that SCLC did not advocate racial exclusivity.

Along with its own initiatives, the SCLC joined other groups in, and sometimes coordinated, protests and voter registration in locations such as Albany, Georgia (1962), Birmingham, Alabama (1963) and St Augustine, Florida (1963–4). It played an important part in the March on Washington and the Selma to Montgomery March in 1965. After the passage of the Civil Rights Act of 1964, the SCLC led efforts to desegregate schools. Campaigns spread northward to Chicago, Illinois (Chicago Freedom Movement, 1966) and to Washington, DC, to put pressure on the US Congress and the White House to legislate to assist people in living in poverty with the Poor People's Campaign in 1968.

The SCLC's influence waned during the mid-1960s, especially following the assassination of Martin Luther King, Jr. on 4 April 1968. As it worked with other groups, it was criticized for its unwavering focus on non-violence. The beginning of the Black Power era combined with the increasing popularity of Black Nationalism clashed with the SCLC's pacifist-integrationist philosophy in the struggle for equal rights.

The Student Nonviolent Coordinating Committee (SNCC)

The Student Nonviolent Coordinating Committee (SNCC) was a grassroots organization that was established in April 1960 in the midst of the college student lunch counter sit-ins. It became the leading force for voter registration in the rural South, areas that had not been targeted by the efforts of the other major civil rights organizations. SNCC leaders put themselves in danger in areas where the KKK was unfettered and where

▲ "We shall Overcome" button from the SNCC

African Americans had been under the political, legal and economic rule of white Americans since the end of Reconstruction. White and African American residents lived in a white supremacist society where the violent suppression of African Americans was commonplace. Unlike cities easily accessible to the national press, rural Mississippi, Alabama and Georgia were out of the spotlight; the publicity that worked in Montgomery, Little Rock, Greensboro and Nashville would not help register African American voters or elevate African American political and economic power in the Deep South's "**Black Belt**".

Black Belt

The rural areas of the Deep South in which African Americans comprised a majority of the population.

The organizing meeting took place in Raleigh, North Carolina. The first office was located in Atlanta, Georgia, within SCLC headquarters. It was Ella Baker who prompted the SCLC to sponsor the Southwide Youth Leadership Conference on 15–17 April at Shaw University, which was attended by 200 college students. Baker was a 56-year-old veteran civil rights activist, a committed and gifted community organizer who had served as an NAACP staffer. She traveled to communities large and small in the South, visiting churches, homes and farms to recruit members and train field organizers, and became the NAACP Director of Branches in 1943. Baker joined the newly formed SCLC in 1957 as its first staff member. She served as its interim director for more than two years, catalyzing and organizing many SCLC activities. However, Baker chafed at the hierarchy and limits of the organization's structure. The SCLC leadership, including Martin Luther King, Jr., hoped the SNCC would become the youth wing of SCLC. Conversely, Baker wanted the Civil Rights Movement to be led from below, not from the top, and in the energy and optimism of the college students who led scores of sit-ins in early 1960, she saw opportunity. The SNCC immediately became an independent organization.

Under the leadership of James Lawson of Vanderbilt University and Marion Barry of Fisk University, the SNCC dedicated itself to the philosophy and methodology of non-violent direct action and the Beloved Community. Other members included James Farmer, John Lewis, Diane Nash and Charles Sherrod. The first major action taken by the SNCC was to combine with CORE to organize the Freedom Rides. After the first ride ended in violence, Nash, from Fisk University in Nashville, Tennessee, took the lead, resolving to complete the rides, which involved many students having to leave college just before exams. Nash forcefully, but politely, ignored pleas from the Kennedy administration to cease, and became the unofficial leader of the new Freedom Riders. On the rides, the students were attacked and jailed, but they did not waver. The courage demonstrated by the Freedom Riders motivated many other students to join the SNCC.

The primary focus of the SNCC in its early years was voter registration. In 1961, Bob Moses, like Baker committed to grassroots organizing, came to the Black Belt of Mississippi. He became the director of the SNCC's Freedom Summer project to register African American voters. Often living in the communities they operated in, SNCC workers and volunteers faced continual violence. However, they also overcame residents' fears of outsiders by listening and following advice, and learning the local customs. African Americans who offered a bed or a meal to these volunteers, or even evidenced an interest in voting, faced severe economic and physical reprisals, including death. Nonetheless, the "One Man, One Vote" campaigns continued.

The SNCC worked with the Council of Federated Organizations (COFO) to organize and participate in Freedom Summer. Its activities prompted the establishment of the Mississippi Freedom Democratic Party (MFDP) and its oldest field organizer, Fannie Lou Hamer, became the MFDP spokesperson. After Freedom Summer, SNCC workers continued voter registration efforts in Mississippi, Georgia, Arkansas, Virginia, South Carolina, Texas and Alabama. The SNCC was a major organizer of the Selma voter registration efforts and the Selma to Montgomery March.

The SNCC did involve itself in cities, too. It organized the Albany Movement to end discrimination in transportation and public facilities, and participated in the March on Washington. SNCCs Chairman John Lewis was involved in the most well-known controversy. Scheduled to speak, the 23-year-old Lewis was, like much of the SNCC's membership, highly critical of what they saw as the Kennedy administration's weak efforts on behalf of equal rights. Lewis, beaten in the first Freedom Ride and arrested more than twenty times, prepared a speech that voiced his objections. He was persuaded to tone down his remarks by A Philip Randolph. His address still made his anger clear, stating that the federal government was *"dominated by politicians who build their careers on immoral compromises and ally themselves with open forms of political, economic, and social exploitation"* (1963). He told the nation that, African Americans *"do not want to be free gradually, We want our freedom and we want it now"*. The young SNCC Chairman closed, urging African Americans to *"stay in the streets of every city, every village and every hamlet of this nation … until the unfinished revolution of 1776 is complete"*.

The SNCC continued its work, but as white supremacist violence continued into the mid-1960s many SNCC activists became disillusioned with non-violence. A major division exposed itself during James Meredith's March Against Fear in 1966, when Stokely Carmichael, a veteran of the Freedom Rides, Parchman Prison and a field organizer for the SNCC, decided he had had enough of being beaten and arrested. When released from jail, he gave his first "Black Power" speech. The same year, the SNCC began to exclude white Americans from some activities and within a year white Americans were expelled and non-violence reduced from an organizing philosophy to a tactic. In 1968, the *N* in SNCC no longer represented *Nonviolent*, but instead stood for *National*, and within two years the SNCC ceased to exist, superseded by the Black Panther Party (BPP).

▲ SNCC Chairman John Lewis, 1964

Rising from the energy, courage and activism of college students, the SNCC was a major force in the Civil rights Movement. Its foundational basis was grassroots organizing, unique among the major civil rights organizations. The SNCC was involved with many major campaigns and events, and its actions resulted in changes in interstate transportation, public facilities, voting rights, numbers of African American elected officials and major federal legislation.

The Nation of Islam (NOI)

With Malcolm X as its nationally recognised spokesperson and charismatic leaders such as Louis Farrakhan, the Nation of Islam's emphasis on Africanism, African identity, racial separatism, righteous living as understood through Islam, economic self-reliance and self-governance made the organization an important force in the civil rights struggle, especially in the urban centres of the North during the late 1950s and 1960s.

The Nation of Islam (NOI) was founded by Wallace D Fard (also known as Fard Muhammad) of Detroit, Michigan, in 1930. Fard was a traveling fabric salesman who combined Black nationalism with an unorthodox interpretation of Islam. The NOI was largely a fringe group during its early years. Fard disappeared in 1934 and Elijah Muhammad took over NOI's leadership. NOI holds that there is no God but Allah, but that Fard Muhammad is the Messiah. The religion teaches that the Black race lived in paradise until Yacub, an evil scientist, created the "white devil", who would rule the earth for 6,000 years.

The NOI was founded to prepare and educate African Americans (Original People) for the struggle to take back the Earth and make it a peaceful paradise again. Under Elijah Muhammad, NOI founded private schools to educate young African Americans in its teachings, because NOI believed that public schools, in the North as well as in the South, were designed to preserve white supremacy. These schools were sometimes harassed by police. The Fruit of Islam (FOI) was created to protect schools and mosques. Muhammad also travelled to various northern cities, setting up NOI mosques. During the 1930s and 1940s, NOI adherents numbered in the hundreds. Followers also visited prisons to spread their faith. It was in prison that Malcolm Little converted to the Nation of Islam and became Malcolm X.

The rise in popularity of the NOI coincides with Malcolm X's time as a minister and its principal spokesperson. From a membership of under 1,000 in 1952, the number of NOI followers increased to reach between 100,000 and 300,000 by the time Malcolm X left the NOI in 1964. The Olympic boxing champion Cassius Clay converted to NOI and took the name Muhammad Ali. The NOI's teachings struck a chord in the midst of increasingly visible white-on-black violence in the years 1954–1965. Its message that racial separatism was necessary for African Americans to gain rights and economic status and stability differed significantly from every other civil rights organization at the time. The lack of government support for civil rights and economic opportunity for African Americans only served to give credence to NOI's message of the "white devil". Also, NOI advocated forceful self-defence, dismissing the concept of the Beloved Community and non-violence.

During the period 1954–1965, NOI differed from mainstream civil rights organizations in another way, too, in that it did not run campaigns to gain voting rights or integrate facilities. Rather it focused on growth, recruitment and spreading its doctrine. Louis Farrakhan joined the organization in 1955, becoming its second most effective speaker. Farrakhan was seen and heard speaking at Mosque No 7 in New York in 1959, in the television special *The Hate That Hate Produced*. The broadcast showed Farrakhan emphatically condemning white Americans:

> *I charge the white man with being the greatest liar on earth! … I charge the white man, ladies and gentlemen of the jury, with being the greatest murderer on earth. I charge the white man with being the greatest*

peace-breaker on earth ... I charge the white man with being the greatest deceiver on earth. I charge the white man with being the greatest troublemaker on earth. So therefore, ladies and gentlemen of the jury, I ask you, bring back a verdict of guilty as charged!

— Farrakhan, 1959

The message repelled white liberals who had supported the Civil Rights Movement and was widely seen as an affront to the integrated natures of the NAACP, SCLC, CORE and SNCC, each of which had been integrated from its inception.

Malcolm X, as well as belittling integrationist civil rights leaders for at best misleading their followers, spoke eloquently for African American separatism. The following excerpts from his June 1963 speech, "The Black Revolution", illustrate Malcolm X's powerful rhetoric and the NOI's objections to the civil rights initiatives of the time:

God wants us to separate ourselves from this wicked white race here in America because this American House of Bondage is number one on God's list for divine destruction today. I repeat: This American House of Bondage is number one on God's list for divine destruction today. He warns us to remember Noah never taught integration, Noah taught separation; Moses never taught integration, Moses taught separation. The innocent must always be given a chance to separate themselves from the guilty before the guilty are executed. No one is more innocent than the poor, blind American so-called Negro who has been led astray by blind Negro leaders, and no one on earth is more guilty than the blue-eyed white man who has used his control and influence over the Negro leader to lead the rest of our people astray....

I must point out that The Honorable Elijah Muhammad says a desegregated theater, a desegregated lunch counter won't solve our problem. Better jobs won't even solve our problems. An integrated cup of coffee isn't sufficient pay for four hundred years of slave labor. He also says that a better job, a better job in the white man's factory, or a better job in the white man's business, or a better job in the white man's industry or economy is, at best, only a temporary solution. He says that the only lasting and permanent solution is complete separation on some land that we can call our own.

— Malcolm X, 1963

The NOI was criticized by other civil rights leaders and groups as being all talk and little action. Malcolm X even commented in his autobiography, *"It could be heard increasingly in the Negro communities: 'Those Muslims talk tough, but they never do anything, unless somebody bothers Muslims'"* (1965). However, civic action was not a part of Elijah Muhammad's apolitical stance: NOI was a religious organization, not a civil rights group.

The NOI's message of African American separatism and nationalism became more popular in the late 1960s and early 1970s. The assassination of Martin Luther King, Jr., amid continuing violence, left many African American leaders and activists questioning whether the goal of integration was a valid one. The Black Power movement and the Black Panther Party both espoused self-defence, black nationalism, and African American self-reliance. The influence of its leading spokesperson, Malcolm X, continued to grow long after his death, as evidenced by the popularity and impact of his autobiography and Spike Lee's biographical film.

Source skills

Source A

An excerpt from Malcolm X's 1963 speech "The Black Revolution."

I charge the white man with being the greatest liar on earth! ... I charge the white man, ladies and gentlemen of the jury, with being the greatest murderer on earth. I charge the white man with being the greatest peace breaker on earth ... I charge the white man with being the greatest robber on earth. I charge the white man with being the greatest deceiver on earth. I charge the white man with being the greatest troublemaker on earth. So therefore, ladies and gentlemen of the jury, I ask you, bring back a verdict of guilty as charged!

Source B

An excerpt from Martin Luther King, Jr.'s speech "I Have a Dream."

There are those who are asking the devotees of civil rights, "When will you be satisfied?" We can never be satisfied as long as the Negro is the victim of the unspeakable horrors of police brutality. We can never be satisfied as long as our bodies, heavy with the fatigue of travel, cannot gain lodging in the motels of the highways and the hotels of the cities. *We cannot be satisfied as long as the negro's basic mobility is from a smaller ghetto to a larger one. We can never be satisfied as long as our children are stripped of their self-hood and robbed of their dignity by signs stating: "For Whites Only." We cannot be satisfied as long as a Negro in Mississippi cannot vote and a Negro in New York believes he has nothing for which to vote. No, no, we are not satisfied, and we will not be satisfied until "justice rolls down like waters, and righteousness like a mighty stream."[1]

Third question – 6 marks

Compare and contrast the views that Sources (A) and (B) express about treatment of African Americans by whites.

Examiner's hint:

Some of the points that you may consider are listed below. Make sure to write one paragraph of contrast and one of comparison. Make sure to use specific evidence from the sources. You can also write about tone and method. Even though the hints and markschemes are in bullet form, you must write in prose.

Comparisons:

- Both are speeches by civil rights leaders using the rhetorical device of repetition and parallel structure

- Both cite violence, Source A calling white people murders and Source B citing "police brutality."

- Source A states that white people are robbers and Source B states that African Americans have been robbed of their dignity.

- Both sources evoke a demand for justice. Source A requests a "verdict of guilty" while Source B says that African Americans "will not be satisfied until "justice rolls down like waters."

Contrasts:

- Source A focuses on general charges against white people while Source B focuses on the conditions of African Americans.

- Source B lists specific circumstances that link to unequal treatment such as lack ability to get a hotel room, while Source B does not.

- Source A calls for justice in a guilty verdict of all white people, while Source B allows for justice with satisfaction of changed conditions.

Or

- Source B condemns all white people while Source B does not state or imply that white people as a whole are at fault.

For further hints, consult the Paper 1 question 3 markbands on page 10.

Full document: Freedom Summer: Mississippi Summer Project

Source A

Robert Moses, a long-time voting rights activist and SNCC field secretary, discussed the some of the reasoning for the Mississippi Freedom Democratic Party in a 1986 interview for the series *Eyes on the Prize*.

INTERVIEWER: SO FOR THOSE PEOPLE WHO DON'T KNOW VERY MUCH ABOUT THIS WHOLE PROJECT HOW, TELL ME MORE ABOUT IT, MORE CONCRETE IN TERMS OF...

Robert Moses: All right, I remember one thing that changed Jim Foreman's mind about the summer project, was the response that he began to get in the friends of SNCC offices to the summer project in the sense that a lot of support was flowing into the offices around the students. That is not only were the students coming down but they were beginning to mobilize and to help mobilize around the country a support effort. One in terms of medical support, we had a whole organization of doctors who came down to Mississippi. Alvin Poussant, headed up that service. Doctors began to explore all the medical conditions in Mississippi. Open clinics, built health stations. Work that has continued till this day. The lawyers. Around the effort on the summer project they organized groups of lawyers... Lawyers from all over the country came down and began to work on the segregation statutes of Mississippi and began to file suits opening up various restaurants, all the public accommodations in Mississippi under the 1964 civil rights act. Church people. Bob Spike with the national council of churches had organized the Mississippi/Delta project and they began to send down church people, some of whom are there to this day, who took part in community organizing and took part in the summer project. The Free Southern Theater. Gil Moses and John O'Neil organized the Free Southern Theater, right there in Mississippi in the context of the Mississippi summer project.

Source B

Robert Weisbrot, a Professor of History at Colby College, explains how the State of Mississippi prepared for Freedom Summer in his book *Freedom Bound: A History of America's Civil Rights Movement* (1990)

Mississippi mobilized for the arrival of civil rights workers as if threatened by a foreign army. Governor Paul Johnson won legislative approval of an increase in the number of state highway patrolmen from 275 to 475. In Jackson the police force grew from 200 to 390 officers. Mayor Allen Thompson bought 250 shotguns and had them loaded with buckshot and mounted on squad cars and motorcycles. The mayor also readied his "Thompson tank," a sis-ton armored vehicle complete with 12-guage steel walls, bulletproof windows, and a submachine gun mounted on the turret. As a final precaution, the state enacted a "bill to restrain movements of individuals under certain circumstances," a euphemism for declaring martial law.

Source C

Clayborne Carson, Professor of History at Stanford University, explains the organizing idea of the Summer Project in his 1981 book *In Struggle: SNCC and the Black Awakening of the 1960s.*

The plans for the Summer Project reflected both SNCC's past development as a protest group and its emergence as a cadre of radical community organizers. SNCC prepared for a decisive test of its integrationist orientation by seeking to mobilize white liberal support outside the South. The complex mixture of idealism and realism that guided preparations for the summer was evident in a prospectus for the project written during the spring. "A large number of students from the North making the necessary sacrifices to go South would make abundantly clear to the government and the public that this is not a situation which can be ignored any longer, and would project an image of cooperation between Northern and white people and Southern Negro people to the nation which will reduce fears of an impending race war." The goal of the project would be to force either Mississippi officials to change their policies or "the federal government to intervene on behalf of the constitutional rights of its citizens."...The project also aimed "to develop and strengthen a home-grown freedom movement that will survive after the 1,000 visitors leave."

Source D

Photographer Steve Schapiro took this photograph of the Mississippi Summer Project students being trained in Oxford, Ohio in 1964 while preparing for potential brutality when working to open Freedom Schools and register African American voters.

First question, part a – 3 marks

According to Source B, how did support increase during Freedom Summer?

First question, part b – 2 marks

What message is conveyed by Source D?

Second question – 4 marks

With reference to its origin, purpose and content, analyze the value and limitations of Source C for a historian studying the goals for Freedom Summer.

Third question – 6 marks

Compare and contrast the Sources B and C on preparations for Freedom Summer.

Fourth question – 9 marks

Using the sources and your own knowledge, assess the reasons for and effectiveness of the Mississippi Summer Project (Freedom Summer).

References and further reading

For historical debate about the Civil Rights Movement see:

Steven F Lawson and Charles Payne, *Debating the Civil Rights Movement, 1945–1968*, Lanham: Rowman & Littlefield Publishers, Inc, 1998.

For a definitive study of 1963–1965 see:

Taylor Branch, *Pillar of Fire: America in the King Years: 1963–1965*, New York: Simon & Schuster, 1998.

For selections from Taylor Branch's trilogy of the Civil Rights Movement see:

Taylor Branch, *The King Years: Historic Moments in the Civil Rights Movement*, New York: Simon & Schuster, 2013.

For an important history of Malcolm X see:

Malcolm X, *The Autobiography of Malcolm X: As Told to Alex Haley*, New York: Ballantine Publishing Group, 1965 & 1999.

For an important autobiography of a major figure of the Civil Rights Movement see:

Ralph David Abernathy, *And the Walls Came Tumbling Down*, New York: Harper & Row, 1989.

For a study on the Student Non-Violent Coordinating Committee see:

Clayborne Carson, *In Stuggle: SNCC and the Black Awakening of the 1960's*, Cambridge: Howard University Press, 1981 & 1995.

For a comprehensive study of the Civil Rights Movement in Mississippi see:

Charles M Payne, *I've Got the Light of Freedom: The Organizing Tradition and the Mississippi Freedom Struggle*, Berkeley: University of California Press, 1995.

For a study of the events leading up to the Civil Rights Act of 1965 see:

Clay Risen, *The Bill of the Century: The Epic Battle for the Civil Rights Act*, New York: Bloomsbury Press, 2014.

For information on the Southern judges in the aftermath of the Brown Decision see:

Jack Bass, *Unlikely Heroes: The Dramatic Story of the Southern Judges who Translated the Supreme Court's Brown Decision into a Revlolution for Equality*, New York: Simon & Schuster, 1981.

Writing the internal assessment for IB History

"Doing history": Thinking like a historian

The **internal assessment (IA)** is an engaging, inquiry-based **2200 word investigation** that provides teachers and students with the opportunity to personalize their learning. You will select, research and write on a historical topic of individual interest or curiosity.

The IA is an essential component of the IB History course. Students in both standard level (25%) and higher level (20%) will complete the same task as part of their course mark. Your teacher will evaluate your final draft, but only a small, random sample of your class' IAs will be submitted to the IB for moderation.

The purpose of the historical investigation is to engage students in the process of thinking like historians and "doing history" by creating their own questions, gathering and examining evidence, analyzing perspectives, and demonstrating rich historical knowledge in the conclusions they draw. Given its importance, your teacher should provide considerable time, guidance, practice of skills and feedback throughout the process of planning, drafting, revising and submitting a final

copy of the IA. In total, completing the IA should take **approximately 20 hours**. This chapter is designed to give both students and teachers some guidance for approaching these tasks.

What does the IA look like?

The IA is **divided into three main sections**. Each of these sections will be explained and approached in more detail later in this chapter. Below is an overview of each section:

1. Identification and evaluation of sources (6 marks)

- Clearly state the topic in the form of an appropriate inquiry question.

- Explain the nature and relevance of two of the sources selected for more detailed analysis of values and limitations with reference to origins, purpose and content.

2. Investigation (15 marks)

- Using appropriate format and clear organization, provide critical analysis that is focused on the question under investigation.

- Include a range of evidence to support an argument and analysis, and a conclusion drawn from the analysis.

3. Reflection (4 marks)

- Reflect on the process of investigating your question and discuss the methods used by historians, and the limitations or challenges of investigating their topic.

Your history teachers can use the IA for whatever purposes best suit the school context, syllabus design or the individual learning of students. Nevertheless, you should be encouraged to select and develop your own question. The IA can be started at any point during the course, however the task is most effectively introduced after students have been exposed to some purposeful teaching and practice in historical methods, analysis and writing skills.

The IA is designed to assess each of the following History objectives:

Assessment objective 1: Knowledge and understanding

- Demonstrate understanding of historical sources.

Assessment objective 2: Application and analysis

- Analyse and interpret a variety of sources.

Assessment objective 3: Synthesis and evaluation

- Evaluate sources as historical evidence, recognizing their value and limitations.
- Synthesize information from a selection of relevant sources.

Assessment objective 4: Use and application of appropriate skills

- Reflect on the methods used by, and challenges facing, the historian.
- Formulate an appropriate, focused question to guide a historical inquiry.
- Demonstrate evidence of research skills, organization, referencing and selection of appropriate sources.

Beginning with the end in mind: what does success look like?

ATL Self-management skills

Throughout the process of planning, researching, drafting and revising your investigation, you should be continually checking the criteria. Ask your teacher and other students to provide specific feedback using the criteria. Continually ask yourself if your work meets the criteria.

Before getting started, you should look carefully at the assessment criteria to appreciate what each section of the IA demands. Teachers will **use the same criteria for both SL and HL**. It is important to have a clear understanding of what success will look like before you invest the time and hard work that this task will require. Teachers will use the criterion found in the IB History Guide to provide feedback to teachers and to assess the final draft. The assessment is based on "positive achievement", meaning that teachers will try to find the best fit according to the descriptors in each criterion. Students do not have to write a perfect paper to achieve the highest descriptors, and teachers should not think in terms of pass/fail based on whether scores are above or below 50% of the 25 marks in total.

To simplify the criterion and to provide some fixed targets for what success looks like, consider using the assessment tool provided on the next page.

Teacher, Peer and Self-Assessment Tool

Criterion A: Identification and evaluation of sources (6 marks)

Suggested word count: 500

Criteria for success	Strengths	Improvements needed
• Does the investigation have an **appropriate question clearly stated?**		
• Has the student selected, identified, and referenced (using a consistent format) **appropriate and relevant sources?**		
• Is there a **clear explanation of the relevance** of the sources to the investigation?		
• Is there detailed analysis and evaluation **of two sources** with explicit discussion of the **value and limitations**, with reference to their **origins, purpose and content?**		

Criterion B: Investigation (15 marks)

Suggested word count: 1,300

Criteria for success	Strengths	Improvements needed
• Is the investigation **clear, coherent and effectively organized?**		
• Does the investigation contain **well-developed critical analysis clearly focused on the stated question?**		
• Is there evidence from a **range of sources** used effectively to **support an argument?**		
• Is there **evaluation of different perspectives** (arguments, claims, experiences etc.) on the topic and/or question?		
• Does the investigation provide a **reasoned conclusion** that is **consistent with the evidence and arguments provided?**		

Criterion C: Reflection (4 marks)

Suggested word count: 400

Criteria for success	Strengths	Improvements needed
• Does the student **focus clearly** on what the investigation revealed about the **methods used by historians?**		
• Does the reflection demonstrate clear **awareness of the challenges** facing historians and/or the **limitations of the methods** used by historians?		
• Is there an **explicit connection** between the reflection and the rest of the investigation (question, sources used, evaluation and analysis)?		

Bibliography & formatting (no marks applicable)

Suggested word count: Not included in total

Criteria for success	Strengths	Improvements needed
• Is the **word count clearly stated** on the cover? (2200 maximum)		
• Is a single bibliographic style or format **consistently used**?		
• Is the bibliography **clearly organized** and **include all the sources** you have referenced or used as evidence in the investigation?		

Getting started: Approaches to learning history

Ideally, you will have opportunities throughout the IB History course to explore and develop understandings about the methods and the nature of history. This will prepare you to better develop the skills necessary for the IA and the other assessment papers in the IB History course. Additionally, these kinds of learning activities provide clear links to TOK.

- Debate controversial historical events and claims.

- Compare and corroborate conflicting sources of evidence.

- Take on, role play or defend different perspectives or experiences of an event.

- Discuss the value and limitations of historian's arguments and evidence.

- Develop criteria for selecting and comparing historical sources.

- Gather and analyze a variety of different kinds of sources (photos, artwork, journal entries, maps, etc.) focused on the same event or issue.

- Co-develop good questions and carry out an investigation of a historical event as a entire class.

- Read an excerpt from a historian's work and identify which parts are analysis, evidence and narrative.

If students better understand that history is more than simply memorizing and reporting on facts, dates and chronological narratives, then they are more likely to be curious, engaged and motivated learners of history. Accordingly, they will more likely develop appropriate questions for their investigation and have a better understanding of how to organize and write effective analysis.

Selecting a topic and appropriate questions

Once you have some general understanding of the IA components and are familiar with the assessment criteria, it is time to select a topic focus. Students often do not know how to begin selecting a topic. Identify a historical topic of interest and get to know it well by conducting some background reading from a general history textbook or an online encyclopaedia. You may find some information that will help you narrow the topic focus quickly. These kinds of sources often outline the differing perspectives, interpretations and controversies that make for an engaging investigation. Well-written textbooks and articles will also include references, annotated bibliographies and footnotes of additional, more detailed sources that will help in the research stage.

After selecting a topic, formulating an appropriate research question can also be very challenging. It is essential that you take the time to carefully think about what kinds of topics help produce good questions for investigations. Before you begin any writing, **you should submit a proposal** to your teacher to ensure that the investigation will be successful.

Some teachers recommend that students write about a topic related to their course syllabus, but there are a countless number of possible topics and you are better off choosing topics that interest you and motivate you to learn. The topic must be historical however, so students **may not investigate any topic that happened within the last ten years.** All investigations will take one of three forms:

1 **An investigation of a historical theme, issue, person or event based on a variety of sources.**

2 **An investigation based on fieldwork of a historical building, place or site.**

3 **An investigation of a local history.**

When selecting a historical topic, students often fail to select a topic that is manageable. For example, examining all of the causes of the Second World War is too broad for the purposes of a 2200 word investigation. Many students also select topics that cannot be researched in depth because there are not enough readily available primary and/or secondary sources.

Investigating a historically-themed film or piece of literature can be very engaging; but many students write better papers when they focus the investigation on a particular claim, portrayal or perspective contained in the work, rather than the entire work itself. Students who choose to investigate a historical site, or to investigate local or community history, often have an opportunity to engage in experiences that are more authentic to the work of professional historians, but these can also produce a lot of challenges when looking for sources. Whatever the topic that you select, it is essential to formulate a good question.

One of the most common errors students make when planning and writing the IA is formulating a poor question about their topic. Formulating a good question is essential for success and helps ensure that the IA is a manageable and researchable investigation. Consider the following criteria when formulating a good question:

1 The question is researchable.	• *There is an adequate variety and availability of sources related to your topic.* • *The sources are readable, available and in a language that is accessible.*
2 The question is focused.	• *Questions that are vague or too broad make it difficult to write a focused investigation limited to 2200 words.* • *Questions that are too broad make it difficult to manage the number of sources needed to adequately address the topic.*
3 The question is engaging	• *Interesting, controversial or challenging historical problems make better questions.* • *Questions with obvious answers (i.e. Did economic factors play a role in Hitler's rise to power?) do not make good investigations.*

Using the concepts to formulate good questions

The IB History course is focused on **six key concepts: change, continuity, causation, consequence, significance and perspectives**. Each of these concepts shape historians' thinking about the kinds of questions they ask and investigate. Therefore, they are helpful to students as a framework for formulating good IA questions. Using the historical thinking concepts, you may be able to generate several good questions about any historical topic that can be eventually focused into successful investigations.

Concepts	Possible investigation prompts

Student's topic

change
- What changes resulted from this topic?
- To what extent did this event, person or issue cause change?

continuity
- To what extent did the topic remain the same?
- Did this event, person or issue cause progress or decline?

causation
- What were the long term, short term and immediate causes?
- What were the factors that caused the event related to the topic?

consequence
- How has this topic had immediate and long-lasting effects?
- How significant were the effects of this topic?

significance
- To what extent is this topic significant? Is the significance of this topic justified?
- What events, people or issues are important to know about this topic?

perspectives
- What different perspectives or interpretations are there about this topic?
- How did people experience this topic?

To illustrate, a student interested in the Russian Revolution might use the concepts to brainstorm the following possible investigations:

Change: *In what ways did the Russian Revolution change Russian society?*

Continuity: *To what extent did Stalin's regime resemble the Tsarist system?*

Causation: *How significant were long term factors in causing the February Revolution?*

Consequence: *To what extent did Stalin's purges affect military preparedness?*

Significance: *How important was Lenin's role in the October Revolution?*

Perspectives: *To what extent did Doctor Zhivago capture the experience of upper class Russians during the Revolution?*

After generating some possible questions, students can bring greater focus to their topic. For example, a student interested in how women experienced Stalinism may narrow the focus to a particular place or event. A student investigating long-term causes of an event may have more success if the question is focused on the significance of a specific, singular cause. For good examples of historical questions, you should consult past Paper 2 or Paper 3 examination questions.

You should notice that many of the questions above include more than one concept. Most good historical investigations will require students to think about perspectives because there will likely be multiple accounts of the issue under investigation, or there will be some controversy between historians. Here are some question exemplars showing how they capture more than one key historical concepts:

- *How significant was Allied area bombing in reducing German industrial capacity during the Second World War? (significance; consequence)*

- *To what extent did Gandhi's leadership achieve Indian independence? (significance; perspectives; causation)*

All successful IAs begin with a well-developed, thoughtful and focused question that is based on one or more of the historical concepts.

Categorize the following questions (Good – Needs Improvement – Poor) according to their suitability as a historical investigation according to the criteria provided above. Suggest ways the questions might be improved.

1   Which Second World War film is the most accurate?

2   To what extent did nationalism play a role in causing the First World War?

3   How did women win the right to vote in the United States?

4   Did Hitler use film for propaganda?

5   In what ways did Stalin start the Cold War?

6   To what extent was the influenza epidemic a factor in the collapse of the Central Powers in 1918?

Common problems when selecting a topic and question:

- Poorly focused question – too broad and unmanageable.
- Obvious question.
- Question is not researchable.

Getting organized: making a plan of investigation

ATL Self-management skills

Create your own plan for completion with target dates and goals. Submit this with your proposed topic and question. Include some initial sources of information you will use.

Completing the IA successfully requires that students **create a plan for completion** that includes several important steps of the inquiry process. Some of the steps may overlap, but it is important that you organize your tasks and stay on track for completion by setting goals and due dates. Your teacher should read at least one draft and give some feedback to ensure that the IA is not plagiarised. A plan of investigation should include the following steps:

1 Planning	• Select a topic and formulate a question.
	• Submit a proposal to your teacher.
	• Identify information sources.

2 Researching	• Gather information sources and evidence.
	• Carefully read and evaluate information.
3 Organizing and processing	• Create notes.
	• Record references using a standard citation format.
	• Create a bibliography.
	• Organize ideas into an outline.
	• Formulate an argument.
4 Drafting	• Write each section of the IA.
	• Revise and edit.
	• Check assessment criteria.
5 Sharing	• Submit a draft for feedback.
6 Revising	• Revise based on feedback from your teacher.
7 Publishing	• Submit final copy to your teacher.
	• Evaluate using criteria.

Getting organized: researching

ATL Communication skills

When supporting historical claims, it is important to make your evidence visible to your reader. Make sure you use a standard bibliographic format to show the reader where your evidence was found. In the discipline of history, the University of Chicago style or MLA style is most commonly used because it provides significant information about the origins of the source, and the endnotes or footnotes format allows the historian to insert additional information about the source where necessary.

Take good notes during the research stage. Post-it notes are helpful to record thoughts and ideas next to key passages as you read and think about the information in relation to the question. Using different coloured highlighters to identify different perspectives on the question as you read can also be helpful. If using borrowed books, take a photo of important pages on a tablet device and use a note taking application to highlight and write notes on the page. Students who make their thinking visible as they read will have a easier time writing later in the process. Create a timeline of the event you are researching to ensure the chronology is clear in your mind.

It is strongly recommended that you record the bibliographic information and page numbers where you find important evidence and analysis. Many students wait until the very end of the writing process to compile their bibliography, but this is much more easily accomplished if the information is recorded throughout, instead of as an afterthought when the draft is finished. There are several easily accessible web sites that provide the most up-to-date versions of **MLA** (www.mla.org), and **Chicago Manual of Style** (www.chicagomanualofstyle.org), which are the two most common formats used for bibliographies in university history departments.

Common problems when planning and organizing an IA:

- Lack of general background knowledge of the topic.
- No feedback on proposed topic and question.
- No plan for completion.
- Inaccurately recording page numbers and references.
- Poorly organized notes; or no notes at all.

Internal Assessment skills

Create a proposal for the IA using the template shown.

Topic:	Student:
Research question:	
Proposed sources:	
Sources (2) proposed for evaluation in Section A:	

Section A: Identification and evaluation of sources

Section A is worth 6 of the 25 total marks. It is recommended that the word count does not exceed much more than 500 words. While this section does not count for a substantial portion of the marks, most students will not be successful without a strong Section A. There are three key aspects of this section.

1   **Clearly state the topic of the investigation. (This must be stated as a question).**

2   **Include a brief explanation of the two sources the student has selected for detailed analysis, and a brief explanation of their relevance to the investigation.**

3   **With reference to their origins, purpose and content, analyse the value and limitations of the two sources.**

Common problems with Section A:

- Question is not clearly stated.
- Relevance or significance of selected sources not explained.
- Student summarizes the content of selected sources.
- Limited analysis.
- Discussion of origins, purpose and content is in isolation to value and limitations.
- Poorly chosen sources.
- Speculates vaguely about the values and limitations of sources.
- Reference to origins, purpose and content is not explicit.

Thinking about evidence: origins, purpose, value and limitations

Because it is built on a foundation of evidence, history is by nature interpretive and controversial.

This is not something many people understand – to them history is simply a long list of dates and dead people. While there are a great many things historians agree upon, there are countless historical questions that are enshrouded in debate and controversy. Since relatively few people personally witness the events they study, how one understands the past depends largely on which sources of evidence are used, and how they are interpreted. Even facts that historians generally agree upon can change over time. Philosopher Ambrose Bierce once said, *"God alone knows the future, but only a historian can alter the past."* Though the past cannot actually be changed, historical memory and understanding is always changing as each generation brings forward new questions, new evidence and new perspectives. This process of changing historical interpretations is referred to as **revisionism**. Revisionist historians are those who challenge **orthodox**, or generally accepted arguments and interpretations.

Besides revisionism, another reason why history is controversial is that accounts or evidence from the same events can differ drastically. People record events from different **origins and perspectives**, and for different **purposes**. Historical evidence might come from a limitless number of possible kinds of sources. Sources that all originate from the same time and place that we are investigating are typically referred to as **primary sources**. The interpretations and narratives that we find in documentaries, articles and books created by historians are called **secondary sources**.

Students often make the error of thinking that primary sources are more authentic and reliable, and therefore have more **value**, and fewer **limitations** than secondary sources. This isn't always the case. Being there does not necessarily give greater insight into events, and indeed, sometimes the opposite is true. Historians can look at events from multiple perspectives and use a wide range of evidence not available to the eyewitness. Students often speculate that a primary source is valuable and significant to their investigation, but have poor reasons in support of this beyond the fact that it is a primary source.

It is important that you understand how to evaluate the value and limitations of sources with reference to the origins, purpose and content of the source. Discussing the origin, purpose and content outside the context of the value and limitations will result in a poor assessment.

Origins	• Where did the source come from?
	• Who wrote or created it?
	• Whose perspectives are represented? Whose are not?
Purpose	• Why was this created?
	• What purpose might this document have served?
Content	• What does the source mean?
	• What does it reveal or contain?
	• How useful is the information? Is it reasonable to believe it is accurate? Can it be corroborated?

Generally, the closer in proximity (place and time) the origin of a primary source is, the more **value** it has to historians. If students can find ways to **corroborate** (support, confirm) a source by other sources, then the source likely has greater value to the investigation. **Limitations** may include any factors that cause someone to question the truthfulness, validity or value of a source.

Keep in mind, that using the term **bias** is not always useful in history – it is important to be able to identify bias, but bias does not necessarily limit the value of a source. Students often make the error of assuming a source is unreliable because they detect bias. Remember that most people will have biased perspectives that are unique to their own experiences, time and place. This does not mean that you should blindly dismiss the evidence they offer us. You should ensure that you explain clearly how the bias affects the value of the content in the source used.

Internal Assessment skills

Use this template for taking notes from each of the sources used in the investigation.

Research Question:		
Source (bibliographic information):		
Primary or secondary source?	How is the source relevant/significant to the investigation?	Origins/Purpose? Value/Limitations?
Page#:	What evidence does the source provide? (quote, paraphrase, describe)	What is your interpretation? How does the content of the source relate to your question? What perspective does it add?

Selecting sources for the IA

One of the challenges to students writing a successful Section A is making sure that they choose two appropriate sources to evaluate. You should be able to clearly and effectively explain why the chosen sources are relevant and important to the investigation.

Often students make the mistake of relying too heavily on non-scholarly sources such as online encyclopaedia articles and general history textbooks. As stated, these are good starting points for finding a topic, but they are not good sources to build your investigation upon. They are especially poor choices to use for detailed analysis in this section. Before selecting sources consider the following:

- You will be expected to discuss as much detail about the origins and purpose of the source as possible. Be sure to choose sources where you can identify as much of the following as possible: when it was created; who created it; why it was created; where it was created. If much of this information is not readily identifiable, you will have difficulty evaluating value and limitations with explicit reference to the origins and purpose.

- Select sources or excerpts of sources that have clear significance to the question. You should be able to clearly, and explicitly explain why the content of the source is important to the investigation. Some students choose sources that are largely irrelevant or vaguely related to the question.

- The investigation should include an appropriate range of sources. As a general rule, you should include both primary and secondary sources, but this may not work with some types of investigations. While secondary sources on a topic are likely to be easily obtained, they often provide less to discuss in Section A. Interviews, personal correspondence, newspaper articles, journals, speeches, letters, and other primary sources often provide students with much more meaningful material to evaluate in Section A. Ideas about origins and purpose come more readily with primary sources than they might when using secondary sources which generally, but not always, strive to present balanced arguments and perspectives.

- Choose secondary sources that reference the evidence the historians used to support their arguments. You will find it less difficult to assess the validity of the evidence the historian uses, or how the evidence is interpreted in the arguments, if the historian has documented the evidence clearly.

- Consider using periodical articles. Many historians write excellent, concise articles on historical topics for peer-reviewed journals. These articles often have rich footnoting and bibliographies that you can use to find additional sources for the investigation.

- Be careful about relying too heavily on general web-based sources. Many online sources are not referenced or footnoted properly so it is difficult to validate information about the origins, purpose and authorship. On the other hand, a great number of rich primary sources can be found online, as well as articles written by respected historians.

- Consider using interviews. Some students have written exceptional IAs based on people's experiences, or by interviewing historians or other people with extensive knowledge and experience. When using interviews, record them as an audio file for reference and accuracy.

Analysing the selected sources

After stating the research question and explaining the two selected sources and their relevance to the investigation, the largest portion of Section A should focus on analysing the two sources. Depending on the sources chosen, they can be discussed simultaneously and comparatively, or they can be discussed separately. Discussing them separately is often more advantageous because you can make the origins, purpose, value and limitations more explicit.

- It is important that any arguments about the value and limitations make specific references to the content, origins and purpose.

- Be careful that the value of a source is not dismissed on the basis of bias without a strong argument about why the bias limits the validity or reliability of the content.

- You should avoid summarizing the content too much. Summarize and describe content only to the extent necessary to construct a strong analysis about the source's value and limitations.

- You should be thorough in examining all aspects of the source's origins including date of origin, cultural context, author's background, publisher or other important details. If little information about the origins is identifiable, it is likely a poorly chosen source for analysis.

Internal Assessment skills

Use the Section A assessment criteria to discuss and evaluate this excerpt of a student's work. Identify where the student has explicitly discussed origins and purpose, and value and limitations.

This investigation will seek to answer the question "What did the Tiananmen Square protest reveal about the democratic sentiments in China between 1980 and 1989?" Democratic sentiments are defined as people's attitudes toward democratic ideals. This investigation will analyze factors that influenced democratic sentiments from multiple perspectives, but will not assess the ethics and justification of the Chinese government's response to the protest.

In order to take into account the opposing views on this event and keep the scope of the investigation manageable, I have made use of a variety of carefully selected sources. Two primary sources will be evaluated …

Source 1: Prisoner of State: the secret journal of Zhao Ziyang[1]

The origin of the source is of great value because the author is Zhao Ziyang, the General Secretary of the Communist Party during the Tiananmen Square Protest (the Protest). Zhao attempted to use a non-violent approach to resolve the protest and spoke against the party's hardliners. After a power struggle, Zhao was dismissed and put under house arrest until his death in 2005. The content of the journal is translated from thirty audiotapes recorded secretly by Zhao while he was under house arrest between 1999 and 2000. The book is published in 2009 by Simon & Schuster, one of the largest and most reputable English-language publishers. The reputation of the author and publisher increases the reliability of this source.

Zhao's purpose for recording these tapes is to publicize his political opinions and express his regret for failing to prevent the massacre. This is valuable because Zhao was not allowed to publicize his opinions while under house arrest, so this source is the only surviving public record of Zhao's opinions and perspectives on the Protest. This source is also valuable because its author, Zhao, was directly involved in the government's decision-making process during the protest. It reveals the power struggle within the Communist Party through the lens of the progressive bloc.

However, its exclusivity may limit its value because there are no counterparts to compare with and to verify its claims. As a translated material, the source may not accurately present Zhao's intentions and may have lost some cultural expressions. In addition, this source may be biased in that Zhao speaks in favour of political reform and democracy, which does not represent the Party's position…

[1] Zhao, Ziyang, Pu Bao, Renee Chiang, Adi Ignatius, and Roderick MacFarquhar. *Prisoner of the state: the secret journal of Zhao Ziyang.* New York: Simon & Schuster, 2009.

Section B: Investigation

Common problems with Section B:

- Too much narrative.
- Poor referencing of sources.
- Limited awareness of different positions or perspectives.
- Listing of evidence instead of integrating analysis and evidence.
- Overuse of quotations.
- Plagiarism.
- Poor organization and arguments that are difficult to follow.
- Few connections to the question and purpose of the investigation.
- Conclusions are not evidence-based.

It is essential that you keep Section B focused on the purpose of the investigation and construct an argument using all of the sources you have listed in the bibliography. No marks are awarded for the bibliography, but an incomplete treatment of your sources, or inaccurate referencing will cost you marks in this section. **Evidence must be integrated** with **very clear critical commentary** that leads the reader to an eventual **evidence-based conclusion** that addresses the question posed in Section A. Students often make the error of simply listing facts they researched, without explaining how they are relevant or relate to their question. The following points should be considered when writing this section.

- The investigation should be carefully organized. The synthesis of evidence and critical commentary should be carefully planned to ensure that there is logic and flow to the section, and that your argument is very clear.

- The type of question you pose for the investigation will determine how you organize your writing. For example, a question that invites comparisons (for example: whether a film portrays an event accurately) will require you to discuss both similarities and differences. "To what extent" questions will require you to discuss both perspectives of "ways no" and "ways yes".

- As you gather evidence and document your thinking in your notes, keep in mind you may need to adjust or change your question. You should give some consideration to planning and writing Section B before writing Section A.

- Where appropriate, discuss different perspectives of the topic. Historians may offer different interpretations, or there may be multiple experiences of an event.

- Quotes should be used sparingly. Most of your writing should summarize and paraphrase the evidence collected and explain explicitly how it relates to the investigation. Too many student papers read as long lists of quotes from sources. Quotes must be explained, or integrated as evidence in support of an argument, and add something specifically and convincingly to your argument.

- Any references to sources, or ideas that are not your own, should be referenced appropriately using endnotes or footnotes. If this is not completed carefully, you risk plagiarizing others' ideas as your own.

- You should avoid writing significant amounts of narrative. Retelling a historical narrative or sequence of events is not the purpose of the investigation. On the other hand, you should demonstrate a clear understanding of the chronology and historical context of the events you are analyzing.

- Your conclusion is essential. The conclusion must offer possible answers or solutions to the question identified in Section A. It should not read simply as a summary of points, but rather as a well-reasoned, convincing, evidence-based closure to the investigation.

- There is no suggested number of appropriate sources required for your investigation. The number of sources you should use depends entirely on your topic and the kind of investigation you are doing. Local or community history, for example, might offer a limited numbers of sources. Interviews or community archives that this kind of IA might require could yield fewer, but very rich primary sources. Wherever possible your sources should be varied and specific, rather than few and general.

Submitting your bibliography

The bibliography – an **alphabetically ordered list of sources** – should be inserted at the very end of your paper. It is mentioned here with Section B because it should be created as part of the writing process, not simply thrown together at the last minute before submitting the paper. This bibliography is not worth any marks but it is an essential component of the paper that is often overlooked or poorly completed. Any sources referenced as evidence in Section B must be included in your bibliography.

Internal Assessment skills

Use the Section B assessment criteria to evaluate an excerpt of this student's investigation. Has the student effectively integrated evidence and critical commentary?

…Sentimentality played a key role in the events leading up to the protest in 1989. Western democracy and parliamentary system were believed to be the panacea for China's social problems. As Zhao Ziyang stated in his memoir: "in fact, it is the Western parliamentary democratic system that has demonstrated the most vitality. It seems that this system is currently the best one available."[1] The death of Hu Yaobang, the former General Secretary of the Party who advocated strongly for democratic reform, created a unified sense of democratic sentiments that united both ideological and practical groups.[2] Hu's successor, Zhao Ziyang, an even more progressive leader, spoke publicly in favour of political reform. Zhao's rise in power gave people an optimistic belief in democracy, and encouraged other progressives to act more openly.

However, contrary to the revolutionary attitudes later in the protest, the democratic sentiment under Zhao's leadership was relatively constructive. Based on the Seven Demands[3] drafted by the protesters, it was clear that, in the beginning of the Protest, protesters did not intend to be anti-governmental or anti-communist; they merely demanded that the Party take actions to end corruption and grant citizens more political freedom.[4] As the leading figure behind the Party's progressive bloc, Zhao was generally in line with the protestors. Internally, he attempted to persuade hardliner party officials, particularly Deng, into making concession with the protestors.[5] He also allowed the media, such as the People's Daily and the China Central Television to bypass censorship and broadcast the protest…

---

[1] Zhao, Ziyang, Pu Bao, Renee Chiang, Adi Ignatius, and Roderick MacFarquhar. "Preface." In *Prisoner of the state: the secret journal of Zhao Ziyang*. New York: Simon & Schuster, 2009. xv.

[2] Meaning the intellectuals and the working class.

[3] Liang, Zhang. "The Tiananmen Papers." The New York Times. https://www.nytimes.com/books/first/l/liang-tiananmen.html (accessed May 26, 2014).

[4] Ziyang, op. cit.

[5] Zhao, Dingxin. *The power of Tiananmen state-society relations and the 1989 Beijing student movement*. Chicago: University of Chicago Press, 2001. 156.

Section C: Reflection

In Section C (approx. 400 words) you have the opportunity to reflect on what the investigation revealed to you about the methods used by historians and the challenges they face when investigating topics like your own. This section is worth the fewest marks (4), but it could make the difference between a good and an outstanding paper. You should no doubt already have an understanding that the study of history is beset with a number of challenges and limitations, some of which have been discussed earlier in this chapter. Section A is designed to give you an opportunity to reflect on this understanding, but it must be focused specifically on the nature of your topic and/or the kind of investigation you undertook, rather than a reflection on the nature of history in general.

> Common problems with Section C:
> - Limited understanding of the nature of history and the challenges facing historians.
> - Limited understanding of the methods historians use to examine and study history.
> - Poorly focused on the challenges specific to the student's topic.

Throughout your IB History course, your TOK and History teachers should provide opportunities for you to think about and discuss the challenges of determining historical truth and understanding.

History can often be determined largely by who writes it, his or her purpose, and the methods he or she decides to use. Consider also that where there is scant evidence, historians often make very authoritative sounding **speculations** – essentially educated guesses – where they fill in gaps in the historical record with judgments they think are reasonable to believe. But often we cannot with absolute certainty verify or prove beyond doubt that their accounts are correct.

Many of the inherent challenges of history stem from problems related to its evidence-based nature. History is also challenging because of how it is used for so many different purposes including political slogans, national narratives, personal and group identity, entertainment, advertising and countless other ways. The past the historian studies is not a dead past. History is living, changing and visible in the present. Therefore, there is no shortage of questions to consider in your reflection section.

- What is history? Is it more creative and interpretive as opposed to scientific and objective?

- How did the nature of your investigation present specific challenges to finding reliable evidence?

- What methods did historians use? How were they limited by time and place? How are they limited by ideology or world views?

- Is it possible to capture the entirety of an event?

- What are the challenges of causation? How far back in time should the historian search for causes? Can immediate causes ever be separated from long term causes?

- How might national identity, cultural norms, values or beliefs affect one's ability to reason and arrive at an understanding of history?

- How might mass culture, the entertainment industry or other powerful forces influence historical understanding?

- Who decides what topics and issues are important to record and study?

- How does bias and editorial selection impact what is recorded and reported on, and what is not?

- In what ways does the outcome of an event determine how it is recorded in history?

- How does technology affect understanding of history, or the methods the historian uses?

- How are value judgements in history determined? For example, how are terms like atrocity, terrorism or revolution treated now compared to the period under investigation? Should historians make moral judgements?

- In what ways does the idea of progress and decline affect our treatment of some historical events?

- What is the role of the historian? Can the historian ever be objective?

- Are all perspectives of history equally valid? If not, how do we determine which have greater value?

- How might knowledge of your investigation be used to solve complex problems in the present? How might it be abused?

In would be far too ambitious for you to consider all of these questions in Section C. It is essential however that you give considerable thought to what you learned about history from your investigation. You should demonstrate clear awareness of the challenges facing historians, and the limitations of specific methods used in investigating topics like your own. In other words, there should be a clear connection between the nature of history as a way of thinking, and your own investigation. For a greater understanding of the nature of history, the following books are very useful.

> E.E. Carr, 1961. *What is History?* Penguin Books. London, UK
>
> M. MacMillan, 2008. *The Uses and Abuses of History.* Viking. Toronto.
>
> J. L. Gaddis, 2004. *The Landscape of History.* New York, Oxford University Press.

Final touches: Wrapping up the IA

The Internal Assessment is arguably the best opportunity IB History students have to maximize their overall course mark. The final assessed mark is entirely in your hands because you control the process of topic selection, research, planning and writing. Before submitting to your teacher for final assessment, make sure you have completed the following:

- Select and thoroughly research a question of personal interest.

- Complete all sections fully, according to the criteria.

- Compare your IA to examples posted on the OCC or in the Teacher Support Materials.

- Include all relevant sources in your bibliography.

- Reference all sources using a consistent, standardized citation format.

- Edit and proofread your work carefully.

- Submit a draft for effective feedback from your teacher.

- Include a title page with your question, name, candidate number and total word count clearly listed.

- Include a table of contents.

Internal Assessment skills

Discuss and evaluate the student example below using the criteria for Section C:

Ever since Deng declared martial law on May 20th, 1989, the Tiananmen Square Protest had been a taboo topic in Mainland China. There are no public records of the Protest, and any discussion regarding the Protest is immediately censored. In the educational system, particularly, the Protest was considered "non-existent". The Party's illegitimate historical revisionism illustrates the extent to which history can be manipulated to influence public opinions. Therefore, historians have the morally imperative role to present a balanced account of the Protest.

However, historians hoping to investigate the Protest face a dilemma: most primary sources are not made public by the Chinese government, and most available sources are from the protestors' perspectives. Historians either have no primary sources to work with, or have a disproportionate number of pro-protest sources. This dilemma is a common problem caused by illegitimate historical revisionism, which made it difficult for historians to remain objective. Government records are not available. Media coverage during the Protest is censored. Government and military officers who gave orders during the Protest are not permitted to publicize their narratives. On the other hand, a large number of sources originate from political dissidents, protesters who sought asylum overseas, and families of protestors who were killed

on June 4th. These sources, although highly valuable to historians, can be biased and unreliable. Therefore, historians should exercise caution when evaluating these sources.

In order to counterbalance the aforementioned dilemma, I purposely limited the number of sources originated from the protestors. I also took advantage of my Chinese proficiency by looking through Chinese newspaper archives and talking with former protestors and former Party officials during the protest. These methods of acquiring evidence should have helped me gain a more balanced understanding of the democratic sentiments during the protest.

Apart from balancing different perspectives, historians who investigate this issue are under social and ethical pressures. If they suggest that there were democratic sentiments within the Party and the Army executing the martial law, many former protesters (especially families of victims who were killed during the June 4th incident) would accuse the historians of downplaying the Party's crime. In addition, the Western world almost unanimously agrees that the June 4th incident was a massacre and that the Party was the antagonist. Historians who propose otherwise are under significant ideological pressure. Therefore, historians should prevent these pressures from influencing the investigation. Any conclusions should be re-examined by other historians to ensure a higher degree of objectivity.

Index